FRANK LLOYD WRIGHT

HOLLYHOCK HOUSE AND OLIVE HILL

BUILDINGS AND PROJECTS FOR ALINE BARNSDALL

Kathryn Smith

New color photography by Sam Nugroho

RIZZOLI
NEW YORK

First published in the United States of America in 1992
by Rizzoli International Publications, Inc.
300 Park Avenue South, New York, N.Y. 10010

Library of Congress Cataloging-in-Publication Data
Smith, Kathryn, 1945–
Frank Lloyd Wright, Hollyhock House and Olive Hill : buildings and projects
for Aline Barnsdall / by Kathryn Smith.
p. cm.
Includes bibliographical references and index.
ISBN 0-8478-1540-4 : $39.95
1. Wright, Frank Lloyd, 1867–1959—Criticism and interpretation. 2. Hollyhock
House (Museum). 3. Theater architecture—California—Los Angeles. 4. Barns-
dall, Aline, 1882–1946—Art patronage. 5. Architects and patrons—California—
Los Angeles. 6. Los Angeles (Calif.)—Buildings, structures, etc. I. Title.
NA737.W7S43 1992   92-10082
720'.92—dc20   CIP

Design by Charles Davey
Printed and bound in Japan

Front cover: View into living room, Hollyhock House.
Photograph by Sam Nugroho.
Back cover: Living room, Hollyhock House.
Photograph by Sam Nugroho.

NOTE

When projects are referred to by their proper name, they are capitalized. The terminology used in this book is that which was used by Frank Lloyd Wright and Aline Barnsdall even though their usage was sometimes inconsistent. The title Hollyhock House was not used until 1932 when Wright introduced it in *An Autobiography.* On the plans, it had been referred to as Owner's Residence or Barnsdall Residence. The first Director's House was renamed Residence A in 1921. Wright is known to have referred to Residence B as Studio Residence B after 1923.

CONTENTS

PREFACE

As the twentieth century draws to a close, it is surprising to realize that understanding of the work and the significance of Frank Lloyd Wright is still in its infancy. There is no other architect in this century who approaches his protean creativity or the grandeur of his ambitions. The closest comparison is to Picasso. Although both masters have become synonymous with the birth of modernism, both elude an analysis of their work that explicates form and meaning and that integrates the various periods of their career to create a comprehensive critical and historical perspective.

Wright has always enjoyed a curious relationship with historians and critics. And perhaps, more than anything else, he has been plagued by modernism. First propelled to European recognition as its prophet in the first decades of the century, he fought hard in the 1920s and 1930s to remain at its forefront even when his own more cosmic vision was pulling him in another direction. At his death, he had succeeded in convincing the skeptics and apologists that he must be taken seriously for his own later work, as much as for his anticipation of the work of a younger generation. In the intervening decades, Wright's reputation has fallen and risen again with the tides of modernism. Ironically, the tables turned in his favor as modernism became discredited and his attributes, which had previously been perceived as sins, made him attractive to a new generation in search of alternative roots. Yet beyond the perception of Wright's importance in light of contemporary theory and taste, determined as it is by the barometer of modernism, are Wright's own intentions and ideas. "Radical though it may be," Wright declared in 1908, "the work here illustrated is dedicated to a cause conservative in the best sense of the word. At no point does it involve denial of the elemental law and order inherent in all great architecture."

Because of Wright's prolific production, there is no definitive documentation, even now, of how many buildings and projects he designed, no precise chronology of their sequence and development, and no description of the circumstances under which they were created. The next two decades will witness an avalanche of books and exhibitions utilizing not only the vast collection of correspondence, drawings, and documents from the Wright Archives, but also research compiled from public sources and individuals still living—family, clients, associates, and apprentices. The completion of a chronology must precede any analysis of his major themes or a critical evaluation of his place in history. Until now, attention has been directed primarily to Wright's great masterpieces, the Prairie houses, Fallingwater, the Johnson Wax Administration

Building and Research Tower, the Larkin Building, and the Guggenheim Museum. This imbalance has reinforced the view, fostered by Wright himself, that he was a genius who worked in a vacuum, without the years of struggle and experimentation that precede the synthesis necessary to create such powerful statements. Of particular significance is the period between the well-known Oak Park Studio years and the last decades of his life, which coincide with the Taliesin Fellowship.

These transitional years are generally associated with Wright's scant executed work, Midway Gardens, the Imperial Hotel (the former demolished in 1929, the latter in 1968), Hollyhock House, and the Los Angeles concrete block houses. In reality, during the decade between 1914 and 1924, Wright was commissioned by Aline Barnsdall to design cultural, residential, and commercial buildings for what constituted a planned community, Olive Hill. The history of this commission is one of the most dramatic in Wright's career, revealing him in all of his guises and presenting a perplexing set of questions, not easily answered.

The most well-known building of this commission, Hollyhock House, is one of the most puzzling of Wright's career. Although it appears to follow logically from the Prairie house type, its exterior and its relationship to its site do not conform to the same canon of principles. Although of conventional construction, its appearance of monumental mass has led to the conclusion that it is a reinforced concrete building and, as such, represents Wright's commitment to the "art and craft of the machine." There is no reference in the archival material that Wright ever intended it so; in fact, the structural system—hollow tile walls and false attic story, framed in wood—is unique in Wright's career.

In addition to these anomalies, the form of Hollyhock House has closed our eyes to other factors of Wright's architecture and has limited our understanding of Hollyhock House itself, which is primarily known in isolation from the much broader original intentions for Olive Hill. Its plan, its siting, even details of its ornamental efflorescence are interpreted in terms of historical sources, in other words, by analyzing Wright's influences. Although these factors are essential to a comprehensive understanding, it is essential to know the building in the context within which it was created—that is, in relation to both its original site for a planned community and to the circumstances under which it was designed and built.

Such a point of view is presented here for the first time by documenting the complete history of all the commissions for Aline Barnsdall, which span a decade of Wright's career. It confirms the notion that the contradictions and ambiguities inherent in Hollyhock House were also manifest in the larger, but less well-known, Olive Hill plan.

I first became aware of Hollyhock House as a student at the University of California, Los Angeles. It seemed an appropriate topic for research because, owing to public interest in it and its accessibility due to the city's ownership, it was a compelling cultural resource for the City of Los Angeles. My early work led to two exciting and unexpected discoveries. First, that the house that had been illustrated and discussed in the general literature on Wright was part of a much larger commission for a whole community, a project that was virtually unknown, although parts of it had been published sporadically, mainly in Europe, in the 1920s. This expanded knowledge was greatly enhanced when I discovered over two dozen Wright drawings and a collection of blueprints in the files of the City's division of Architects and Engineers, Department of Recreation and Parks, in 1973. These drawings not only supplemented the material in the Archives of the Frank Lloyd Wright Foundation, but contained another major discovery as well: Wright had designed a second house for Aline Barnsdall on a spectacular site in Beverly Hills.

What had begun as work toward a graduate degree, now at the University of California, Santa Barbara, with David Gebhard, grew into a larger study that encompassed an entire decade in Wright's career. This tumultuous period was inextricably entangled with the history of the design and building of the Imperial Hotel in Tokyo, Japan. It gradually became evident that it would not be possible to evaluate or analyze the buildings and projects for Barnsdall without first gaining a greater knowledge of Wright's whereabouts and state of mind at the time. The results of this research appeared as an article in the June 1985 issue of *The Art Bulletin*.

It is not only possible, but probable, that Hollyhock House will be interpreted in many ways. This study is concerned above all with the context within which the building was designed and built and with the themes of the overall commission for Olive Hill. Undoubtedly, one of the greatest themes was the powerful duality of architecture and nature. For the projects at Olive Hill, the haunting mysteries of natural forces and elements were conveyed through the evocation of sacred mountains, streams, pools, waterfalls, hearth fires, and the dome of the sky—the edge between heaven and earth. Wright's buildings and landscape occupied this realm and sought to reconcile the two. At this point in his career, he drew on inspiration from Japan, Mesoamerica, and China. Clues are evident not only in the details and forms of the buildings themselves, but in references and techniques used in the presentation drawings. By the 1930s, these references would be completely synthesized in his art. Perhaps Wright's greatest discovery during this period was of the expressive power of water as a metaphor, which now seems to supplant fire (the hearth) to elucidate the meaning of his architecture. It was to be a major theme for the remainder of his career.

What do the buildings and projects for Aline Barnsdall, including Hollyhock House, reveal of Wright's design process during this decade? They show Wright struggling with opposing forces: classicism subjected to geometric abstraction on the one hand, and the primarily non-Western sacred landscape tradition on the other. In addition, there is a second duality: complex interior space shaped and given continuity not by the light, articulated screen of the Prairie house but increasingly by solid plastic wall surfaces, sometimes of concrete. And in the later buildings—Barnsdall's Beverly Hills house and the Little Dipper—he also sought to reconcile the technology of modernism with the traditional role of buildings as conveyors of meaning. Wright then was developing the themes that would inform the last third of his mature career and produce masterpieces such as Fallingwater, Taliesin West, the Johnson Wax Administration Building, and the Guggenheim Museum. Although the Prairie house remains the focus of critical attention and public popularity—because by posing a more limited number of questions, its resolution was more complete—the projects and buildings for Aline Barnsdall demonstrate that Wright not only abandoned a suburban practice when he departed Oak Park, but redefined his ambitions on an even grander scale.

ACKNOWLEDGMENTS

This book could not have been undertaken, or completed, without the aid, encouragement, and cooperation of Olgivanna Lloyd Wright and the members of the Frank Lloyd Wright Foundation. I owe special gratitude to Bruce Brooks Pfeiffer, Director of Archives, who gave generously of his time, invaluable experience, and good humor during the research and writing of this book. I must also thank Richard Carney, Indira Berndtson, Oscar Munoz, Penny Fowler, Greg Williams, and all the members of the Taliesin Fellowship.

I am deeply indebted to the friends and families of Aline Barnsdall and/or Frank Lloyd Wright who have been good enough to entrust me with their personal recollections, advice, and unpublished material: Lloyd Wright and his son, Eric Lloyd Wright; Pauline Schindler and her son, Mark Schindler; Michael and David Devine; Edmund Teske; Viroque Baker; Ellen Van Volkenburg; and Sheldon Cheney.

I am particularly indebted to Robert Sweeney whose encouragement, understanding, help, and presence cannot be measured. I owe more than I can readily express to Esther McCoy, whose generosity and wisdom proved invaluable; to Edgar Kaufmann, Jr., Henry-Russell Hitchcock, Barbara Giella, Donald Kalec, Jonathan Lipman, Jack Quinan, and Thomas Heinz for their support and generous assistance.

The institutions that own Wright drawings or related documentation were all extremely helpful. I would particularly like to thank David Gebhard, Director of the Architectural Drawing Collection, University Art Museum, University of California, Santa Barbara; Virginia Kazor and Earl Sherburn, Cultural Affairs Department, City of Los Angeles; W.H. Crain, Curator, Harry Ransom Humanities Research Center, University of Texas at Austin; Nicholas Olsberg, Gene Waddell, Stephen Nonack, Pamela Kratochvil, and Brent Sverdloff of Special Collections, the Getty Center for the History of Art and the Humanities, Santa Monica, California; and Ann Cager, Lloyd Wright Collection, Special Collections, University of California, Los Angeles.

Additionally, aspects of this study have been associated with my teaching at the Southern California Institute of Architecture and I would like to express appreciation to Michael Rotondi and Margaret Crawford for their encouragement. I especially wish to thank Eulogio Guzman, who contributed immeasurably to this work. His dedication and perseverance in completing a reproduction of Wright's 1919 plan for Olive Hill, and other drawings, provided an invaluable contribution. And to Masami Tanigawa, Thomas Hines, Lionel March, Francis Naumann, Dion Neutra, William Jordy, and Mary Jane Hamilton, who provided information or assistance, my warmest thanks are due.

Sam Nugroho and Marvin Rand, despite the difficulties of a number of photographic problems, also gave generously of their expertise. I gratefully acknowledge the contributions of David Morton, Rizzoli International Publications, whose enthusiasm for Hollyhock House made this book possible in its present form; Charles Davey, for the book design; and Noel Millea for her editing.

The research for this book was made possible in part under a grant from the Graham Foundation for Advanced Studies in the Fine Arts, Chicago, Illinois. Writing of the text was supported by grants from the National Endowment for the Arts and the National Endowment for the Humanities in Washington, D.C., both Federal agencies.

And finally, I am grateful to my husband, Randall H. Kennon, whose confidence has been unfailing even at the darkest moments. My thanks go to him for his patience, understanding, and encouragement.

Olive Hill, 1945 (photo by Edmund Teske)

To Randy

South Michigan Avenue, Chicago, Illinois, circa 1910 (courtesy The Art Institute of Chicago). Left to right: Auditorium Building, the Fine Arts Building, The Chicago Club.

PART ONE PRELUDE TO

HOLLYHOCK HOUSE
AND OLIVE HILL
1915–1919

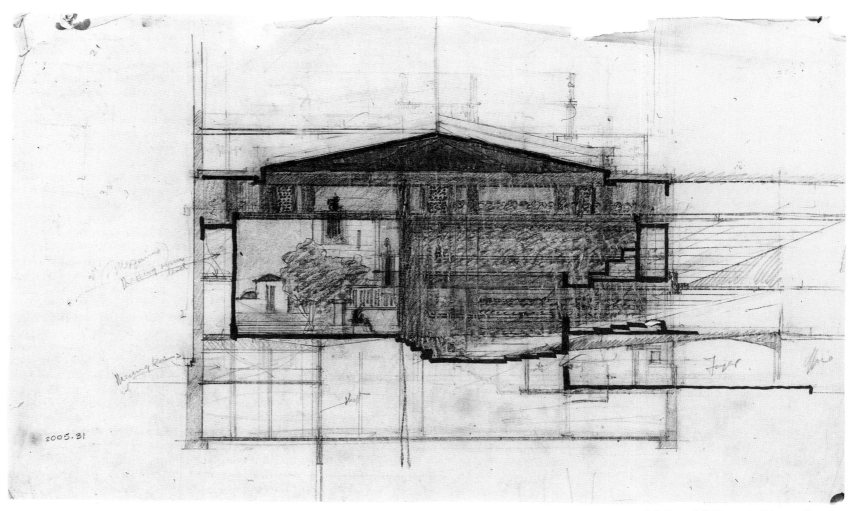

1-1. Barnsdall Theater I, Chicago, Illinois, circa 1915, longitudinal section (courtesy of the Frank Lloyd Wright Foundation)

CHAPTER 1

CHICAGO AND THE FINE ARTS BUILDING

As the threat of war hung over Europe in the beginning of 1914, Aline Barnsdall (fig. 1-2), the daughter of one of America's richest oil tycoons, launched her career in the American theater. She did not begin with the idea of designing a new kind of theater in collaboration with the most progressive of American architects, Frank Lloyd Wright, but when she chose Chicago as the location for her work, it was probably inevitable that they would eventually meet.

Inspired by the growing avant-garde movement that challenged commercial theater, which she had witnessed in productions from Germany to England, Barnsdall vowed to create an American interpretation of "the newer expression of the drama."[1] Sometime before the summer she founded the Players Producing Company, in partnership with Arthur Bissell, taking a two-year lease on one of the theaters in the Fine Arts Building. She settled into a flat at 5502 Everett Avenue in Hyde Park, one block from the Midway Plaisance, the site of the 1893 Columbian World's Exposition.[2]

Her choice of location could not have been more propitious. Not only was Chicago experiencing the birth of its own literary, artistic, and architectural traditions, but Barnsdall was sharing the Fine Arts Building with what was to become the most important American dramatic experiment to emerge from Europe's theatrical revolution. The Chicago Little Theatre had been started in 1912 by Maurice Browne and Ellen Van Volkenburg, who were inspired by the Irish Players at Dublin's Abbey Theatre. With a company of amateurs, the Little Theatre had, in two seasons, established a critical reputation for performing classical Greek drama, Shakespeare, and the work of contemporary Europeans such as George Bernard Shaw, August Strindberg, and Henrik Ibsen. Although always short of funds, Browne and Van Volkenburg had managed to create a loyal following among both the literati and the social elite of Lake Shore Drive.

After only a short acquaintance (probably dating from no later than the beginning of 1915), Barnsdall offered to provide Browne and Van Volkenburg with a larger and more modern theater.[3] It is not likely that Barnsdall had purchased a site, but she approached Frank Lloyd Wright (fig. 1-3) with the commission for a multi-storied theater building that would also include artists' studios. According to Wright, it was Henry Blackman Sell who introduced them, and in later years Barnsdall recalled irreverently, and without explanation, that their first meeting took place in Mrs. Potter Palmer's garage, not her drawing room or ballroom.[4] As publicist for the Fine Arts Building, Sell had probably met Barnsdall by the late summer or early fall of 1914. He had more than passing knowledge of Wright—he had spent late 1914 and early 1915 writing reviews of Wright's work: first of his book *The Japanese Print,* which appeared in the January 1915 issue of *The Little Review;* and then of his newly completed Midway Gardens for the May issue of *International Studio.*

In late 1914, Wright was in a crisis in his personal and professional life. He had established an independent practice in the Chicago suburb of Oak Park in 1893. Over the next fifteen years, he devoted himself primarily to the complete transformation of the American single family dwelling. His innovations were primarily spatial as he sought to break up the compartmentalization of the Victorian "box." He created a house with strong horizontal lines that appeared to hug the earth; a pinwheel plan that rotated around the chimney core, an anchoring vertical axis; and a flow of interior space, joining rooms together at the corners, creating taut diagonal movement. This domestic architectural revolution resulted in the Prairie house, which as a type was virtually complete by 1902. From 1903 until 1909, Wright pursued two other directions. One was an increasing level of geometric abstraction that began to transform traditional architectural elements such as walls, windows, and roof into pure planes of either solid or void. This interest was coupled with an exploration of the use of concrete for both public and residential buildings, which produced Unity Temple (1904–1906) and the "Fireproof House for $5000" (1906).

After these achievements he made an abrupt break in 1909. He closed his studio and left his family. He and Mamah Borthwick Cheney, a former client, traveled to Germany where Wright prepared the drawings for a deluxe portfolio of his work published by Ernst Wasmuth in 1910. On their return several months later, they left Oak Park for Wright's newly built country house and studio, Taliesin, in Wisconsin. Scandal ensued anew when Wright's first wife, Catherine, refused to grant a divorce, but the couple continued to live together in the rural Wisconsin community of Wright's maternal relatives. With a resulting substantial loss of commissions and increased financial burdens, Wright struggled to create a new life with Mamah Borthwick. But on August 15, 1914, this chapter in Wright's life ended with finality when Borthwick, her two children, and four of Wright's employees were murdered, and the residential section of Taliesin burned to the ground by a deranged servant.

Although Wright immediately began rebuilding, in the interim he moved to 25 Cedar Street in Chicago while maintaining offices at Orchestra Hall. His staff included his second-eldest son, John Lloyd Wright, who had returned to Chicago from San Diego in 1913; a former draftsman from the Oak Park studio, Harry F. Robinson; and a newcomer, Russell Barr Williamson. Wright's years of notoriety and his absence from the country had distanced him from his former clientele, the middle class families of Chicago's suburbs, and cut deeply into the volume of his work, but he had several large jobs—including a housing development in Glencoe for his lawyer, Sherman Booth; the invention of a residential building system (the American Ready-Cut System) for Arthur Richards; and a new building for the Imperial Hotel in Tokyo. Barnsdall, with her great wealth and artistic idealism, offered Wright the chance to produce another important public building and ease his financial crisis at the same time.

Barnsdall's wealth originated with her grandfather William Barnsdall, a shoemaker who had come from England in the early 1800s and settled in Titusville, Pennsylvania. In 1859, when Colonel William Drake drilled the first oil well, Barnsdall and a partner immediately followed with a second, and Barnsdall went on to even greater fortune by building the first oil refinery.

His son Theodore Newton entered the oil business eight years later, when he was sixteen. Without completing his formal education, he drilled his first well and, using his own capital, went on to open additional fields, expanding beyond Pennsylvania into New York, Ohio, West Virginia, Indiana, and Kentucky, and eventually into Texas, Oklahoma, and Alaska. Possessed of imagination and a natural instinct for business, he became one of the leading producers in the

1-2. Aline Barnsdall, circa 1914 (courtesy of Security Pacific Photograph Collection)

1-3. Frank Lloyd Wright, circa 1918 (courtesy of the Architectural Drawing Collection, University Art Museum, University of California, Santa Barbara)

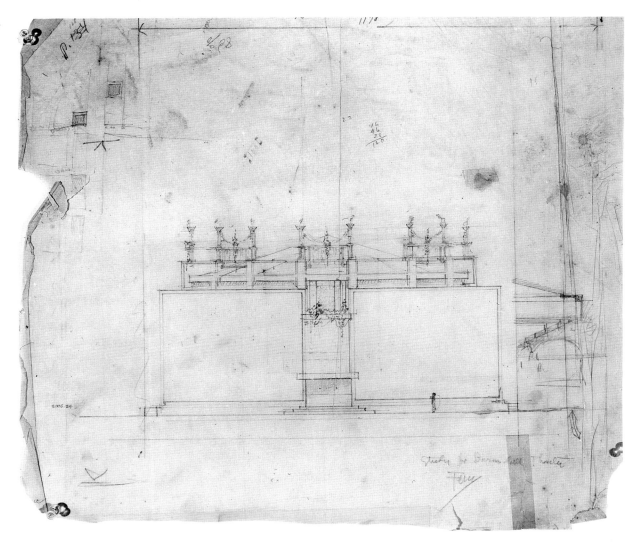

1-4. Barnsdall Theater I, Chicago, Illinois, circa 1915, elevation (courtesy of the Frank Lloyd Wright Foundation)

natural gas industry and eventually expanded into mining coal, iron, zinc, silver and gold. As a grown man, T.N., as he was commonly known, stood six feet four inches tall and weighed 250 pounds. He wore a full mustache and, with his barrel chest and great height, presented a commanding appearance. His robust physique allowed him to carry out his business with unflagging energy. Although he had a large house on fourteen acres of land in Pittsburgh, he rarely spent time there. He was constantly catching trains in pursuit of his business interests throughout the United States, Mexico, and Canada, or touring Europe.[5]

Louise Aline Barnsdall, the elder of his two daughters, was born on April 1, 1882. She received her education in Pittsburgh and then went on to travel in Europe. By her midtwenties, her interest in the theater drew her to a year of study with the actress Eleanora Duse, who persuaded her to give up acting and go into production, where her talents would serve her best. No doubt Duse's suggestion was prompted by her impression of Barnsdall's potential. Norman Bel Geddes, who met Barnsdall a few years later, vividly recalled that she "was a fascinating woman; not attractive or appealing, but fascinating: far from easy to describe." He found her to be "erratic, unpredictable, contrary, stubborn, generous, and a dozen other things as anyone [he had] ever known, only more so."

As a supporter of both social causes and the arts, he perceived that "she had a violent passion against convention; was one hundred per cent rebel; would give vast sums of money to anything revolutionary, not because she was sympathetic to the principles involved, but because it was challenging easy conformity." And with regard to the theater, he discovered that

she had a mad desire to be creative, but wasn't: consequently [she] did the next best thing and is to be commended for it. She associated around her the best talent in the specialized area she was interested in.[6]

However, her dealings with people in the theater were sometimes frustrated because

she had complete confidence with no social graces, behaving like the rough self-made man her father was. She was very serious with a sense of humor that peaked out mildly. Never made the least effort to be ingratiating, craved affection, but was unable to do anything about it.[7]

Despite Barnsdall's passion for the theater and her considerable financial resources, both necessary for her role as producer, she lacked a clearly defined artistic point of view. Although her conservative friends thought "she was well on [her] way to perdition" when she read Gordon Craig's theories on the theater "with many thrills and not much understanding" while studying in England, she proudly announced that she "succeeded in doing a nice, conventional thing with [her] first production in spite of past thrills and admirations."[8]

However, with her third play, an adaptation of Lewis Carroll's *Alice's Adventures in Wonderland* in February 1915, Barnsdall achieved both a critical and commercial success.[9] She received national recognition when the play—written, designed, and performed by local talent—arrived in New York for a two-month run after it closed in Chicago. It caused the *New York Times* to remark, "'Alice in Wonderland' now to be shown in matinees at the Hudson is Chicago's contribution to the new art of the stage."[10] But by this time, Barnsdall's attention was distracted by a new challenge: her plans to build a theater for the struggling, but critically acclaimed, Chicago Little Theatre, both her closest rival and her ideal.

Interviewed many years later, Van Volkenburg recalled attending a meeting with Barnsdall, Browne, and Wright in his office on the eighth floor of Orchestra Hall. In his autobiography, Wright remembered his first impressions of Aline Barnsdall: "Her very large, wide-open eyes gave her a disingenuous expression not connected with the theater and her extremely small hands and feet somehow seemed not connected with ambition such as hers."[11]

Barnsdall probably expressed an interest in commissioning a building similar to the Studebakers' Fine Arts Building. In the late 1890s, Charles C. Curtiss, who had become the building manager, had convinced the Studebaker family to remodel their company building into ground floor theaters and upper floor studio space for artists and musicians. When the building opened, it was equipped with two ground floor music halls, one of which was converted into a popular theater within a few months; special sound-proof music studios; and a banquet hall on the top floor with a view of Lake Michigan across the lakefront park. Curtiss, who had built a reputation by successfully combining art and business, proved to the Studebakers that the Fine Arts Building could be profitable. No doubt this factor had tremendous appeal to Barnsdall, who sought to protect her family's wealth with careful investments. She would also have been attracted by the quality of past and present tenants, including Francis Fisher Browne's *The Dial,* the most influential literary publication of its day; Margaret Anderson's *The Little Review;* and the printer Ralph Fletcher Seymour, who printed Wright's books as well as Harriett Monroe's *Poetry* (which introduced T.S. Eliot, Ezra Pound, Vachel Lindsay, and Carl Sandburg, among others).[12] Barnsdall would have been especially intrigued by the fact that the rent of the studios could support the building if a play failed; thus, the entire venture more than paid for itself while still supporting the arts.

Wright's plan for the Chicago Little Theatre was an abstract form of a circle circumscribed within a square structure, sixty feet on a side (figs. 1-5 and 1-6), for a site eighty feet in width, which, Wright later recalled, he considered "a desperate pinch."[13] His scheme was a tremendous advance over the converted storage room the Chicago Little Theatre was occupying at the time. The seating capacity was enlarged substantially from 91 to 450, in orchestra seating parallel to the stage, a dress circle, and semicircular balcony with three semicircular boxes above. Instead of the tiny stage at the Fine Arts Building (only fourteen by twenty feet) that was obstructed by a structural column on the right, Wright's plan included an elevator stage with two revolving tables for three-dimensional scenery that opened to the auditorium with four steps. These innovations, suggested by Browne and Van Volkenburg, had been introduced elsewhere before 1900, but Wright's scheme boldly unified the stage and auditorium as one space (fig. 1-7) separated only by partition walls terminating in columns that framed the stage and supported the ceiling.[14] The rear of the stage was enclosed by a semicircular cyclorama the same height as the partition walls. A band of delicate ornament formed an upper frieze on all four sides of the space, creating a

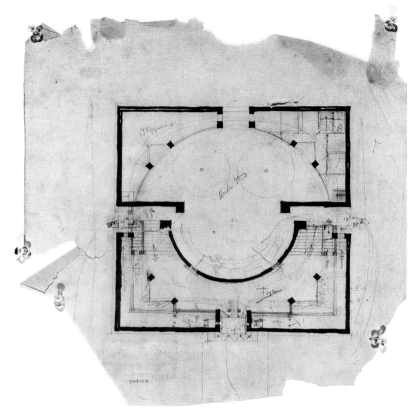

1-5. Barnsdall Theater I, Chicago, Illinois, circa 1915, ground floor plan (courtesy of the Frank Lloyd Wright Foundation)

18

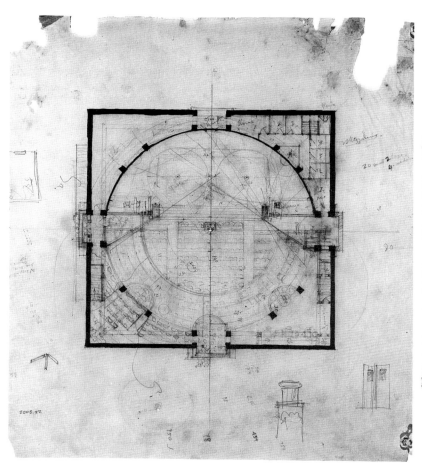

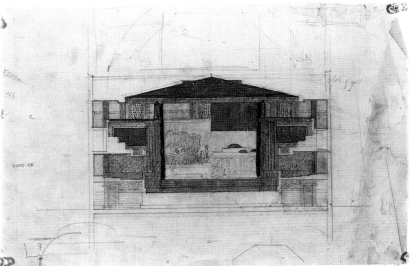

1-6. Barnsdall Theater I, Chicago, Illinois, circa 1915, orchestra and balcony plan (courtesy of the Frank Lloyd Wright Foundation)

1-7. Barnsdall Theater I, Chicago, Illinois, circa 1915, cross section (courtesy of the Frank Lloyd Wright Foundation)

continuous surface. The decorative scheme of black marble, gold leaf, and gold cloth was rich and bold.

The few surviving sketches show Wright responding to Barnsdall's request by placing the theater at the base of a building that accommodated studios occupying perhaps one or two stories above (fig. 1-1). He also sketched a front elevation (fig. 1-4) and a longitudinal section depicting how the building would appear if it were freestanding. His initial concept shows a cube pierced by a central entrance, with flat, planar walls surmounted by a row of torches and garlands resting on an open screen base. These sketches may have been done either at the time he submitted the scheme to the Chicago Little Theatre or later when he was revising it for Barnsdall.

Certainly, Barnsdall, Browne, and Van Volkenburg would have been aware that Wright had apprenticed in the office of Adler and Sullivan during the years when that firm had established a reputation for theaters and concert halls — the Auditorium Building, McVicker's Theater, and the Schiller (later Garrick) Theater, all in Chicago, prominent among them. It is noteworthy that Wright's first theater owes almost nothing to these earlier designs. Unlike the Adler and Sullivan buildings, which combined Dankmar Adler's technical brilliance for acoustics and mechanical equipment with Louis Sullivan's skill at ornamental composition, Wright's theater relied on the manipulation of interior space to create a new theatrical experience.

Barnsdall's reaction to Wright's plan is unrecorded. In the meantime, national attention began to focus on California, the site of two major expositions, and Barnsdall's wanderlust beckoned her farther west.

2-1. Wright's staff and a consultant, 1918 (courtesy of Katharine Floto Loverud). *Left to right:* William E. Smith, R.M. Schindler, Arato Endo, Goichi Fujikura, Julius Floto. Floto was a consulting engineer on the Imperial Hotel; the other four were draftsmen who helped prepare drawings of Barnsdall's theater and house that spring. The group is standing in front of the entrance to the Studio at Taliesin, Spring Green, Wisconsin.

Before plans for the Chicago Little Theatre had advanced beyond the preliminary stage, Barnsdall began to change her mind. The spring and summer of 1915 passed and Barnsdall spent her vacation in California, probably on the occasion of the two fairs, the Panama-California Exposition in San Diego and the Panama-Pacific International Exposition in San Francisco. On her return to Chicago, she decided to move to San Francisco and build her own theater there. She announced her plans to Browne and Van Volkenburg and asked them to join her, but Van Volkenburg later recalled they declined on the grounds that they did not want to be "pioneers a second time."[1]

By November 30, 1915, Barnsdall had conceived her idea. She wanted to settle in San Francisco and use it as a production center from which to tour along the California coast, with plans to take one or two plays to New York every other year. She wanted to do "five or six productions each season that [would] be as brilliant as anything done in New York with a couple of months of what would be clearly understood as an 'experimental season' when smaller rarer plays would be tried and young artists would have the opportunity of trying out their ideas freely." After proving herself as a producer she then vowed, "If this succeeds and I am determined it will, I will then be in a position to build." But with perhaps some premonition of the very ambitious nature of her dream, she reflected, "This looks like a big order for one fairly young person, but I think with good organization, it can be done. All I ask is to cover expenses after the production is on."[2]

Barnsdall was preparing to depart for San Francisco where she was planning to open in the summer or fall of 1916. Although she had neither a site nor a company, she wanted Wright to execute the design as soon as possible. On December 10, 1915, she announced that she was working on plans with "one of the most, if not the most, original architects in this country."[3]

By the time she decided to build her own theater, Barnsdall probably knew quite a bit about Wright. Certainly, she would have seen the Wasmuth portfolio of 1910 and been impressed by Wright's reputation in the progressive architectural circles of Europe. She probably had seen, or even read, the publications and books (in a very different vein) that he had produced with Mamah Borthwick, including translations from the Swedish social philosopher Ellen Key, *The Morality of Women, Love and Ethics,* and *The Torpedo under the Ark; "Ibsen and Women."* As a supporter of both Margaret Sanger, the birth control advocate, and Emma Goldman, the political anarchist, Barnsdall would have been sympathetic to Wright's advocacy of unconventional social ideas. Of course, it

CHAPTER 2

THE PLAYERS PRODUCING COMPANY

would have been impossible for her not to have heard often of Wright's personal life. At the time of her arrival in Chicago, the newspaper headlines had broadcast news of the murders and fire at Taliesin throughout the Chicago area. Just as she was making plans with Wright to design her theater in San Francisco, another scandal revealed that he was living with a new companion, Miriam Noel. A packet of Noel's letters had been stolen by Wright's housekeeper who sold them to the Chicago newspapers while she simultaneously attempted to have the police prosecute Wright under the provisions of the Mann Act. Barnsdall would not have been dissuaded by Wright's unconventional personal life since they were alike in many ways. In fact, Wright's description of her could have applied equally well to himself: "She was neither neo, quasi nor pseudo. She was near American as any Indian, as developed and traveled in appreciation of the beautiful as any European. As domestic as a shooting star."[4]

During Barnsdall's year in Chicago she would have had many opportunities to tour Oak Park, to see the houses illustrated in the Wasmuth portfolio firsthand, and to visit Unity Temple, one of Wright's most important public buildings. She might even have been invited to Taliesin, which was nearing the end of its rebuilding after the fire. It is certain that she had been to the Midway Gardens, a few blocks away and across the Midway Plaisance from her flat in Hyde Park. An indoor-outdoor entertainment center, laid out with a music pavilion, outdoor seating, and a restaurant, it was Wright's most recent building and the only one he had built that was comparable to a theater. Henry Sell, who had introduced Barnsdall to Wright, had written of the Midway Gardens: "Here...the forms of the three arts, architecture, sculpture and painting, are found proceeding from and determined by the same mind. Everything, from the intricate complications of the commodious kitchen to the comfortable dining-rooms, where every guest has an unobstructed view of the cabaret...to the polychromatic panels...came from the brain of this versatile builder of buildings."[5]

Although it was probably the reputation that Wright had forged with the work of the Oak Park studio that persuaded Barnsdall to commission him, he had moved on and was now exploring new ground. It was the Wright of Taliesin, not Oak Park, that Barnsdall hired. In his buildings from 1914 onward, Wright was increasingly interested in modern construction and materials (especially reinforced concrete), in organizing the building process as an ordered system (analogous to machine manufacture), and in integrating ornament and architectural elements. He was also deepening his interest in preindustrial cultures such as the Japanese, the Chinese, the pre-Columbian, and the American Indian. Wright

was after more than stylistic parallels; he was trying to recapture the spirit of a direct connection to nature. More than anything else, this aim would set him at odds with the European modernists, who, in reaction to the sentimentality of the nineteenth century, turned to the future as represented in the reality and the image of the machine. In contrast, Wright used technology to reach back to a period when man was not master over nature and the elements, but was in tune with them and even dominated by their mysterious power.

Barnsdall probably met with Wright several times before her departure for California in February 1916, but with her plans so indefinite, the scheme could not proceed much further. Her departure for California coincided with the arrival at Taliesin of Aisaku Hayashi, the general manager of the Imperial Hotel in Tokyo.[6] Although Wright had been to Tokyo in 1913 when he made preliminary drawings for a larger and more modern building to replace the hotel's nineteenth century building, Hayashi's visit was intended as a prolonged stay: a more detailed scheme was being prepared for the final approval of the hotel's board of directors. Confident that he already had the job, Wright declared to his friend and former client Darwin Martin on February 28: "I am not going to Japan for at least a year and then only for a few months at a time to keep in touch with the progress of the work—which will not start for ten or twelve months at least."[7]

More than one year after the tragedy at Taliesin, Wright's practice was still slow. Antonin Raymond, who joined Wright's studio in May 1916, worked primarily on perspective drawings for the American Ready-Cut System catalog. He left after some months because, as he recalled, "There was hardly any work in the office." He added, "The work he performed on paper was tremendous, but actual building for clients was very scarce, practically non-existent."[8] But more than at any other time in his career, commissions were drawing Wright away from the Midwest, from Chicago and from Taliesin, where he had been rooted since his teens. The way to Japan was west, and California was a point of embarkation for the Orient. "Yes, I was eager to go," he wrote years later, "for again I wanted to get away from the United States. I still imagined one might get away from himself that way—a little....But at this time I looked forward to Japan as refuge and rescue."[9]

By the summer of 1916, Barnsdall, settled in a rented house in Mill Valley across the bay from San Francisco, was struggling to put her season together. She was becoming impatient for her own theater and had decided to build her own house as well to better serve her role as producer. Her frustration grew as she spent months trying to rent a building in San Francisco only to find that independent companies were at the mercy of commercial producers who controlled the theaters.

By July 27, 1916, Barnsdall's impatience to see her ideas realized outweighed her progress. Although she admitted that she was still looking for land, and hoped to acquire property within two months, she urged Wright to complete the plans for the theater. She wrote him, "This is the psychological moment and if I do not grip it and build a theatre within the next six months somebody else will." Yet she could not act without her father's approval. She still wanted a building with studios. She implored:

> You will put your freest dreams into it, won't you! For I believe so firmly in you[r] genius that I want to make it the keynote of my work. Can't you give it the grace of the Midway Gardens, with the added lift and color they never achieved. Things done in the theatre will always have a certain lightness, piquancy and grace, so it should have lovely golds that take the sun!
>
> Can you give me a rough idea of cost and what is expected of me and when? It must not be a large theatre not over a thousand but exquisitely perfect in detail. You can't build a model until you see the site can you? Please let me know all these details. I'm so eager![10]

Wright's reply has not survived, but as the months passed, Barnsdall was drawn into the preparations for her season in the fall.

In that same summer of 1916, Barnsdall, frustrated with San Francisco, turned to southern California and rented the Egan Dramatic School, which she renamed the Los Angeles Little Theatre. The previous fall, she had contacted Norman Bel Geddes, then a twenty-two-year-old commercial artist living at home with his parents in Detroit, Michigan, and known as Norman Geddes. She was interested in producing his play *Thunderbird,* based on an American Indian theme. Although they had never met, after an exchange of letters between October and December 1915 Barnsdall offered Geddes a contract to stage the play in California himself. As a result of this sudden success he had married Helen Belle Sneider and, in a romantic gesture, marked the occasion by hyphenating her middle name to his first name. Immediately thereafter he began calling himself Norman-Bel Geddes.[11] Within a few weeks, because of a sudden change in Barnsdall's company, Bel Geddes—in his first theatrical job—took over as stage and lighting designer for the entire season. By October 1916, the Players Producing Company also included a director, Richard Ordynski, and several actors (among them Elaine Hyman, whose stage name was Kirah Markham) from the Chicago Little Theatre.

That fall, for the first and only time in her life, Barnsdall was on the verge of accomplishing her most important professional goals. Despite her stated preference for original American material, her one major play, Bel Geddes's *Thunderbird*, was canceled as the opening production for lack of a proper cast. She then proceeded with a season of primarily European plays that included *Nju* by Ossip Dymov, *The Shadowy Waters* by William Butler Yeats, and *The Widowing of Mrs. Holyroyd* by D.H. Lawrence. Although she attracted movie actors and directors such as Charles Chaplin, Cecil B. deMille, and Gloria Swanson to her audience, she did not achieve a popular success. The most notable achievement of her only solo season as a producer was her discovery of Bel Geddes as a scenic designer. Steeped in the theories of Gordon Craig, Mario Fortuny, and the European avant-garde, Bel Geddes introduced experimental lighting and flexible, three-dimensional stage sets.

Before Wright was able to proceeed with the plans, Barnsdall set in motion a series of events that would lead to the permanent termination of her work in the theater. On the one hand, it was clear that she was motivated by genuine idealism, as Bel Geddes certainly knew firsthand. He recalled years later that

> [Aline's] single purpose was to make it possible for worthwhile talent to work under the proper conditions....She believed that the young inexperienced

talent for which she had such a strong instinct would receive inspiration in a fine theatre and develop better when liberated from worry about room and board. As a matter of fact she thought freedom from considerations would encourage ability in any field. She was willing to back those who attracted her attention even outside her main preoccupation with the theatre for she was interested in people, especially the underdog.[12]

No one in the company had benefited more from Barnsdall's encouragement than Bel Geddes, yet he was aware that something was lacking. He searched for an explanation:

> Perhaps our incomplete lack of appreciation [of Aline] was due to [her] lack of leadership. Although she enjoyed and was absorbed by people, she lacked security in handling them and was one of the loneliest persons I have ever known. Even though she was a means to an end for all of us, the uncertain manner caused by her loneliness in turn caused most of the company to avoid her away from the theatre. Her great heart could be burning with passion, but her undemonstrative manner conveyed frigidity. None of the people in the company felt any genuine warmth for her thus her loneliness only grew.[13]

Finally Bel Geddes was able to pinpoint what set Barnsdall apart from others and prevented her from attaining her goals:

> Being overconscious of her great inherited wealth as a girl of great beauty is too aware of beauty, she was unsure of herself in every way except her wealth. She believed that everyone knew this and that they were secretly only interested in her money. She dressed plainly, never discussed money except when she thought someone was trying to take advantage of her. She was sincere in her desire to use it for the betterment of others. In this she was thwarted by several persons, due again to her lack of instinct for working with people. Aline had another characteristic in common with other women of wealth and ideals I came to know—when things did not go as they had planned, after putting up a short skirmish they gave up.[14]

Bel Geddes began to notice that while Barnsdall was removed from others, she was growing closer to one member of the company. He recalled:

> By the time our season had reached the latter part of January [1917], Ordynski had become the dominating influence....Ordynski's romantic success with Aline was only partly due to his being a charmer. There was no love affair between them at first. She just had respect and admiration for the way he handled his job. Also though there was the recollection of Isadora Duncan who had children by Maurice Maeterlinck and Gordon Craig. Aline wanted a child. She had told us so several times and about Isadora Duncan. So that mild admiration for Ordynski coupled with his charm and conversation for the first few weeks and her need and desire for a personal masculine interest as she frankly told him led after a distinct understanding that no marriage would ever be involved to a pathetically [sic] mild affair. Within its brief duration, she returned from one of the motor trips pregnant and happy. They were unmarried, but she was going to have the baby and made no effort to conceal the father's identity. The baby born some months later was a beautiful child with her mother's red hair and named Aline Elizabeth Barnsdall. Although the only name I ever heard her called was "Sugar."[15]

Ordynski, who had worked closely with Max Reinhardt, began also to affect Barnsdall's artistic resolve. He influenced her to change her final production and present *Everyman*, a contemporary translation of a medieval morality play. Ordynski staged the play in a large church auditorium as a spectacle, in a style imitative of his mentor. At the end of the run, Barnsdall terminated her season and released her company. On February 7, 1917, Elaine Hyman, who at the time was briefly married to Wright's eldest son, Lloyd, confided in a letter to her father-in-law:

[Aline Barnsdall] really has no actual conception of what she wants to do with a theatre at all. She has vague illuminated moments, but the flashes that come in then are eternally slipping away on close contact with people she puts in power to execute them....And she wants so much to go on. Yet I scarcely believe I could endure the strain of a second season with her.[16]

A few weeks later, Barnsdall's father, T.N., died unexpectedly in Pittsburgh.[17] For the remainder of the year, Barnsdall was preoccupied with the birth of her baby and settling her father's estate. She and Frank Lloyd Wright had seen each other infrequently in the last year. The Imperial Hotel had moved more quickly than Wright had anticipated, and by the beginning of 1917 he was in Tokyo.

Undoubtedly, the new building for the Imperial Hotel was more important to Wright than the Barnsdall commission. He was turning fifty and had completed only one major public building, Midway Gardens, since his return from Europe. The job in Japan was like a dream come true. It allowed him to live and work in the culture he admired most; it gave him an opportunity to acquire Oriental art, especially Japanese woodblock prints, and to learn more about the buildings, gardens, and customs that had attracted him for so long. More important, he would be able to produce a building with modern technology while still expressing the organic principles of an architecture close to nature. On the other hand, Aline Barnsdall posed very different problems. She longed for something she had great difficulty defining. She had little notion of how to proceed with an architect, and her faith in Wright outweighed her sense of what he needed to realize his buildings.

Further jeopardizing Barnsdall's project was the settlement of T.N. Barnsdall's estate. By the beginning of 1918, it was apparent to Barnsdall, who had moved to Seattle to have her baby, that she would have to postpone building again. "When will your time be in demand on the Tokyo Hotel," she wrote to Wright on January 4, 1918, "and how soon will you be free. I won't be ready for a year, but when I do it can be done quickly. I want to start spring of 1919, but can you? Everything seems so vague, designs, etc."[18]

Wright had spent four months in Japan, returning to Taliesin on May 17, 1917, to prepare the working drawings for construction of the Imperial Hotel. Despite his original estimates, the construction of the hotel would occupy his time for four solid years. Most of that time he would spend in Japan, with annual visits to the United States of several months' duration. The longest uninterrupted period that he would spend in the United States until his last Pacific crossing in the summer of 1922 would be the last six months of 1917 and the first ten months of 1918. To Barnsdall's misfortune, it coincided exactly with the legal entanglements surrounding her father's estate.

During that time, Wright, reestablished at Taliesin and with a Chicago office in the Monroe Building, was surrounded by a new group of assistants (fig. 2-1). Robinson and Williamson had left, and John Lloyd Wright was in Tokyo. Thirty-year-old R.M. Schindler had arrived in February 1918 to join two Japanese architects, Arato Endo and Goichi Fujikura, at work on the Imperial Hotel drawings. As a student in Vienna, Schindler had been so impressed by the Wasmuth portfolio that in 1914 he had accepted a three-year position in the Chicago firm of Ottenheimer, Stern and Reichert in hopes that he would meet and perhaps work for Wright before returning to Austria. Eventually Wright would send him to Los Angeles where he later established a practice as a leader in modern architecture and lived until his death in 1953. Wright's studio staff also included William Smith, known as Will, from Ottawa, Canada, who acted as Wright's secretary and general assistant.

Barnsdall's disappointments with her Los Angeles season did not dissuade her from her ambition. With time to think, she considered her mistakes and planned to make changes, some of which affected the design of her theater. She wrote Wright a letter that has been lost, but his undated reply makes clear that she suggested the studios be eliminated.

Yes, the theatre will be more simple and monumental, and the first cost less if the studios are eliminated and your limit of $250,000 grounds and buildings would cover it safely. It was only in an effort to make the rent of the theatre a negligible quantity that the studio proposition would have any merit. In that case it would have considerable [sic] and I had planned the thing so the theatre was not hurt by it. In case the studios were built I had hoped to get one side of a city block extending as far back to the usual alley. A 99 year lease on a piece of ground like this—

The theatre will take less ground of course 90 feet will do—in width on the street and at a desperate pinch 80 feet would allow us to work if that happened to make a great difference in location. The depth should be anything from [135 or 175, number illegible] up....[19]

Barnsdall's experience in Los Angeles had also convinced her that she needed two performing spaces: a small experimental theater, where unproven talent would try out before moving on to bigger and more important productions, and a larger theater.[20] She reached this conclusion after casting amateurs and professionals together in the same play where she observed the "sure touch of the very experienced professional shows the very unsure touch of the inexperienced amateur."[21]

She was also struggling with the problem of artistic direction and control of her productions. Bel Geddes, still in Los Angeles, was urging her to let him take over, but she was reluctant to commit herself. "The organization of the company, its standard, choice of plays, decorators, actors, etc. must be my personal expression—the thing on which I stand or fall," she had explained to him earlier. "Otherwise I should not be more than a figurehead—a thing I should not consent to."[22]

Bel Geddes was eager to continue his lighting experiments, but Barnsdall was now even more hesitant to set a specific direction for her theater. She made it clear to him that he first had to prove himself. "I am putting ten thousand dollars aside for experimental use in the smaller theatre," she wrote, "and I am willing to hand that over to you for an eight weeks experiment in a small way."[23] She was willing to allow him to install a lighting system, and if his productions were successful, it would "open sesame to the large theatre the following season...on a larger scale."[24] She was willing to allow him to have complete control over the funds, except for the box office receipts which would be set aside for the next experimental season. No doubt with Ordynski in mind, she confided, " I am going to try and think of the good as a whole, in the future, and have no personal admirations or prejudices."[25]

Despite her struggle, Barnsdall still wanted her own theater. Wright had explained to her on more than one occasion that he needed enough time to develop the plans. Although she had vacillated and postponed the project repeatedly, now she was not willing to wait. Wright's reluctance was becoming a source of tension between them. In her 1918 New Year's letter, she enclosed a check for $2,500.[26]

THEATRE, OLIVE HILL 2005,01

CHAPTER 3

BARNSDALL THEATER

3-1. Barnsdall Theater II, circa 1918, sketch of exterior (courtesy of the Frank Lloyd Wright Foundation)

With no site or definite location, and with Barnsdall's fluctuating artistic point of view and no permanent company, by March 1918, Wright was put in the position of designing what was almost a theoretical building. Although she had said that she wanted the theater to reflect her convictions about the drama, Barnsdall also had implored Wright to put his "freest dreams into it." He revealed later, "I had wanted a theatre of my own ever since when, as a boy, I read of Wilhelm Meister's puppet-theatre in the attic of the house Goethe designed for him."[1] Although Wright's scheme contained several ideas that had been suggested by Browne and Van Volkenburg, it was primarily a new interpretation of a theatrical space consistent with his radical experiments in the Oak Park studio.

Wright elaborated on his earlier idea of a circle within a cube that enclosed both actors and audience in a unified space. He enlarged the initial cube (now 100 feet on a side) by appending a rectangular volume (50 by 80 feet) containing the entrance with foyer and balcony seating above and two narrow lateral rectangular volumes of 90 feet by 15 feet (rear measurement), which united the two masses of the building (figs. 3-2 and 3-3). The seating was thus increased from almost 450 in the earlier scheme to 1,500, including Wright's calculation of 100 people in standing room.

Wright further refined his bold concept of interior space by eliminating the columns framing the stage so that the stage and auditorium were separated only by partition walls, rising twenty feet to a ceiling thirty-five feet in height (figs. 3-6 and 3-7). The partition walls continued visually behind the stage as a semicircular cyclorama, or "hemi-cycle," as Wright called it. The columns were replaced by posts capped by incense burners (fig. 3-4), sculptural objects of a winged figure seated on a sphere. A series of steps leading from the stage down into the orchestra further integrated the theater spatially. A dressing room gallery occupied three sides of the area behind the stage (fig. 3-3). Actors' entrances were through doors concealed to the left and right of the stage behind the partitions. Among the most unusual features were two small balconies in front of and behind each of the twenty-foot partition walls. Presumably the front balcony, facing the auditorium, was for use by an actor speaking directly to the audience. But the rear balcony, not visible to the audience, was intended for the conductor of an orchestra that Wright placed in a musicians' gallery behind a perforated half-octagonal screen above and behind the cyclorama. Behind the musicians were places for two organs (fig. 3-5).[2]

Wright retained the elevator stage, but enlarged the area below ground significantly for wardrobe and scenery fabrication and storage (figs. 3-2 and 3-7).

3-2. Barnsdall Theater II, 1918, ground floor plan (courtesy of the Frank Lloyd Wright Foundation)

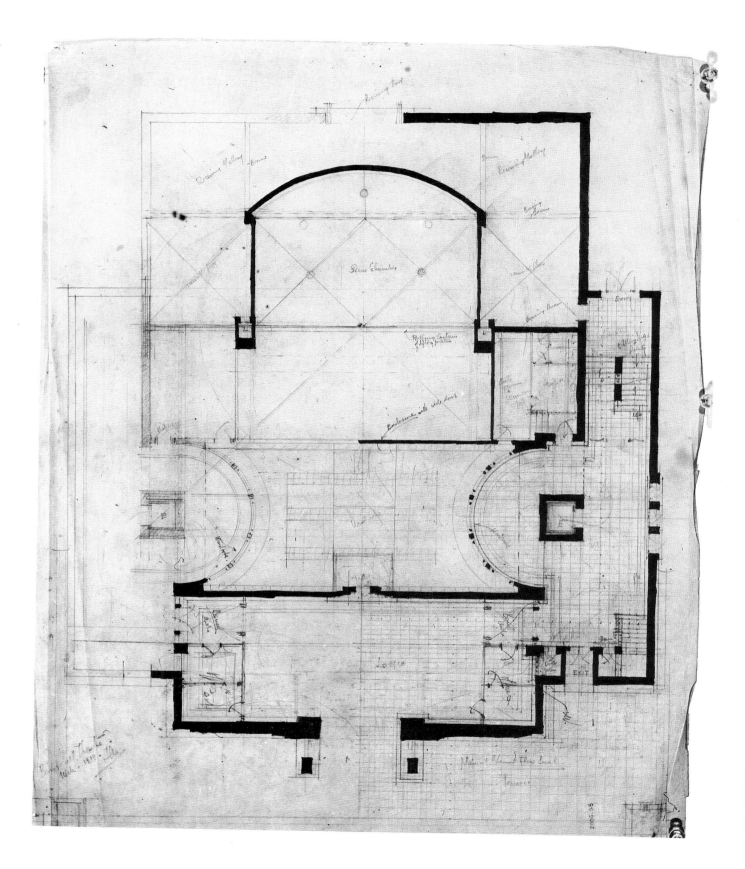

3-3. Barnsdall Theater II, 1918, balcony plan (courtesy of the Frank Lloyd Wright Foundation)

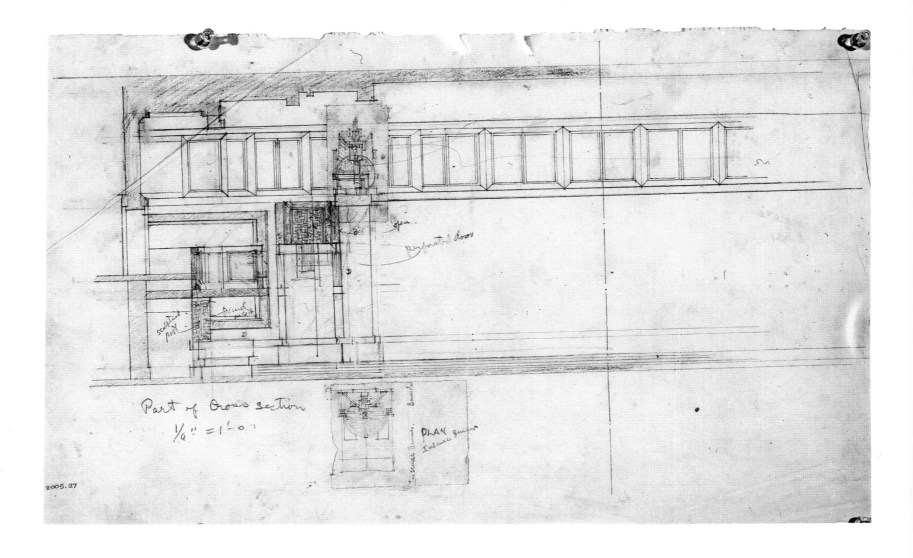

Part of Cross section
1/8" = 1'-0"

PLAN

2005.27

Orchestra seating was parallel to the stage, but the upper levels were altered to allow an increased number of boxes on three sides, parallel and perpendicular to the stage, with balcony seating behind and directly opposite the stage (figs. 3-3 and 3-7).

Despite additions and changes throughout the preliminary design process, there are no indications on either the drawings or models of Wright's introduction of a lighting system. Any analysis of the innovations of this theater would indicate that lighting was essential, yet Wright seemed to make no provision for it.

On the exterior, the building was conceived as a monumental cubic solid crowned by an octagon and joined to a lower secondary mass by two projecting side wings (figs. 3-1 and 3-8). The flat, planar walls were outlined with decorative bands, and the crown was surfaced with perforated geometric ornament (figs. 3-1 and 3-14).[3]

Wright's theater brought the audience and players together in a new spatial relationship. By eliminating nineteenth-century conventions—the proscenium arch and the fly towers housing the flat scenery and backdrops—Wright had simplified the stage, restored the actors and scenery to three dimensions, and brought the audience more actively into the experience of the play. His ideas were consistent with the new movement in the theater associated with the theories of Gordon Craig in England and Adolphe Appia in Germany. Both sought to return to earlier, even ancient, values of the theater by redesigning the theatrical space as well as stagecraft. Like Craig, as early as 1902, Wright eliminated footlights, wings, and borders; the stage was placed in front of a cyclorama with plain and geometric surfaces above and to the sides.

Wright's design was preceded by Appia's visionary theater, the Hall at the Hellerau Institute in Germany, adapted in 1911 by Heinrich Tessenow from Appia's suggestions, where the audience and actors achieved an intimacy with the elimination of the proscenium arch and the addition of a revolutionary new concept of lighting (fig. 3-10). Appia's Hall, which was designed for performances of eurythmic exercises by students of Emile Jaques Dalcroze, was conceived as one room with the audience seated on one side, and performers moving against an abstract geometric stage set on the opposite side. The walls and ceiling of the Hall were completely covered with linen that concealed thousands of electric bulbs, creating a diffused light. With neither a proscenium nor a curtain, changes between scenes and expressive moments of the performance were marked with modulations of light.[4]

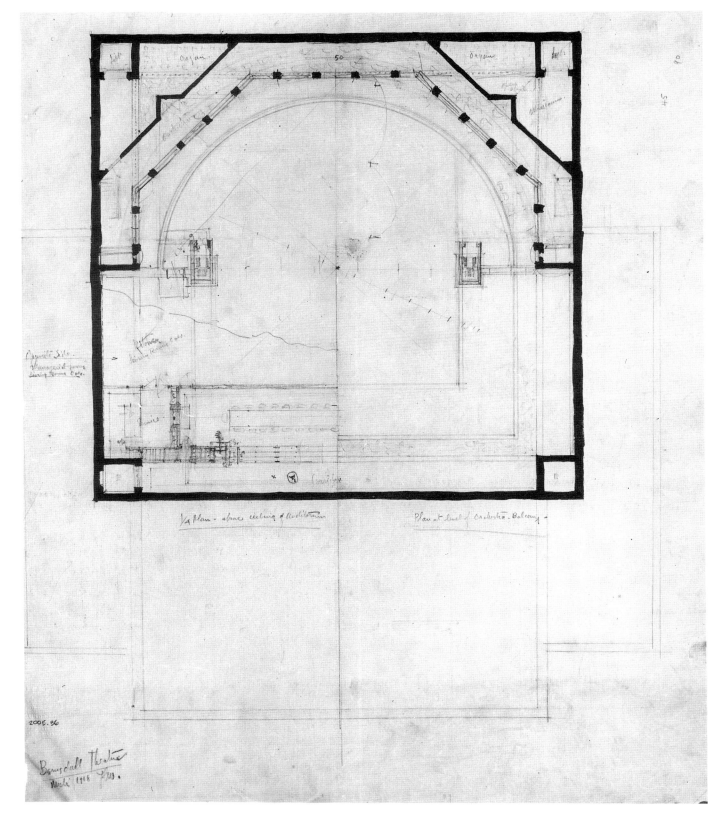

3-4. Barnsdall Theater II, 1918, section detail (courtesy of the Frank Lloyd Wright Foundation)

3-5. Barnsdall Theater II, 1918, orchestra and balcony plan with quarter plan above ceiling of auditorium (courtesy of the Frank Lloyd Wright Foundation)

It is highly probable that Wright had heard of these theories and precedents from either Barnsdall or Browne and Van Volkenburg. Festivals held at Hellerau in the summers of 1912 and 1913 had been widely attended by people in the theater throughout Europe—Barnsdall herself might have been present. In addition, examples of the new stagecraft, including designs by Gordon Craig, had been exhibited in Chicago in 1914 on a national tour.[5]

But Wright's Barnsdall Theater, which was a revision of his drawings for the Chicago Little Theatre, designed as early as February 1915, most closely resembles Norman Bel Geddes's Theatre #6, first published in his own magazine, *Inwhich*, in June 1915, but designed in 1914.[6] Theatre #6 unites the auditorium and stage—without a proscenium arch—under one domed ceiling, a surface used to reflect a variety of changing effects of electric light, bringing to mind the experiments of Appia and Mario Fortuny with lighting and sky domes around the turn of the century (fig. 3-13). Scenery changes, taking place in a basement with the use of a mechanical stage, would be made by simply dimming the lights. Bel Geddes's design, like Wright's, reflects the theoretical change taking place in the theater as a result of the theories of Craig, Appia, Reinhardt, and their followers in the United States, such as Maurice Browne. Bel Geddes's theater celebrates the use of lighting and is especially suited to the sets and scenery he was creating at the time.

Although both Wright's and Bel Geddes's theaters are alike in the notion of the stage and auditorium under one ceiling, they differ in many other respects. The *parti* of each is square, but Bel Geddes placed his stage and orchestra seating on the diagonal, leaving a larger area for circulation and foyer (figs. 3-11 and 3-12). On a more fundamental level, Bel Geddes was creating a theater that could incorporate the technical advances of a new type of stage design that would soon propel him to national prominence, whereas Wright was continuing an exploration of spatial possibilities that he had initiated in his Prairie houses. Wright's concept for the Barnsdall Theater exploded the two boxes that had traditionally contained the audience and actors. His spatial idea united them under the same continuous horizontal ceiling plane that was visible from both sides over the two freestanding vertical planes that did not enclose, but separated the stage from the auditorium. But Wright's design went even farther as he began to assume the role of artistic director in his elaboration of details that provided a new stagecraft and thereby implied a new kind of drama. Unfortunately, no evidence survives to document the conversations between client and architect regarding the plays to be performed. Wright's theater was far from a neutral space that could be used for a variety of dramas. On the contrary, it seemed suited to symbolic rather than realistic or commercial drama, for performances to music, perhaps even opera, with organ accompaniment, rather than primarily the spoken word. With the addition of incense burners, Wright seemed to be creating a sacred rather than secular ritual that recalled the origins of theater in sacred dance.

Despite their significant differences, the resemblance between the two projects was similar enough that both Wright and Bel Geddes mentioned it to Barnsdall. By December 10, 1915, during their initial correspondence, Barnsdall had written in passing to Bel Geddes that she was working with an architect designing a new theater. Bel Geddes replied on December 14 by sending her a copy of the June *Inwhich,* offering his design to her. On April 7, 1916, she asked for another copy, but by May 16, irritated that it still had not arrived, she informed him, "you will remember I wanted Frank Lloyd Wright to read it to assure him it was fundamentally different than his idea."[7] By July 4, Barnsdall told Bel Geddes that she was frightened to learn that he believed Wright had stolen his idea. Although the matter seems to have been dropped, for there is no further correspondence at that time on either side of the argument, the letters do substantiate the fact that Wright's design was well formulated by late 1915.

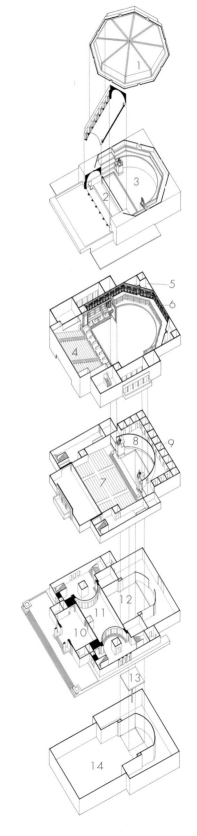

1. Octagonal Crown
2. Library
3. Preparatory Theatre
4. Balcony
5. Organ
6. Musicians Gallery
7. Auditorium
8. Hemi-Cycle
9. Dressing Rooms
10. Foyer
11. Wardrobe
12. Scene Chamber
13. Mechanical Stage
14. Scene Storage

3-6. Barnsdall Theater II, 1918, exploded interior perspective (drawing by Eric Stultz). Wright's drawings were not all consistent in detail or dimensions. Some conjectural decisions were made to unify the various levels.

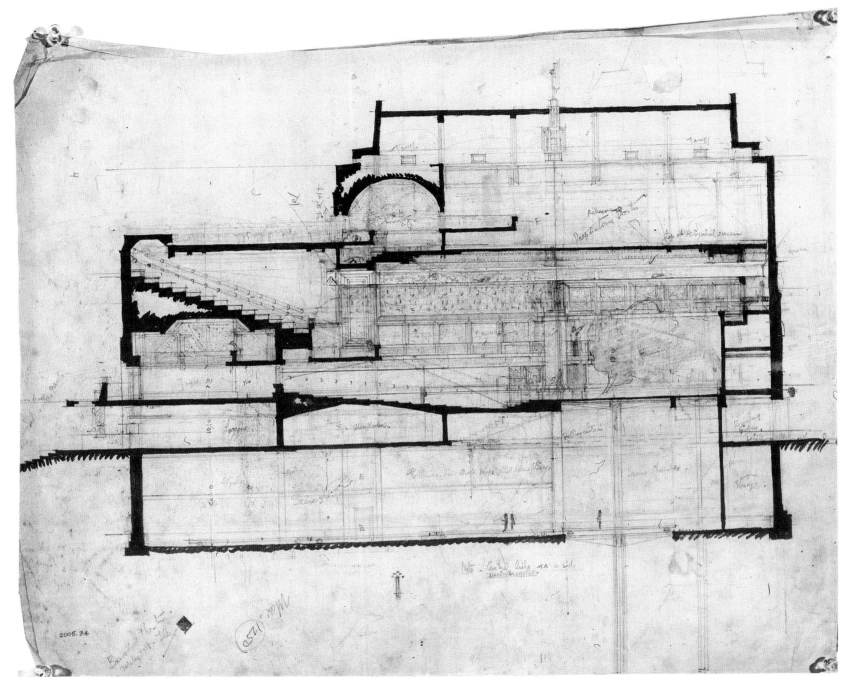

3-7. Barnsdall Theater II, 1918, longitudinal section (courtesy of the Frank Lloyd Wright Foundation)

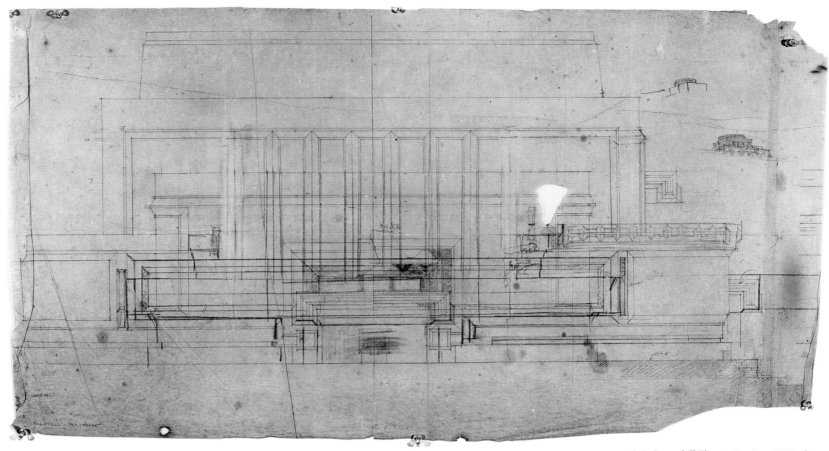

3-8. Barnsdall Theater II, circa 1918, front elevation (courtesy of the Frank Lloyd Wright Foundation)

However, the dispute was revived again, several years later, when Claude Bragdon published Bel Geddes's Theatre #6 in the September 1922 *Architectural Record*. Schindler wrote Bragdon that Wright had designed a theater that contained the essential ideas represented in Bel Geddes's design, implying that Bel Geddes had derived them from Wright.[8] Bragdon passed the letter along to Bel Geddes, who drafted a reply. On October 2, 1922, Bel Geddes informed Bragdon that his theater was designed as early as 1914, predating Wright's, that indeed Wright's scheme did contain the same essential ideas, and that Barnsdall had seen Bel Geddes's magazine. Stopping short of accusation, Bel Geddes simply closed by stating that Barnsdall had shown him Wright's plans to solicit his comments.

I know Miss Barnsdall would verify my statement, and I believe Mr. Wright would. I have no reason to be sure with regard to him, because I am not certain he is aware of the part I have played with regard to his theatre. He knows I have designed several theatres, and he was informed of the essential features of "Number Six" when he and Miss Barnsdall started to work. The only time I met him we discussed his own work and not the theatre. At that time he was very private with his plans and resented suggestions from everyone. All of mine that reached him went through Miss Barnsdall.[9]

There the controversy ended, with Bel Geddes unaware, since Barnsdall apparently never informed him, that Wright had proposed his idea in a different form for the Chicago Little Theatre before Bel Geddes had met her.

Over the next three years most of Wright's attention would be spent in an attempt, first, to resolve the complex levels of the upper floors, and, eventually, to fit the building to the site Barnsdall acquired. Numerous plans and details were made, erased, and redrawn in an effort to integrate Barnsdall's changing programmatic requirements and the topography with Wright's spatial intentions and the dimensions of the structure (see Appendix 1). In the 1918 scheme, the third floor was devoted to Barnsdall's request for an experimental theater, which Wright labeled the Preparatory Theatre. The two-story space, square in plan, was devoted to the smaller theater on the lower level and, above, a balconied banquet hall with apartments to either side for Barnsdall and the manager (fig. 3-5).

In contrast to the complicated levels of the building's interior and the subtleties of its spatial relationships, the exterior was massive and one of the most monumental of Wright's career. It recalled two earlier buildings: one by Wright, his Oak Park Studio of 1898, and one by Louis Sullivan, the earlier Wainwright Tomb of 1892. Like the Oak Park Studio (fig. 3-16), the central mass of the build-

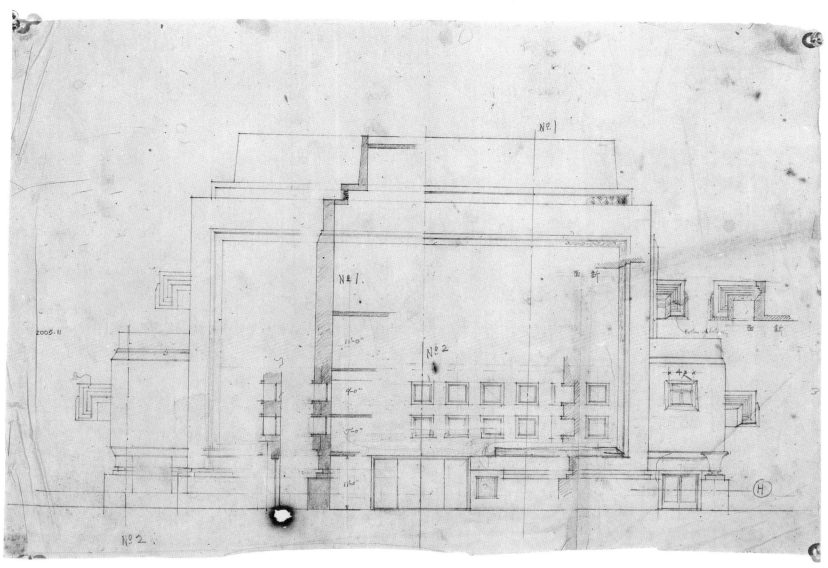

3-9. Barnsdall Theater II, circa 1918, rear elevation (courtesy of the Frank Lloyd Wright Foundation)

ing was a cube surmounted by an octagonal drum (fig. 3-14), lit by a clerestory, although only in the experimental theater. It is clear, as well, that Wright had the Wainwright Tomb in mind, especially when he began to address the composition of the surface and ornament. Sullivan's building, a solid cube capped by a semicircular dome, contrasted the planar surface with a rich band of ornament on all four sides (fig. 3-15). The ornament formed a continuous line following the upper edges of the cube and door frame. Although Wright increased the scale of the Wainwright Tomb to a five-story building, he used a similar treatment in contrasting the planar surface and the ornament, but subtle variations indicate Wright's quite different intentions. While Wright was interested in framing the major openings, he also was intent on dissolving the corners of his massive block. Using the bands of ornament much as he had used wood trim on the interior of Unity Temple, he emphasized the plasticity of his design by framing the building's corners, thereby denying their solidity. The other major similarity between the two buildings—the cubic mass topped by a geometric dome (Sullivan's is circular, Wright's octagonal)—is illuminating because it reveals the original source: as previous critics have pointed out, Sullivan based his design on the *qubba*, an Islamic tomb for a saint, often found in North Africa.[10]

After completing plans, a section, and several studies of the exterior, Wright apparently became concerned about whether either the theater or the house would proceed. Although his letter to Barnsdall, then living in Seattle with her baby, has been lost, her reply indicates he attempted to communicate his apprehension. He apparently warned her that he would need time to develop his design, and he also inquired about her seriousness about building. On May 30, 1918, she responded:

> I can't say anything more definite about the theatre at present—not until the estate is settled (fall) —then I am going to build it as soon as I can. You say you need time to work at it, so go ahead and please have the plans in such form so that we can go over them when I'm in Chicago the *last of June* and take them with me to go over again and again until I get the new forces of interior in *relation* to the work to be done in it. I will know when it can be built by the end of summer. The house I can build in the fall, if its [*sic*] cost is not over $25,000. You say "if you are in earnest." I think I've proven that by holding to the idea for so long. How can I be with no *real* money behind me just at present![11]

She revealed some of her vacillation and hesitancy when she explained:

> The baby is a problem. She must have her chance to grow up into a strong happy free minded young woman. This climate agrees with her—its [*sic*] wonderful how strong and [illegible word] she is growing—I may have to begin here instead of L.A. It makes no difference—"A thing of beauty is a joy anywhere." Seattle is virgin soil not spoilt by "art movements." I am [illegible word] here. I want to get the estate settled but they won't be ready before the last of June. Don't be afraid to let me have the plans. I won't let anybody see them if you don't wish it.[12]

By the summer of 1918, Wright was booking passage for Japan to begin construction of the Imperial Hotel that fall. Preparations were being made in Tokyo to begin clearing the site, with completion scheduled for two years later in 1920.

As the weeks drew closer to Wright's departure, Barnsdall wrote to him on October 8, 1918, about a site that she was considering in Los Angeles. She wanted to meet him to review the plans, but she did not know if she could get away. "It depends upon Sugar Top's nurse staying," Barnsdall wrote, "and she can't tell until about the 16th." Even if she would not be able to meet him, she wanted him to make the necessary arrangements. "I will give you a letter to my lawyer," she explained, "and between you you may be able to get permission to build, especially as I won't take the ranch if I can't build and the owner is a banker and should have some influence."[13]

3-10. Heinrich Tessenow with Adolphe Appia, Hall, Hellerau Institute, 1912–1913 (Richard C. Beacham, *Adolphe Appia, Theatre Artist*)

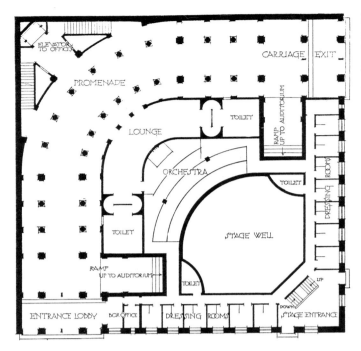

3-11. Norman Bel Geddes, Theatre #6, 1914–1915, first floor plan (*Architectural Record* 52, September 1922)

3-12. Norman Bel Geddes, Theatre #6, 1914–1915, auditorium plan (*Architectural Record* 52, September 1922)

There is no record of whether Wright and Barnsdall met in Los Angeles that fall. But presumably before Wright departed they agreed that a plaster model with removable sections revealing the interior of the theater would be built in Japan under his supervision (figs. 3-14 and 3-17).

During the next three years, Barnsdall never gave up her desire to build the theater; indeed, she continued to refer to it throughout the 1920s, but her priorities began to change and Wright's drawings never progressed past preliminary designs. Although she complained about the vagueness of the drawings, she did not seem to understand that Wright could not proceed with detailed working documents indicating materials, structure, and mechanical systems when she had not purchased a site or even decided on a city. Later, after she purchased property, her energies quickly shifted to the residential and commercial aspects of the general plan. As a result, one can only speculate on the materials Wright intended to use. The only published reference, which appeared in *The Western Architect* in April 1923, was to "concrete monolithic block," obviously reflecting Wright's concerns in 1923, but not contemporary with the design. The form of the building indicates poured-in-place concrete, probably of a character similar to that of Unity Temple.

As the theater began to assume a lesser place in Barnsdall's mind, her house took on greater importance. While the theater plans were being prepared in 1918, Wright was also proceeding with his design for Barnsdall's house.

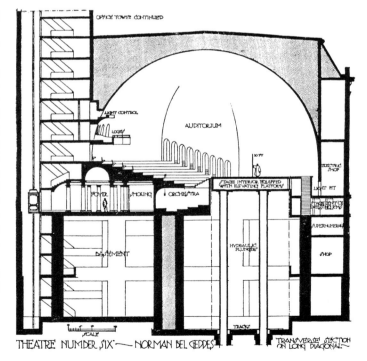

3-13. Norman Bel Geddes, Theatre #6, 1914–1915, section (*Architectural Record* 52, September 1922)

35

3-14. Barnsdall Theater II, circa 1918, exterior of model (Lloyd Wright Studio Archives). Although the model was broken in transit when Wright shipped it from Japan to California in September 1919, photographs, presumably taken in Japan, have survived. The ornamented crown was to be perforated, allowing light into the experimental theater.

3-15. Louis Sullivan, Wainwright Tomb, 1892 (photo by Richard Nickel, courtesy of the Richard Nickel Committee, Chicago, Illinois)

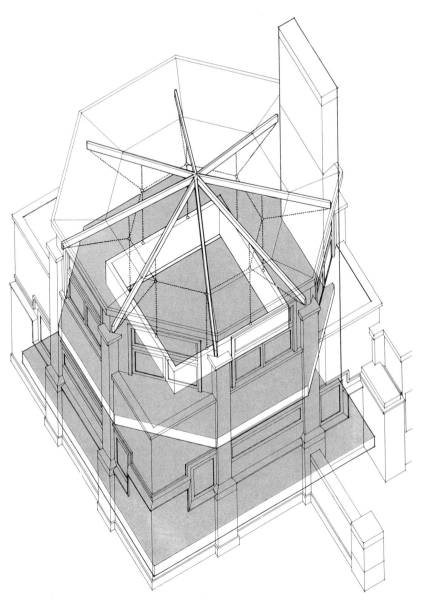

3-16. Axonometric of Oak Park Studio, 1898 (courtesy of Frank Lloyd Wright Home and Studio Foundation)

3-17. Barnsdall Theater II, 1918, interior of model (collection of the author). The top floors have been removed and the ceiling over the theater tilted up to reveal details of the stage and auditorium. View toward the hemicycle (cyclorama) with the octagonal screen in front of the musicians' gallery.

CHAPTER 4

BARNSDALL HOUSE / HOLLYHOCK HOUSE

4-1. Barnsdall House, circa 1916–1918, rendering (collection of the City of Los Angeles, Departments of Recreation and Parks and Cultural Affairs)

A few months after her arrival in California in 1916, Barnsdall had begun to think of building her own house. Originally, it was to have been an extension of her role as head of the Players Producing Company, and presumably Wright made sketches sometime that year.[1] In his published memoirs, Norman Bel Geddes recalled two meetings when the design of Barnsdall's house was discussed, one in the summer of 1916 in Chicago and one in the fall in Los Angeles.[2] But after disbanding her troupe, and with the birth of her baby in 1917, Barnsdall's priorities had begun to change. Although she continued to discuss building the theater, what she really needed was a place to raise her daughter. Wright was undoubtedly reluctant to design a house without at least seeing the site or receiving a topographical map of the land. However, over a two-year period between 1916 and 1918, he produced a general scheme for the house, which he refined after she acquired her property and during construction.

Reconstruction of the design development of the house is limited by the fact that so few drawings from this period have survived. It is inconceivable that Wright would have proceeded without executing plans and sections; however, none have survived to record the evolution. It is only possible with the remaining drawings—elevations and perspectives—to speculate how far the design had advanced by the time of Wright's departure for Japan in October 1918. It is clear that the floor plans, general massing, and relationship of the interior to the exterior, including the gardens and potential views, were all determined before Barnsdall purchased a site.

Antonin Raymond remembered drawings of the house in the Taliesin studio during the spring and summer of 1916. The earliest phase of the design, recorded in three development drawings identical in size and format and remarkable in revealing the origins of Wright's idea, may date from this period. The elevations depict a building organized around an interior garden court, with a central axis bisecting the living room, and two minor axes crossing at the front and rear with two auxiliary wings joining the axes at a ninety-degree angle. Wright's first concept (fig. 4-2) depicted a late Prairie house reminiscent of the unsupervised 1915 E.D. Brigham House in Glencoe, Illinois (fig. 4-5). The central section of a two-story living room consisted of a band of first-floor windows surmounted by an ornamental frieze. This central section was flanked by vertical strip windows, each one set between a narrow and a solid corner pier; overall was a red-tile hip roof. But Wright was no longer satisfied with the Prairie house grammar; he focused his attack on the terminals. In the next scheme (fig. 4-3) the hip roof was replaced by an extension of the ornamental frieze as a wide band above the wall

4-2. Barnsdall House, circa 1916–1918, front elevation (collection of the City of Los Angeles, Departments of Recreation and Parks and Cultural Affairs)

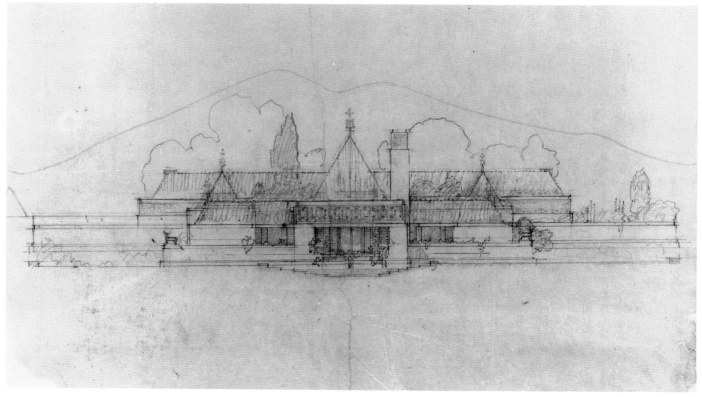

4-3. Barnsdall House, circa 1916–1918, front elevation (collection of the City of Los Angeles, Departments of Recreation and Parks and Cultural Affairs)

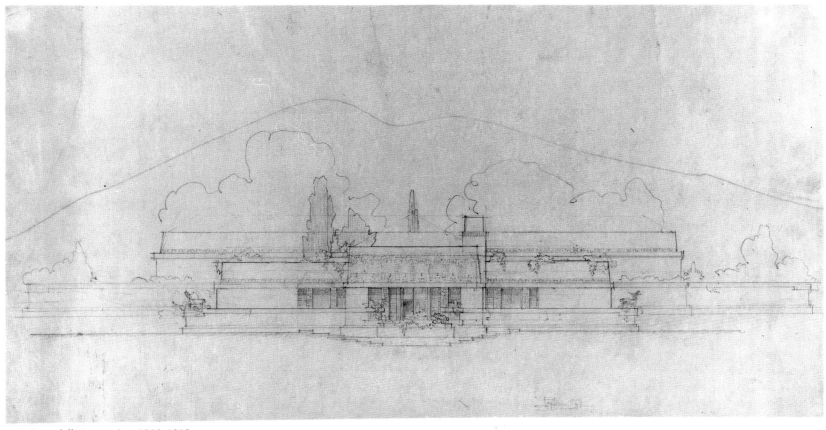

4-4. Barnsdall House, circa 1916–1918, front elevation (collection of the City of Los Angeles, Departments of Recreation and Parks and Cultural Affairs)

plane and a high-pitched roof set within the walls. Finally (fig. 4-4), Wright dispensed with the roof altogether, and canted and heightened the frieze, creating an attic story. The movement from the alternating planes of solid and void in the Prairie house to the hollowed mass of Wright's houses of the 1920s was bridged in the three preliminary drawings. Despite the evolution these drawings reveal— from the articulation of the Prairie house to the more plastic character of poured concrete— there is no evidence to either prove or disprove that the form followed from Wright's choice of material and structure.

What does seem certain is that pre-Columbian elements, which appeared in details of Wright's houses as early as 1893, had become the major reference for the exterior massing. After the building of Taliesin, pre-Columbian elements began to appear with greater frequency until 1915, when Wright recalled the Temple of the Three Lintels at Chichen Itza in the elevation of the A.D. German Warehouse in Richland Center, Wisconsin. Although historical revival styles for residential and public buildings had been popular since the turn of the century, Wright's use of pre-Columbian motifs was more profound than a nostalgic evocation of an exotic past. The profile of the Barnsdall House is massive, with a weight and monumentality that evokes a deeper connection to the solidity of the earth than the earlier Prairie houses. Many years later, Wright explained the relationship between his philosophy of organic architecture and the buildings of the Toltec, Aztec, Mayan, and Inca:

4-5. E.D. Brigham House, 1915, unsupervised, Glencoe, Illinois (photo by Thomas A. Heinz)

41

4-6. Barnsdall House, circa 1916–1918, rendering (courtesy of the Frank Lloyd Wright Foundation)

4-7. Barnsdall House, circa 1916–1918, rendering (courtesy of the Frank Lloyd Wright Foundation)

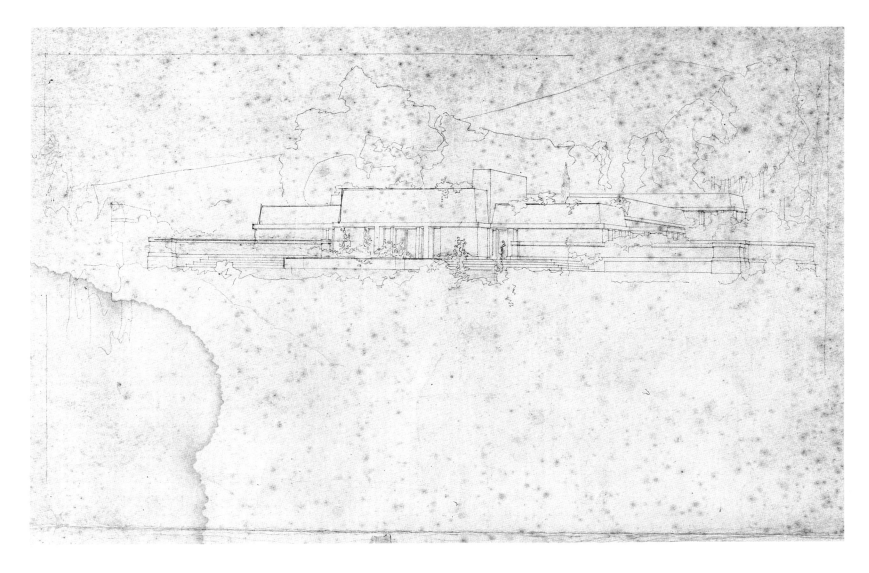

Those great American abstractions were all earth-architectures: gigantic masses of masonry raised up on great stone-paved terrain, all planned as one mountain, one vast plateau lying there or made into great mountain ranges themselves; those vast areas of paved earth walled in by stone construction. These were human creations, cosmic as sun, moon, and stars! Nature? Yes, but the nature of the human being as he was, then. *Entity even more cosmic* had not yet been born.[3]

A clue to Wright's intention to create an architectural reference to a symbolic mountain can be found in all the drawings made for Barnsdall before her acquisition of a site. Wright placed the building, theoretically designed for a flat lot, in an imaginary setting on axis with the base of a gently sloping mountain. In so doing, he recalled the work of Hokusai, one of his favorite Japanese printmakers, in his famous *Thirty-six Views of Fuji*. Although Wright conceived of the Barnsdall House as a Mayan mountain, it is probable that he was also recalling his impressions of Mount Fuji:

From infancy, a sort of subjective contemplation, the minds and hearts of the Japanese are fixed upon the great calm mountain God of their nation—the sacred Fujiyama brooding in majesty and eternal calm over all. They deeply worship as the mountain continually changes moods, combining with sun and moon, clouds and mist in a vast expression of elemental beauty the like of which in dignity and repose exists nowhere else on earth.[4]

Many years later, Schindler remarked, "Although [designed] in a very interesting and personal language..., [the Barnsdall buildings were] trying to give themselves local roots by the introduction of Mayan motifs."[5] Schindler's suggestion that Wright's use of Mayan elements was intended as a contextual response to the culture and climate of Los Angeles has been repeated often. There are several reasons why it is necessary to probe deeper for a more satisfactory explanation. First, Wright used the same imagery in many locales: for the German Warehouse and the Phi Gamma Delta Fraternity, both in Wisconsin; for parts of the Imperial Hotel in Japan (inspiring the legend that Wright originally created the design for a hotel in Mexico City); for the Yamamura House in Japan; and for parts of Taliesin West and the Pauson House in Arizona. Second, when Wright made the drawings, Barnsdall had not chosen Los Angeles as the location. Al-

4-8. Barnsdall House, circa 1916–1918, rendering (collection of the City of Los Angeles, Departments of Recreation and Parks and Cultural Affairs)

though he had some reason to believe she would probably live in California, her first preference was San Francisco, and for a time she considered Seattle.

It is more probable that the choice was determined by formal and symbolic considerations. Based on European and non-Western models, Wright had created a new style during the Oak Park period that developed not toward nature, but into a decorative suburban type. Later rejecting the city and ultimately suburbia, Wright sought a more expressive architecture. In the decades of the teens and twenties, he took the risk of creating a series of unresolved compositions to move beyond the convention of the Prairie house toward a greater evocation of nature. Formally, the change was parallel with the movement from decoration to geometric abstraction in his ornament and from the locally referential to the universal in metaphor. To Wright, the Mayan temple represented a symbolic mountain, and in Oriental art, mountains are perceived as cosmic pillars, shafts connecting heaven and earth. It is likely that Wright was searching for a metaphor for this vital connection between the dualities of nature.

The next series of drawings showed how advanced the scheme became before Barnsdall purchased property. The first two renderings revealed a building that was close to the design as built (figs. 4-6 and 4-7), a U-shaped plan terminating at the rear with a bridge wing. Seen from the front, the building appeared to rest on a raised platform that served as a spacious flagstone terrace, accessible from the living room through a pair of french doors. Details such as a trellised pergola, two glass-enclosed rooms, and pools at the front, rear, and side were clearly visible. A three-car garage terminated a long wall at the side. At this point, the centrally placed living room was wider than it was long, and the scale indicated a low building that seemed to hug the ground.

Wright's celebration of the expressive space of the Prairie house had evolved into an interest in a smooth wall plane punctuated by deep openings for windows and doors. Some years later, he wrote that he felt the silhouette of the Barnsdall House represented a type "adaptable to California conditions," and that type was to be made from concrete.[6] Although he used a contextual argument to rationalize his form, he accomplished the same results with other materials in other regions. Thus, for all of Wright's later allusions to technological experimentation, the Barnsdall House was as much dedicated to traditional architectural values as it was informed by modernist idealism. And if it is accurate to say that

4-9. Barnsdall House, circa 1916–1918, side elevation (collection of the City of Los Angeles, Departments of Recreation and Parks and Cultural Affairs)

his original intention was to use concrete, then the only reference to cost—made in May 1918 when Barnsdall wrote her architect that she could build the house by the fall if the figure did not exceed $25,000—seems ominous.

The next drawing in the sequence revealed two significant changes (fig. 4-1). The living room was extended forward to meet the flower box overlooking the front pool. Access to the terrace was moved to the sides, and small staircases led up to tiled roof terraces above the living room and one wing. The last two surviving drawings, a perspective and a side elevation (figs. 4-8 and 4-9), show the building as it was later rendered in working drawings, with the exception of several changes that were made to accommodate it to the eventual site.

No doubt by the spring of 1919, Wright wondered if Barnsdall would ever commit herself by purchasing land, but on reaching Tokyo, he became totally absorbed in his work in Japan. By the time T.N. Barnsdall's estate was settled, Wright's mind was on the construction of the Imperial Hotel and his own per-

sonal affairs. "I have been much occupied," he wrote Louis Sullivan, "nearly every moment. When not engaged in preparations for building, all Japan seems [to be] hunting me up with the enticing 'Nishikiye' [literally, "brocade pictures," or full-color woodblock prints] which are a pursuit in themselves absorbing and financially devastating."[7] Finally, in the early summer of 1919, beset by problems—the construction of the hotel's foundations seriously behind schedule, his relationship with Miriam Noel in an explosive stage, and on the verge of illness, Wright received word that Barnsdall had at last purchased property. But when he asked his Chicago office to send him a set of the drawings for Barnsdall's house, Schindler replied that they had none, adding that he assumed Barnsdall had taken them all.[8]

Wright had been out of the country for over eight months and Barnsdall was, no doubt, anxious to meet with him. When she was informed that he was not returning immediately, she made plans to sail for Japan.[9]

East Hollywood looking southeast toward Hollywood Boulevard, circa 1901 (courtesy of California Historical Society/Ticor Title Insurance, Los Angeles, Department of Special Collections, University of Southern California Library, negative #6558). Olive Hill can be seen near the horizon at the extreme right.

PART TWO

OLIVE HILL GENERAL PLAN I 1919

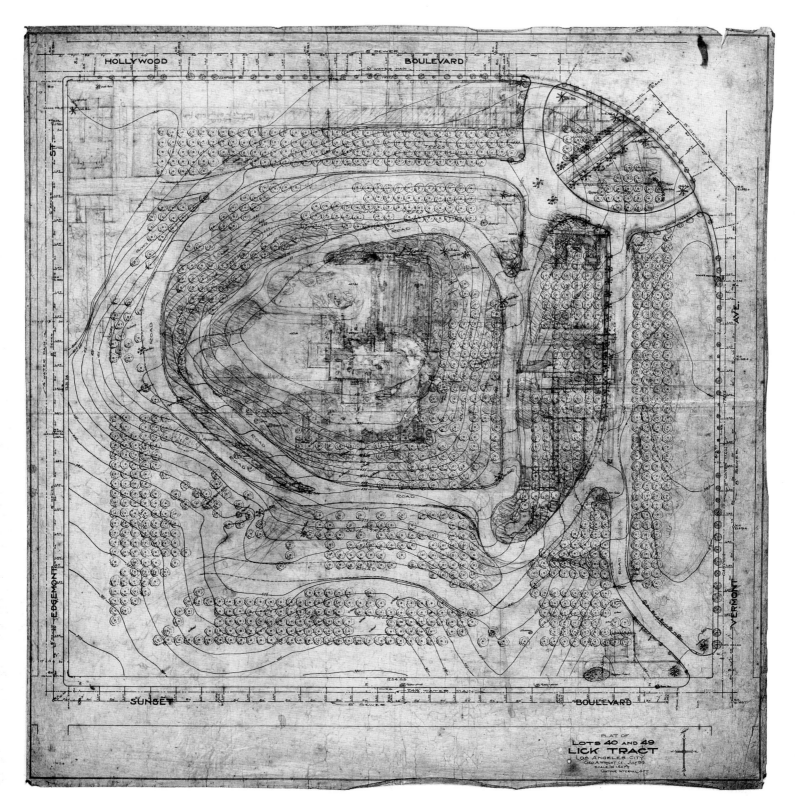

48

CHAPTER 5

OLIVE HILL GENERAL PLAN I

CL (CENTER LINE)
↓

→
MAJOR AXIS

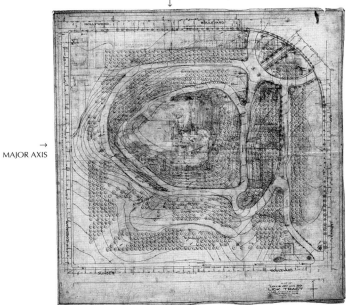

5-1, 5-2. Topographical map of Olive Hill, July 1919 (courtesy of the Frank Lloyd Wright Foundation). Wright's first scheme in 1919 was drawn in graphite pencil over this survey; the stream was colored blue. In 1920, he returned to this drawing to sketch in the buildings that were added along Hollywood Boulevard as well as Residences A and B, to the northeast and west of Hollyhock House, respectively. Arrows indicate Wright's major axis and center line of Berendo Street.

By the beginning of summer 1919, Aline Barnsdall was ready and eager to build. Despite the doubts and reservations she had expressed in the past about the size and cost of her building projects, the California site she purchased (a thirty-six-acre plot) far exceeded anything that she and Wright had initially discussed. Olive Hill, as it was known locally, was a prominent geographical feature on the sprawling plain of the rapidly developing town of Hollywood. From the base of the Hollywood Hills, the orthogonal grid of one-story bungalows and two-story shops extended south until it met a gradual slope that rose ninety-five feet above street level. In the 1890s, this undivided tract of land had been laid out with dirt roads and planted with an orchard of olive trees, an exotic plant originally imported from the Mediterranean by missionaries (fig. 5-1). Noted for its spectacular views of the Pacific Ocean to the southwest and the emerging downtown of Los Angeles to the east, it was a conspicuous landmark in the community, inspiring speculation that it might become a public park. In fact, Easter sunrise services had been held there annually for several years before Barnsdall acquired it. Despite the local interest, Olive Hill was far enough from downtown Los Angeles and, more important, from the growing business center of Hollywood, to inspire doubt about whether it would make a successful location for a public building. It had been for sale at $10,000 an acre for several years, but it was not until Barnsdall made an offer of $300,000 ($8,330 an acre) in cash that the property was sold.[1]

Although Barnsdall was no doubt frustrated by Wright's absence and the lack of working drawings that would have allowed her to proceed, the delay gave her an opportunity to contemplate her property and create her own vision. A few days after the deed was recorded, Barnsdall disclosed her plans to the newspapers. She had never before discussed building more than the theater and her own house, but she now revealed that, in addition to those two buildings, she planned to erect apartment buildings, houses, and cottages. Apparently, the size of her property and the real estate potential of the area encouraged her to expand her scheme. She did not announce how many additional buildings there would be or where they would go, but she had decided that the theater would be located on the east slope facing the street and her house would be placed on the crown of the hill. She disclosed that her architect was Wright and that complete plans for the theater and her house had not been developed because the site had only recently been purchased, but she did unveil drawings for the house. The *Los Angeles Express* characterized it as "modernized Aztec style, as near as it can be described."[2] When questioned about the style of the remaining buildings,

Barnsdall responded, "Why not leave that all to the individual judgement of the architect when he sees the land—why shouldn't Mr. Wright evoke a new type of architecture peculiarly fitted to Southern California without borrowing from any other country?"[3]

The newspapers reported that Barnsdall was aware of the local interest in Olive Hill. "Mr. Wright believes that a California house should be half house and half garden," she was quoted as saying, "and I am strongly of the same opinion. I, therefore, require much room for my own home, but I propose to keep my gardens always open to the public that this sightly spot may be available to those lovers of the beautiful who wish to come here to view sunsets, dawn on the mountains, and other spectacles of nature, visible in few other places in the heart of the city."[4] In a rare display of public self-revelation, Barnsdall provided insight into the deeper conflicts behind her actions:

> I don't want to do it. I know it will take time, agony of spirit and all that liberty which my gypsy soul adores, but it is something I simply have to do. Whether it's a success or a failure, the responsibility of the effort lies with me, and cannot be evaded. Personally, I prefer to vagabond through the world amusing myself with my friends, my studies and my love for the out of doors. I have struggled with this inborn conviction without avail. I seem forced to try, at least, to create a domicile fitting for the art which is, I believe, destined to help form the taste and ideals of the world, and I shall put every ounce of energy and experience and thought I have in the doing.[5]

Barnsdall had made plans to sail to Japan immediately to meet with Wright and to return with him in September. It is doubtful that she made this trip, however, for in the next few weeks she commissioned Walker and Eisen, a prominent local architectural firm, to design a house for Olive Hill. Undoubtedly her growing irritation at Wright's absence motivated her to contemplate another choice of architect. The drawings, dated August 15, 1919, proposed a one-story house in the Spanish Colonial Revival style with a concrete foundation, hollow tile walls, plaster exterior, and tile roof. The five-bedroom, three-and-a-half-bath house was estimated to cost $300,000.[6] Whether Barnsdall was influenced by the estimate, or by the news that Wright had taken ill in Japan in late July and early August but was making plans to return to the United States with a model of the theater, she did not carry through with the Walker and Eisen design.

Wright had been out of the country for ten months, and when his ship docked in Seattle in early September 1919 he did not go directly to Taliesin. Instead, he made plans to meet Barnsdall in Los Angeles.

By the fall of 1919, Wright's practice was concentrated in Japan. The Imperial Hotel was scheduled to open in a little over a year, but the foundations were still being dug. The ambitious nature of his design, together with the difficulty of introducing the Japanese to modern materials and methods, was prolonging construction and necessitating his close supervision on the site. The delays were contributing to Wright's precarious financial situation. As a result, he had begun to buy Oriental art, primarily Japanese woodblock prints, with the prospect of selling to collectors or museums on his return to the United States. "I tried to increase my fee," Wright explained to his friend, Darwin Martin, "by mixing my brains with my money, buying things I knew the quality and value of—cheap—hoping to realize a good profit on them when I came back."[7] But eager as he was to go east to sell prints, Wright was aware that his practice in the United States had dwindled to almost nothing and for that reason alone, Barnsdall was an important client whom he could not afford to disappoint.

Wright's visit to Olive Hill may not have been his first. Toward the end of his life, he told Lloyd Wright that Barnsdall had acquired Olive Hill on his advice.[8] It is possible that this was the site she had asked him to see in the fall of 1918.

5-3. Olive Hill crown looking north toward the Hollywood Hills, 1919 (courtesy of Michael Devine)

5-4. Olive Hill, looking up Berendo Street toward the Hollywood Hills, 1926 (courtesy of California Historical Society/Ticor Title Insurance, Los Angeles, Department of Special Collections, University of Southern California Library, negative #6575).

But now, a year later, she explained her vision for the hill, her ideas for the location of the theater and her house, and her plans for new buildings. She outlined a program that amounted to zoning her site for both public and private use. In addition to the theater and her own house at the top of the hill, she was requesting a furnished house for the yet unnamed director of the company and an apartment building to house the actors and provide a source of income. The cost for all four buildings, including the landscaping and Wright's fee, was not to exceed $375,000, only $75,000 over Walker and Eisen's estimate for one house alone.[9]

Progress on the design of the theater was delayed when the plaster model (figs. 3-14 and 3-17) that Wright had ordered in Japan was broken in transit to the United States. Wright proposed having another made on his return to Tokyo, but Barnsdall urged him to have it done in Los Angeles before he departed again in December. Barnsdall's attention then shifted to her house and the general plan for Olive Hill. She made it clear that she wanted to choose the colors and finishes for her house so they would harmonize with her favorite furniture and rugs. Before Wright left for Wisconsin, they agreed to put these points into a written contract. Barnsdall remembered later that Wright promised her color drawings of the interior elevations of her house and the master plan, "dozens of them," by the end of October if she came out to Taliesin.[10]

Wright must have been surprised to learn that a few days later, Barnsdall was off to San Francisco trying to get a reservation on a ship leaving for the Pacific. When her only hope was a cancellation, she explained to him in a letter dated September 24, 1919:

I so need to get away—new countries always freshen my mind and renew me. If I can't do this, I'll come east the middle of October and go over everything with you.

I had to get away to think and then it was very clear to me that to have a new model made in Japan [is] extravagant of money and time. I can't wait.

If I have to wait much longer I'll give it up—I will pay for the model and use it to get the idea and for exhibition purposes. Why two models when any five hundred dollars means so much? The man said he could construct it from plans and with your help in December he can have it finished before you leave. As this was the projection of an idea as well as a building I considered the model as a part of the "preliminaries" and I could not accept or reject the idea until I had seen the model. If the new model is started by the end of October—it will be finished by the end of December and I can have it with me for a month or six weeks before I sail.

I read the contract...will you object to my changing the payment of the last 2 1/2% to when the buildings are completed and ready for occupancy? That was the first form you gave me and it is more clear cut than "the balance in installments as the work progresses as certified by the architect."[11]

Barnsdall offered Wright the use of the Director's House until the theater was finished and asked him if he would write an article explaining his "organic idea with illustrations of its practical expression" that could be sold at the theater as a souvenir. In a more introspective mood, she continued: "I don't know what I am going to do about Sugar Top. I don't do anything but feel responsible hence worry about the socks, ankles and sniffy colds—when I'm with her, I'm good for nothing. The minute I get away I forget her existence and I think of nothing but the theatre. The delays fill me with forebodings—"[12]

The events of the next few months added to the growing tension between Barnsdall and Wright as they both traveled around the country. Weeks went by before Wright began to work on her plans. First, he was off to New York to sell Japanese prints and to rehire Antonin Raymond to return with him to Japan. He hoped Raymond would return to Taliesin in time to execute Barnsdall's drawings. Her concern began to show when she wrote him from Scottsdale, Arizona, that she was turning over the details of their contract to her business manager,

51

5-5. Diagram of existing conditions, Olive Hill, before Wright's 1919 plan (drawing by Eulogio Guzman). Wright both adhered to and ignored the natural and preexisting features of the site. When the area was subdivided by city streets, the natural hill created an almost perfectly square superblock; the grove roads were laid out in order to plant and tend the olive trees. A dot (•) indicates those trees that Wright retained in his plan and a dash (–) indicates those that he planned to remove.

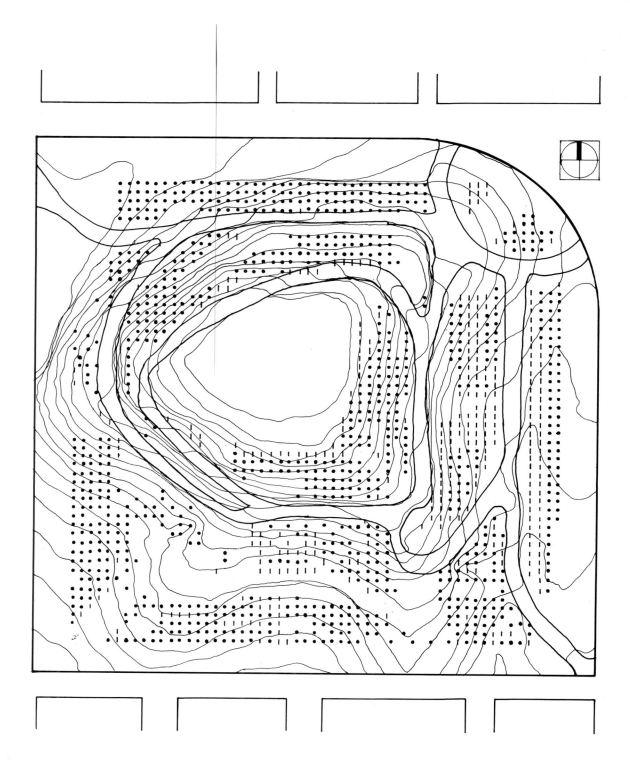

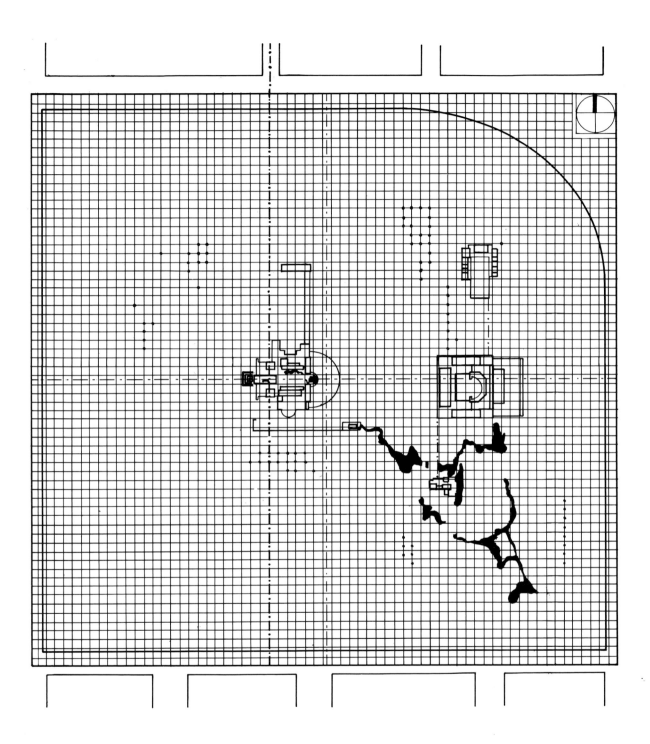

5-6. Diagram of Wright's plan of Olive Hill, 1919 (drawing by Eulogio Guzman). Wright based his twenty-foot planning grid on the grid of olive trees. However, the olive grove was not planted precisely in some areas, varying from eighteen to twenty feet on center. In Wright's drawing the grove became more standardized to the planning grid. The longitudinal axis of Hollyhock House was placed on the major east-west axis of Olive Hill, with the minor axis through the public rooms (music room, living room, and library) on the center line of Berendo Street extending north to the Hollywood Hills. The general plan of the buildings was based on the theater as the center of rotation, creating a pinwheel of three spokes radiating to the south (Director's House), west (Barnsdall House) and north (Actors Abode). The watercourse was laid out in response to the topography. A dot (•) indicates olive trees that Wright planned to add to the site.

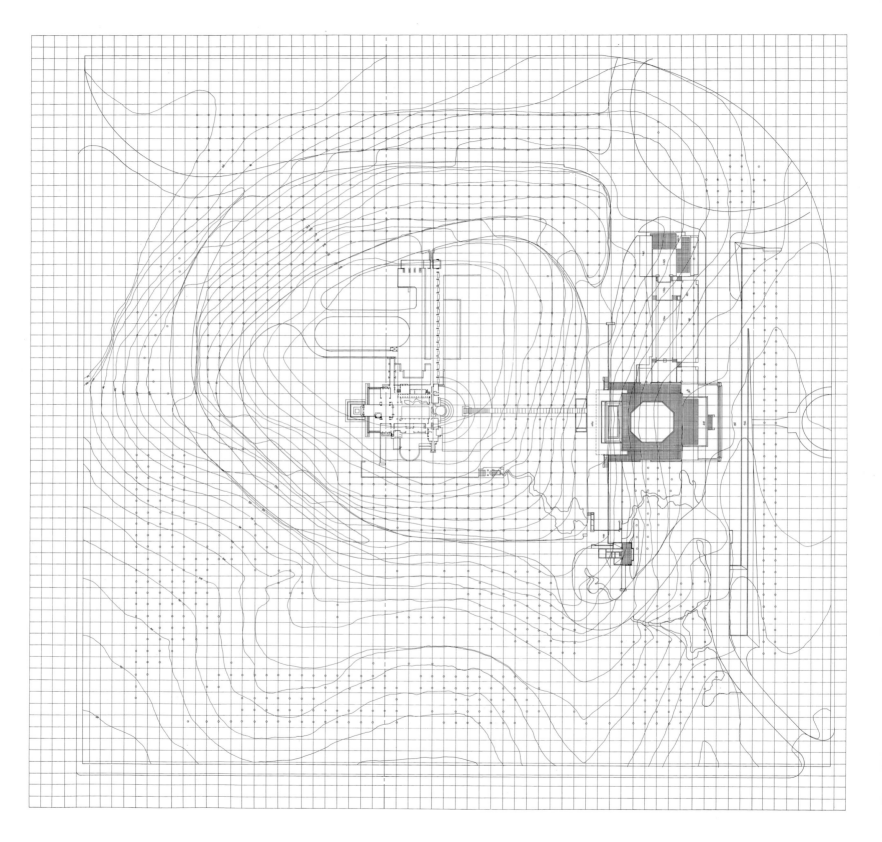

5-7. Olive Hill general
plan I, 1919 (redrawn by
Eulogio Guzman). With
the theater on the right,
north is at the top of the
sheet. The original draw-
ing has been lost. This is
a reproduction of
Wright's drawing based
on a blueprint that
survived (fig. 5-8).

5-8. Olive Hill general
plan I, 1919, blueprint
(courtesy of the Frank
Lloyd Wright
Foundation). The 1920
Water plan was later
redrawn over this
blueprint in red and
yellow pencil.

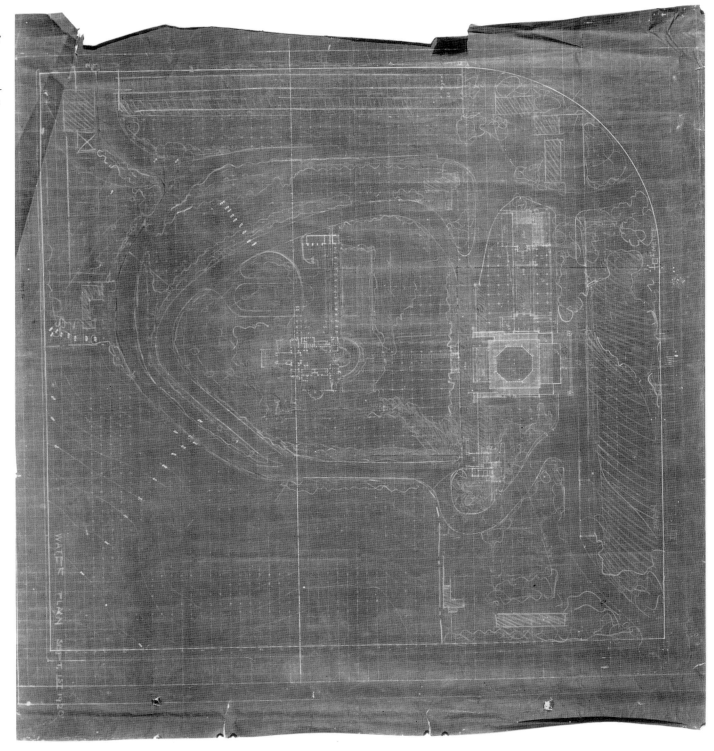

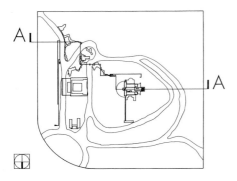

1. Waterfall
2. Director's House
3. Stream
4. Waterfall
5. Spring House
6. Pool
7. Hollyhock House
8. Pool

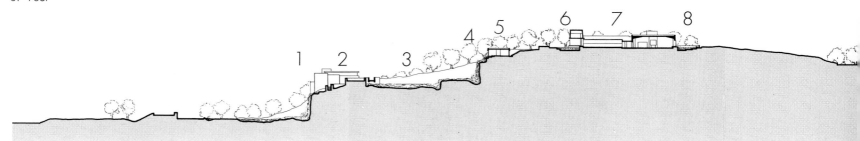

Clarence Thomas. "It is simpler for you and him to discuss the interpretation of the contract than for you and me," she proposed. "We have something too wonderful to get done to waste time and jeopardize it in discussion." Her impatience to see progress was evident when she spoke of the theater: "I want to be here to see the model grow. I want to see the dressing room portion before it is covered. Seeing just a portion of the broken model stimulated me to work out a plan that will prove quite fascinating and original and handle a difficult problem. I'm beginning to see people walking about in it. I want to see more and more of it."[13]

By October 3, back in Los Angeles, she cabled him inquiring when the drawings would be ready. Almost three weeks later (about October 23) shortly after Wright had returned to Taliesin from New York, Barnsdall arrived in Chicago. Wright explained that Raymond was not there yet and the drawings were not ready. He persuaded her to return in November, but her irritation was evident when she replied that she would "rather waste time in [New York] than Chicago."[14] The next day, October 24, Wright and Schindler caught a train heading for Taliesin.[15] With his departure for Japan less than two months away, Wright had little time to design two new buildings, redesign the theater and house for

the hillside conditions, push the master plan and all four buildings through working drawings, and prepare for construction in an unfamiliar locale.

Although Wright was probably as exasperated with Barnsdall as she was with him, he must have been inspired by the site. Olive Hill, with its gently rising slopes, groves of trees, and rural character, was the type of natural setting that was sympathetic to his ideas about man and nature. The hill was reminiscent of his reference to a symbolic mountain in the massing of her house, as well as of the promontories that had appeared in the background of his earlier renderings; and at times, he was reminded of the site of Taliesin.

Olive Hill was almost a perfect square—1,231.28 feet running north-south parallel with Vermont Avenue and Edgemont Street; 1,254.55 feet on the east-west axis parallel with Hollywood and Sunset Boulevards (fig. 5-5). The groves of olive trees were planted in rows that varied from eighteen to twenty feet on center, forming an abstract orthogonal grid over the irregular topography. Two primary entrances, from the northeast and southeast corners, led in to grove roads that encircled the hill in gentle curves.

Sketching in pencil over the topographical map, Wright began his plan by complying with his client's request to place her house on the crown of the hill

5-9. Olive Hill general plan I,
1919, section
(drawing by Eulogio Guzman)

in the one flat area on the site (fig. 5-2). First, he bisected the square by drawing a major axis along the east-west line. With the living room facing west, Wright placed the longitudinal edge of the house along this axis. He then placed a cross axis through the living room wing on the center line of Berendo Street, noting simply "CL" (center line) in pencil at the top of the sheet. Although it was not indicated on the drawing, this axis provided a direct line of sight to a peak of the Hollywood Hills to the north (figs. 5-3 and 5-4). After establishing these two coordinates, he located the theater on axis with Barnsdall's house at the base of the hill facing east toward Vermont Avenue. The Director's House was placed to the south of the theater, projecting forward on line with the theater's western edge. The Actors Abode, as the apartment house was designated, was placed forward of the theater at the eastern edge. The pinwheel geometry used the center of the theater's cubic mass as the point of rotation, with the three buildings extending to the south, west, and north around it.

Dissatisfied with details of this scheme, Wright struggled through several erasures before he determined the final organization. He shifted Barnsdall's house twice until its major longitudinal axis was on line with the major axis of the site.

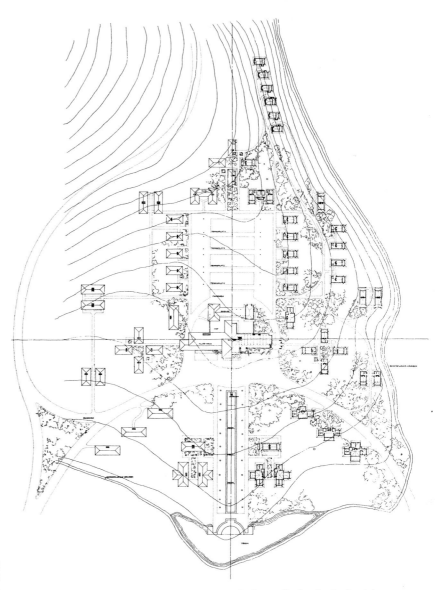

5-10. Como Orchards, Darby, Montana,
1908 (*Ausgeführte Bauten und Entwürfe*,
Wasmuth, 1910, pl. 46)

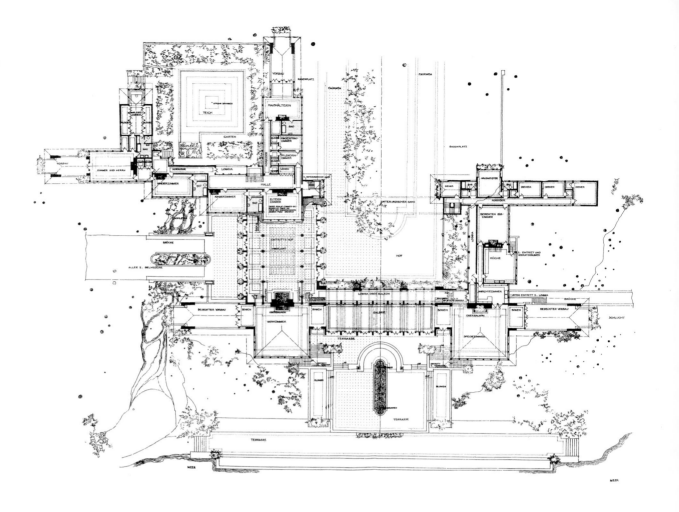

This movement put the center point of the rear circular pool within a few feet of the center of the site (fig. 5-6), but it meant abandoning the idea of placing the entire building on a flat pad; one wing now straddled the southern slope.

In contrast to this dynamic orthogonal geometry, Wright, responding to the topography, introduced a man-made watercourse that took the form of a meandering natural stream forming waterfalls and ponds as it cascaded down the slope and met flat ground. Flowing from northwest to southeast, the stream originated at a Spring House at the southeast corner of the retaining wall of Barnsdall's house, then wound its way south of the Director's House, where it flowed into a pond before it was channeled under the road to emerge at the steepest drop on the site. From there, a waterfall tumbled down the hill and was split by an island, creating two branches of the stream.

When the plan was laid out at a scale of one inch to forty feet (on a drawing that has survived only in blueprint, figs. 5-7 and 5-8), Wright used a twenty-foot square grid, coinciding exactly with the grid of the olive grove near the hilltop, but deviating from it on the periphery. The major axis of Barnsdall's house lay directly on the east-west axis of the square site as Wright had finally determined it on the topographical map. On this drawing (figs. 5-7 and 5-8), Wright indicated only one definite axis, the north-south one, which extended through the living room wing of the house. This clear line of sight led to the crest of a hill, as he had imagined it in his preliminary drawings, and strongly suggests that Wright intended all three of these rooms to be free of walls or full-height partitions.[16]

Yet the drawing clearly indicates a partition wall between the library and the living room. It is possible that Barnsdall insisted on this wall to ensure quiet and privacy for her study. The theater is now pushed off axis, one bay to the south, reinforcing the original pinwheel geometry of the first sketch, which remains the organizational principle unifying the community (fig. 5-6).

Further unifying the two zones, public and private, Wright moved the course of the stream north between the theater and the Director's House, creating a dramatic two-tiered waterfall entrance to the latter building (figs. 5-6 and 5-9). Recognizing the director's importance to the theater community, Wright also placed a reflecting pond directly in front of the building where it would be visible from the road. With this change, however, the stream no longer fed into the steep waterfall at the southeast corner, the one feature that took maximum advantage of the contours of the site. Leaving the waterfall in isolation, a remnant of the original idea remained unresolved.

With the Olive Hill scheme, Wright introduced water as a major expressive and symbolic element of his plan. Although he had used pools and fountains before 1919, the fireplace, symbolizing the familial gathering place, had been the expressive element of the Prairie house; the water features were primarily decorative. But beginning in 1908, as Wright began to outgrow the limitations of the suburban single family residence, he sought to create a more universal expression of the relationship between architecture and nature. All of the water features of Olive Hill had appeared in earlier Wright schemes, such as University

5-12. Harold McCormick House, rendering, 1908 (*Ausgeführte Bauten und Entwürfe*, Wasmuth, 1910, pl. 59)

Heights at Como Orchards near Darby, Montana, and the Harold C. McCormick House, both 1908; and Taliesin, 1911–1914. At Olive Hill, however, he combined them in new ways, creating a powerful synthesis.

All three of these earlier projects have in common the integration of buildings and water elements, both natural and man-made, but at University Heights and Taliesin, Wright was also addressing the idea of community. University Heights, located on a gently sloping site with views over hundreds of acres of apple orchards to Lake Como and the Sapphire Mountains, was a summer vacation retreat for professors from the University of Chicago.[17] Like his Olive Hill plan, Wright's plan for University Heights superimposed a formal axial scheme, with a central clubhouse and cabins symmetrically placed to either side, over the irregular contours of the hill (fig. 5-10). To integrate the buildings with the landscape, Wright had placed on axis a long, rectangular, cascading pool that flowed into the irrigation pond created by the canals encircling the site. Yet the two poles, architecture and nature, remained unconnected, and the sense of community was expressed by the order of classical planning.

With the Harold C. McCormick House on a bluff overlooking Lake Michigan in Lake Forest, Illinois (figs. 5-11 and 5-12), Wright had faced similar problems, but his solution was different. The plan's orthogonal geometry, with primary and secondary U-shaped courtyards, combined with the massing of the lakefront elevation to create order and to provide integration with the natural site. To further reinforce this theme, Wright had visually and symbolically connected the building and the landscape with water. From a square pool in the smaller courtyard, water spilled over an outlet and down a natural ravine into the lake below. The sight and sound of the water could be experienced more immediately through an opening in a bridge connecting the entrance hall with the bluff opposite the ravine.

Turning away from suburbia and toward nature, Wright had found that water, like no other element, isolated the opposite poles he was struggling with and attempting to reconcile. Water, because it takes the form of its container, can assume either a geometric shape or it can be free-form, as in nature, becoming the conduit of *dual* meaning. Reacting to gravity, on a flat plane, it can be still; or in a line, it can ripple and move; from a height, it picks up speed and falls with a rush of energy. Water is essential for life, and it connects the earth with the heavens through evaporation and precipitation. In the McCormick House, Wright had used the metaphor of water to juxtapose pairs of complementary opposites: the house and the lake, geometry and natural forms, architecture and nature. And with the introduction of the stream, the unifying element, the two were reconciled.

In 1910, Wright had left suburbia for good by building a new house, studio, and farm in the valley of his maternal family in rural Wisconsin. The Lloyd-Jones Valley, the site of Taliesin and its surroundings, shared much in common with Olive Hill: a hilltop site, groves of trees, fields in orthogonal grids, and farm roads that conformed to the terrain (fig. 5-13). The valley was also a community containing the original homesteads of his grandparents, uncles, and aunts; his sister's country house, Tan-y-deri; Unity Chapel, the family chapel and graveyard; the boarding school operated by two of his aunts, Hillside Home School; and the adjoining windmill, Romeo and Juliet (fig. 5-14). The major difference was that water was naturally present at the base of the Taliesin hill in the form of a spring-fed stream that wound its way through the valley until it met the Wisconsin River to the north. Originating at his Uncle Thomas's farm just above his grandfather's house, the stream flowed nearby each of these sites, visually connecting them. It was the unifying topographical feature in the valley and an important metaphor for the family community.

In every aspect of the design of Taliesin—its siting, materials, colors, and textures—Wright had responded to the natural elements of the surrounding landscape in a way that surpassed any building he had designed up to that point in his career. The Taliesin legend is a tale of the birth of a poetic voice, and it was no coincidence that Wright chose it to symbolize his new life. Signifying a rebirth, Wright's Taliesin seemed to emerge from the hill in the same way that the head of the mythical Welsh poet appeared from the leather bag that concealed his infant body.[18] Nature provided the poetic elements in the Lloyd-Jones Valley, and Wright merely played upon them.

The one alteration that Wright had made to the natural waterway at Taliesin, in 1911, was the construction of a dam at the base of the hill below his house, which created two important water features—a waterfall and a pond.[19] The dam was a continuation of the wall that formed the entrance gate to the property, and, as a result, the waterfall and the flat surface of the pond mirroring the house above were the first glimpses of Taliesin the visitor received.

All the water elements of the Olive Hill plan were present in the landscape surrounding Taliesin: the stream springing from a source, a pond, and a man-made waterfall. At Olive Hill, however, the watercourse was integrated with the architecture, whereas at Taliesin the relationship was less direct. When presented with the opportunity to design his own stream, Wright, recalling the McCormick House, brought the two more intimately together.

At Olive Hill, although Wright sought to unify the plan of the community by contrasting the axial organization with the romantic twists and turns of the stream, the matter of circulation—bringing people into and around Olive Hill—did not reflect the realities of the growing automobile-dominated spread of Los Angeles. Wright provided two semicircular entrances to the hill, a formal entrance for pedestrians on axis with the theater, and another for cars at the northeast corner; however, there is a conspicuous absence of provision for parking. Evidently, Wright, who had spent little time in Los Angeles up to 1919, believed that most theater-goers would arrive on foot or by public transportation. The Pacific Electric Railroad's "Big Red Cars" created a network of public transportation lines throughout the greater Los Angeles area, but the automobile was gaining in popularity and Wright failed to incorporate it in his plan.

By locating the buildings according to Barnsdall's wishes and in accord with formal axial organization, Wright was forced to adjust the plan of each building to the sloping terrain, creating problems that plagued him as well through the design of the two adjacent buildings, the Director's House and the Actors Abode.

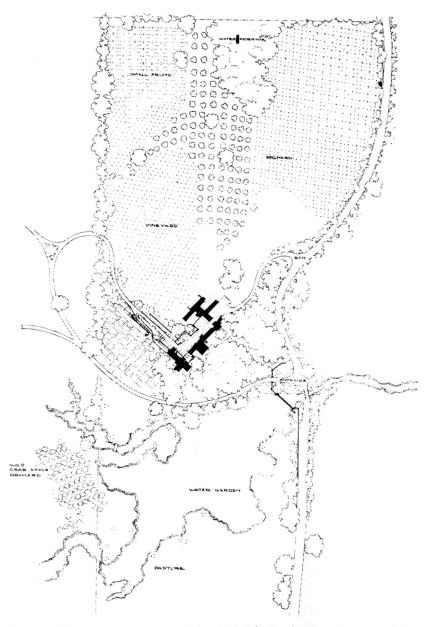

5-13. Taliesin, plot plan, 1911–1914
(*Western Architect* 19, February 1913)

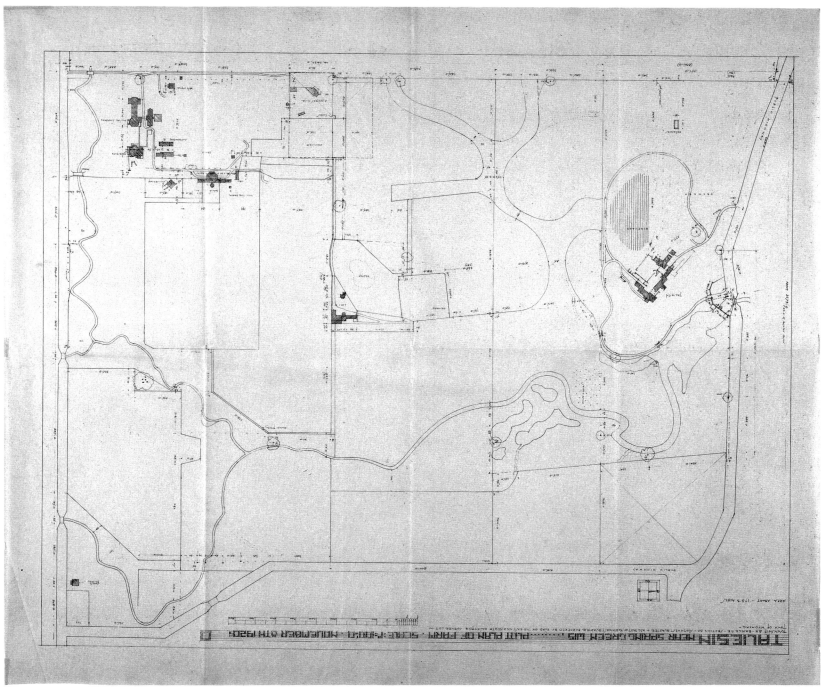

5-14. Lloyd-Jones Valley, plot plan, 1920 (courtesy of the Architectural Drawing Collection, University Art Museum, University of California, Santa Barbara). This drawing is printed upside down to conform to fig. 5-13. The legend reads, "Taliesin near Spring Green, Wis., Plot Plan of Farm, Scale : 1" = 100', November 8, 1920, Township 8N, Range 4E, Section 30, Southwest quarter + adj. part of northwest quarter bordered by road on the east and north excepting corner lot, town of Wyoming, area about 175.5 acres." This drawing by Schindler was made to survey Wright's increased land holdings (mentioned in Chapter 11). With Taliesin on the right, Hillside Home School, Tan-y-deri, and Romeo and Juliet are clustered at the upper left.

5-15. Conceptual sketch of Vermont
Avenue elevation, 1919 (courtesy of the
Frank Lloyd Wright Foundation)

5-16. Vermont Avenue elevation, 1919
(courtesy of the Frank Lloyd Wright
Foundation)

5-17. Study for aerial perspective of Olive Hill, 1919 (courtesy of the Frank Lloyd Wright Foundation)

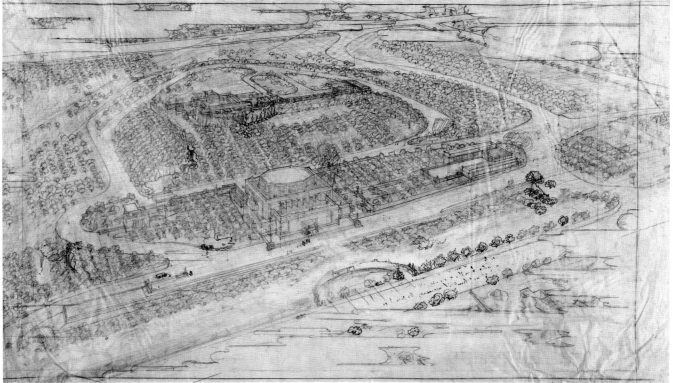

5-18. Olive Hill, 1919, aerial perspective (courtesy of the Architectural Drawing Collection, University Art Museum, University of California, Santa Barbara)

6-1. Director's House, rendering showing front (east) facade, 1919 (courtesy of the Architectural Drawing Collection, University Art Museum, University of California, Santa Barbara)

CHAPTER 6

DIRECTOR'S HOUSE

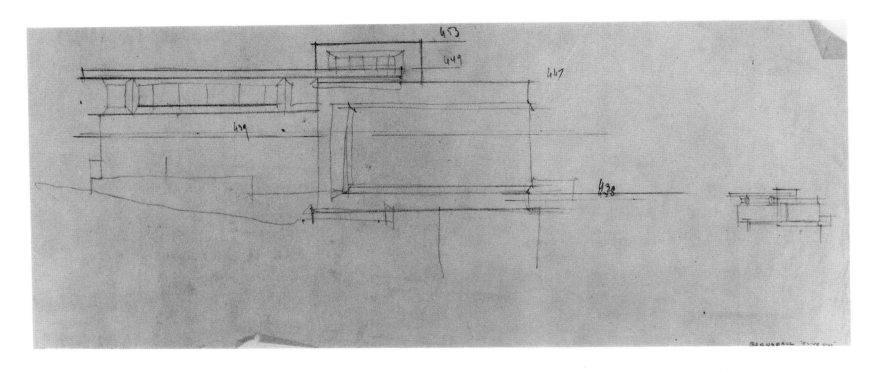

6-2. Director's House, preliminary sketch, 1919 (courtesy of the Architectural Drawing Collection, University Art Museum, University of California, Santa Barbara)

It is impossible to know whether Wright was influenced by the fact that he would be the first tenant, but for the Director's House he was inspired to create a unique design that anticipated one of his greatest masterpieces, Fallingwater, at Bear Run, Pennsylvania. He sited the Director's House into the hillside and, to symbolize the artistic focus of the community, designed a double waterfall bracketing the pedestrian entrance to the theater. The idea recalled the plans for both the McCormick House and Taliesin, but Wright's man-made water elements for the Director's House were the most lyrical he had yet proposed.

Under tremendous time pressure to present Barnsdall with "dozens of drawings," Wright was working under unusual conditions in the fall of 1919. It is conceivable that after producing some preliminary sketches, he instructed Schindler to lay them out in a format resembling a presentation drawing or a rendering.

Whether this hypothesis is correct or not, the only drawings for the Director's House that survived are in Schindler's hand, and any trace of Wright's conceptual drawings has disappeared (figs. 6-1 through 6-5). However, it is absolutely certain that the Director's House was designed before Wright departed for Japan in mid-December 1919, and it is unlikely that he turned sole design responsibility over to Schindler. In addition, the preliminary drawings have been erased and reworked, indicating that Wright revised them. It is safe to say that he was responsible for the design but left Schindler to work out certain details to fit the topography.[1] In January 1920, after Wright's departure for Japan, Schindler drew four sheets of working drawings following the preliminary design, with slight modifications to details.

The plan of the Director's House, drawn on a four-foot square grid, was characterized by its complex spatial relationships and the intricate zoning of private, public, and service areas (fig. 6-6). The house had a rooftop terrace and two living floors over a garage (fig. 6-7). The truncated T-plan was organized with the private rooms, bedrooms, and study on the major axis, and the public rooms, living room, and dining room placed longitudinally on the minor axis. A stair hall rose through the center of the building as a vertical core joining the two horizontal volumes of the house in an interlocking composition. There were three forms of entry: through the central hall to the study three steps above, or after a turn, to the living room; by automobile into the garage and up a flight of steps into the hall; or by a service stair connecting the maid's room to the kitchen.

The fireplace in the living room was off center near the entry, opposite five glazed doors that led to an exterior balcony. The dining room, kitchen, and guest bedroom were on the floor above, with the dining room on a balcony open to the living room below. Two bedrooms and a bath were three steps above this level. The central stairwell rose through the roof as a tower with movable glazed openings on four sides. The lantern roof washed the stairway with light throughout the day, ventilated the interior, and provided access to a roof terrace with views of the theater across the stream to the north (see figs. 5-16 and 5-18). In addition to serving as a chimney and providing circulation, lighting, and ventilation, the central core was a dynamic interlocking composition of horizontal and vertical space.[2] The vertical thrust of the stair, accentuated by overhead light, contrasted with panels of slatted screens that allowed space to penetrate horizontally from one level to the other.

From the exterior, the building was conceived as three intersecting volumes: a solid block and an open block hinged together by a tower (fig. 6-8). The public rooms, which faced the street, were closed on two sides, and open only through five narrow french doors on the front elevation. The bedroom wing presented an entirely different appearance. The tripartite division of a solid footing, a band of ribbon windows on three sides, and a flat, projecting roof conveyed the feeling that the glass disappeared and the roof floated over the base. To screen the rooms facing the street for privacy and to open the bedroom wing facing inward to light and views, the two wings were treated very differently in their massing. The front elevation, lying on the same plane as the theater, repeated forms from that building (figs. 5-16 and 5-18); the baseline and top line of the wall were recessed, creating a flat, projecting plane. These edges were further emphasized by a band of continuous ornament that wrapped around corners and openings. Although Wright, like Louis Sullivan, looked to Islamic architecture for inspiration, he transformed surface and decoration by juxtaposing plain surfaces and complex decoration to dematerialize the mass and create a plastic surface. In contrast, the rear wing recalled the treatment of wall, window, and roof on the lateral wings of the 1912 Coonley Playhouse in Riverside, Illinois.

The Director's House was the only building integrated into the man-made watercourse. Wright shifted the stream so that it ran directly along the northern edge of the house, forcing him to choose between making a visual statement—

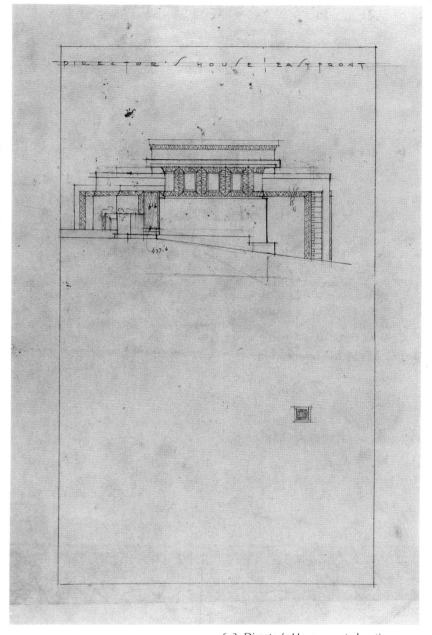

6-3. Director's House, west elevation, 1919 (courtesy of the Architectural Drawing Collection, University Art Museum, University of California, Santa Barbara). This drawing is mislabeled.

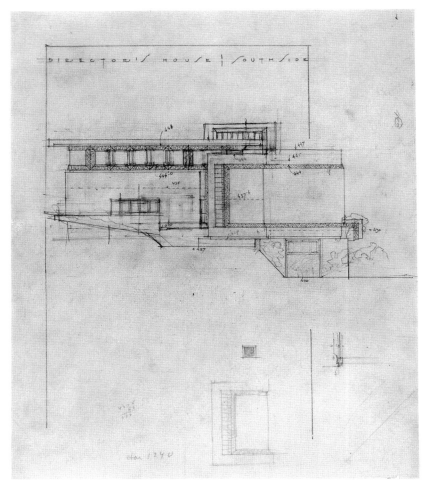

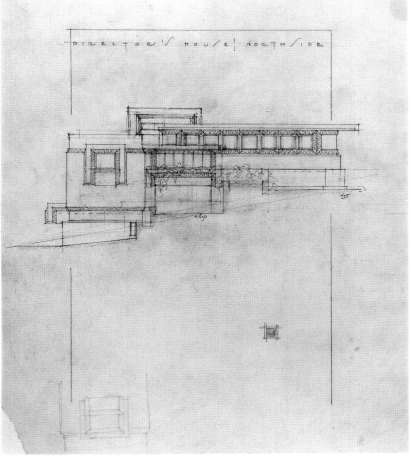

6-4. Director's House, south elevation, 1919 (courtesy of the Architectural Drawing Collection, University Art Museum, University of California, Santa Barbara)

6-5. Director's House, north elevation, 1919 (courtesy of the Architectural Drawing Collection, University Art Museum, University of California, Santa Barbara)

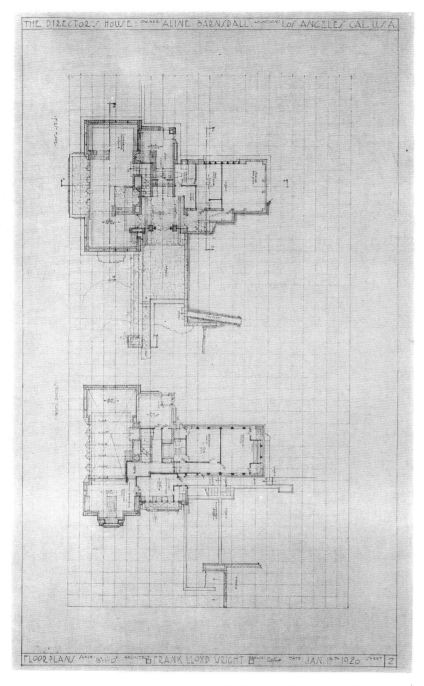

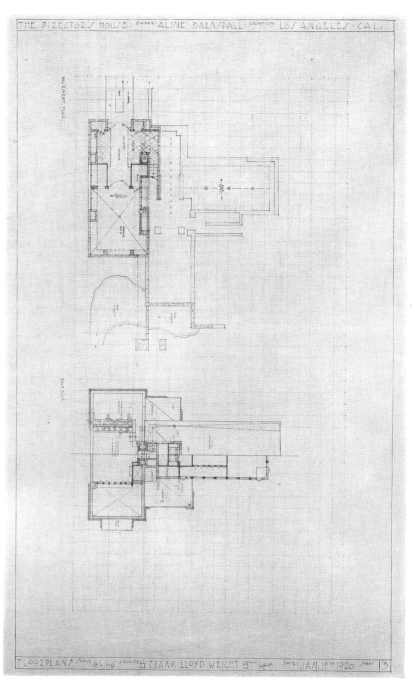

6-6. Director's House, floor plans,
January 15, 1920 (courtesy of the
Architectural Drawing Collection,
University Art Museum, University of
California, Santa Barbara)

6-7. Director's House, floor plans,
January 15, 1920 (courtesy of the
Architectural Drawing Collection,
University Art Museum, University of
California, Santa Barbara)

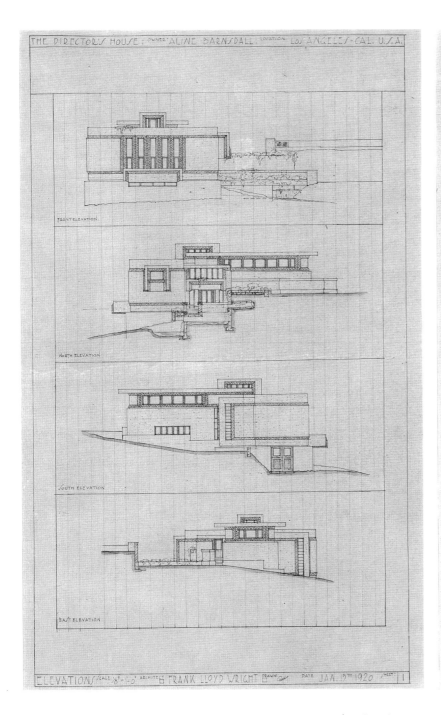

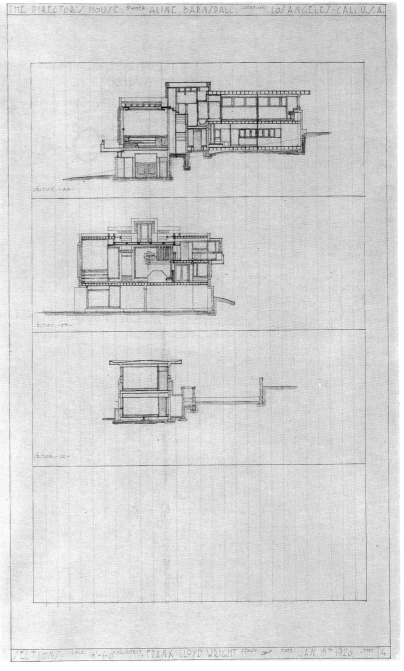

6-8. Director's House, elevations, January 15, 1920 (courtesy of the Architectural Drawing Collection, University Art Museum, University of California, Santa Barbara). Two elevations are mislabeled. The front elevation is the east elevation; the east elevation is actually the west elevation.

6-9. Director's House, sections, January 15, 1920 (courtesy of the Architectural Drawing Collection, University Art Museum, University of California, Santa Barbara)

6-10. Director's House, perspective (drawing by William Rozner and Eulogio Guzman)

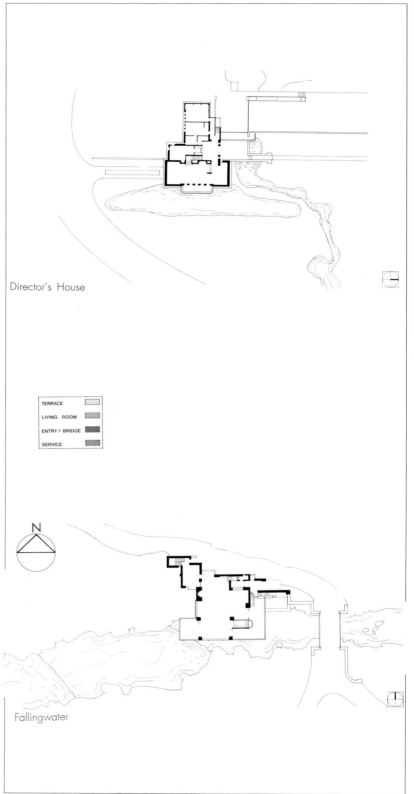

Director's House

TERRACE	
LIVING ROOM	
ENTRY / BRIDGE	
SERVICE	

N

Fallingwater

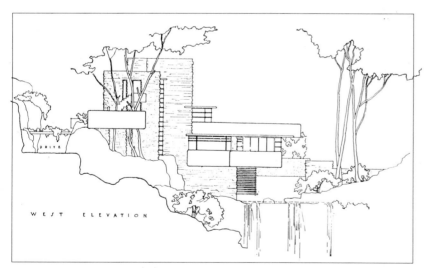

WEST ELEVATION

6-11. Fallingwater, west elevation (courtesy of the Frank Lloyd Wright Foundation)

6-12. Diagrammatic comparison of the Director's House and Fallingwater (drawing by William Rozner and Eulogio Guzman). Note that above the Director's House, Wright has created an opening in the terrace to provide a view of the flowing stream. This element is reminiscent of the McCormick House (see fig. 5-11).

a steep waterfall to the south that conformed to the natural topography — or creating a symbolic waterfall entrance similar to the one at Taliesin. Wright chose to bring the visitor to the house across a narrow bridge, only two feet wide, that opened to a terrace, fourteen by twenty-four feet. Four feet west of the bridge, Wright created a waterfall channeled through a culvert one and a half feet wide, falling five feet below to a small pond. From the pond the water spilled over a dam to a drop of three feet, and continued to meander down the hill out of sight (fig. 6-10). The double waterfall entrance served several purposes. Visually, the first waterfall, a more dramatic cascade of water, would create a moving sculptural form for the visitor. The second waterfall was visible only at a distance as a sheet of falling water. Both waterfalls could be heard from the bridge, but one would be visible and the other mysteriously just out of sight. To further heighten the effect of water, Wright added a mirroring pond to the front elevation. Both major elements of Taliesin, the waterfall entrance and the mirroring pond, were incorporated in Wright's design for the Director's House, but it is important to note that when he was designing both the buildings and the water elements, he made a direct connection between the two.

Like the entrance to Taliesin, the double waterfall in the Olive Hill plan celebrated and announced the visitor's approach to the community's center of creative imagination. It seems safe to say that because water symbolizes life and falling water creates energy, Wright believed that the waterfall entrance was the perfect metaphor for the pulsating heart of the community. Although he used waterfall entrances, both natural and of his own creation, increasingly after Olive Hill (at the Tahoe Summer Colony and House C at Doheny Ranch, both 1923, and at the Gordon Strong Automobile Objective in 1925), it was not until fifteen years later when he was taken to the site of Edgar Kaufmann, Sr.'s country house at Bear Run, a stream in Pennsylvania, that Wright would have a site like that again (figs. 6-11 and 6-12).

At Bear Run the stream flowed in the opposite direction, from east to west; the falls were steeper (twenty-five feet and ten feet), so more dramatic, and fell at an angle to each other, the first predominantly to the south, the second to the west; and the water cascaded over huge broken rock ledges instead of concrete retaining walls. The Kaufmann house, Fallingwater, was a powerful synthesis of Wright's modernism and tradition. It was anchored in the rock of the hillside but it seemed to spring out in flight over the roaring waterfall below. The mass of the concrete and stone played against the transparency of the glass and water, its man-made forms integrated with nature. One powerful building summarized Wright's philosophy of architecture.

When he sited Fallingwater, Wright chose not to repeat the elements of the Director's House (fig. 6-12). Both buildings are approached by a bridge that spans a stream, but at Fallingwater, Wright placed the bridge above the house and away from the falls, which do not become an experience of entry. The house was placed on the north side of the stream facing south, and the front elevation was turned ninety degrees to face the stream and dramatically cantilever over it. The consistent orthogonal geometry of the Director's House was replaced by subtle and essential diagonals resulting in a more dynamic composition; at Fallingwater, Wright placed the orthogonal geometry of the house at a 30/60 degree angle to the line of the first falls.

But the major difference between the two buildings is how they were meant to be experienced in relation to the waterfalls. At the Director's House, the waterfalls were seen primarily on entering or leaving (fig. 6-10), whereas at Fallingwater, they could be heard and glimpsed from the house, but only seen in full view from a vantage point downstream on the opposite bank (fig. 6-13). At Fallingwater, Wright obviously felt that it was more important to integrate the house and the falls without the intrusion of the bridge.

6-13. Fallingwater (photo by Christopher Little)

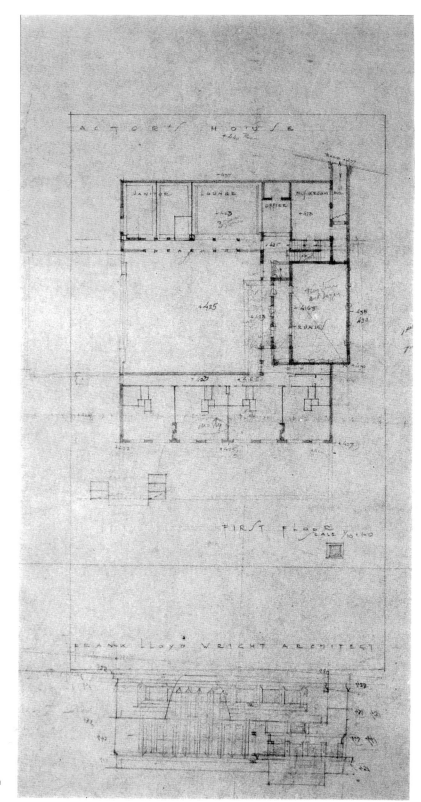

7-1. Actors Abode, plan, 1919 (courtesy of the Architectural Drawing Collection, University Art Museum, University of California, Santa Barbara). Note at the bottom of the sheet an elevation has been drawn upside down.

ACTORS ABODE

The attention lavished on the Director's House seems to have left little time to work out the plan for the Actors Abode, the least resolved building in the Olive Hill plan. The sketches, in Schindler's hand, represent no more than a conceptual scheme for rooms and common spaces in a U-shaped *parti* (fig. 7-1). The hastily rendered plans indicate that little thought was given to issues of siting the building into the sloping contours of the hill, providing natural daylight in the rooms, or circulation.

The drawings prepared in the fall of 1919 proposed a three-story building organized around a central courtyard that opened to the south, facing the theater (figs. 7-1, 5-16, and 5-18). On the ground floor, the central section, separated from the two side wings by staircases, was devoted to trunk storage, with public and service rooms—the office, lounge, music room, and janitor's suite—in the west wing, and four housekeeping rooms, each with kitchen and bath, in the east wing. The second and third floors were identical, with one large suite in the center flanked by six single rooms on the west and four housekeeping rooms to the east. With no regard for the terrain, the building was backed into the hill, requiring a solid retaining wall at the rear. The public spaces, as well as the janitor's suite, were almost completely enclosed by solid walls on three sides, with only small openings on the east and north to bring in light. The courtyard entrance was on axis with the trunk storage, and there was no thought to screening the rooms for privacy or providing views.

There is no record of Barnsdall's reaction to the first scheme, but in the next set of drawings, also in Schindler's hand, the building was revised (figs. 7-2 and 7-3). The five sheets of plans, elevations, and sections, drawn on a four-foot square grid in May 1920, while Wright was in Japan, reflect the struggle to adapt an arbitrary *parti* to the irregular site. The simplistic organization of three equal floors was revised: the east wing was lowered to two floors, but one was placed below ground to house the service areas of storage, laundry, and utility rooms. With the services removed from the public ground floor, the office and lounge (the social and business centers) were moved to lie in a logical position on axis with the entrance, with the music room adjacent in its original location, the northwest corner. The single and housekeeping rooms were flipped 180 degrees in plan and reduced from twelve to eight in number, while the suites were increased by one; but more important, the plan was clarified in the zoning of the public, private, and service areas. There was an attempt to bring more light into the rooms on the ground floor by creating light wells on the west and north.

The building was now terraced, with the west wing two floors taller than the east wing. Roof terraces were added to both wings with vistas to the east and south toward the theater. Repeating an idea from the Director's House, a stair tower rose between the central section and the west wing, joining the two and emerging as a lantern roof for ventilation. The exterior mechanically repeated the surface treatment of the theater and Director's House with a band of ornament outlining the window and door openings, and recessed and projecting wall planes.

The theater zone lying on the minor axis now had three buildings all related in their exterior surface treatment; Barnsdall's house, some two years in design, had to be integrated into a community that did not exist at its inception (figs. 5-15, 5-16, 5-17, and 5-18).

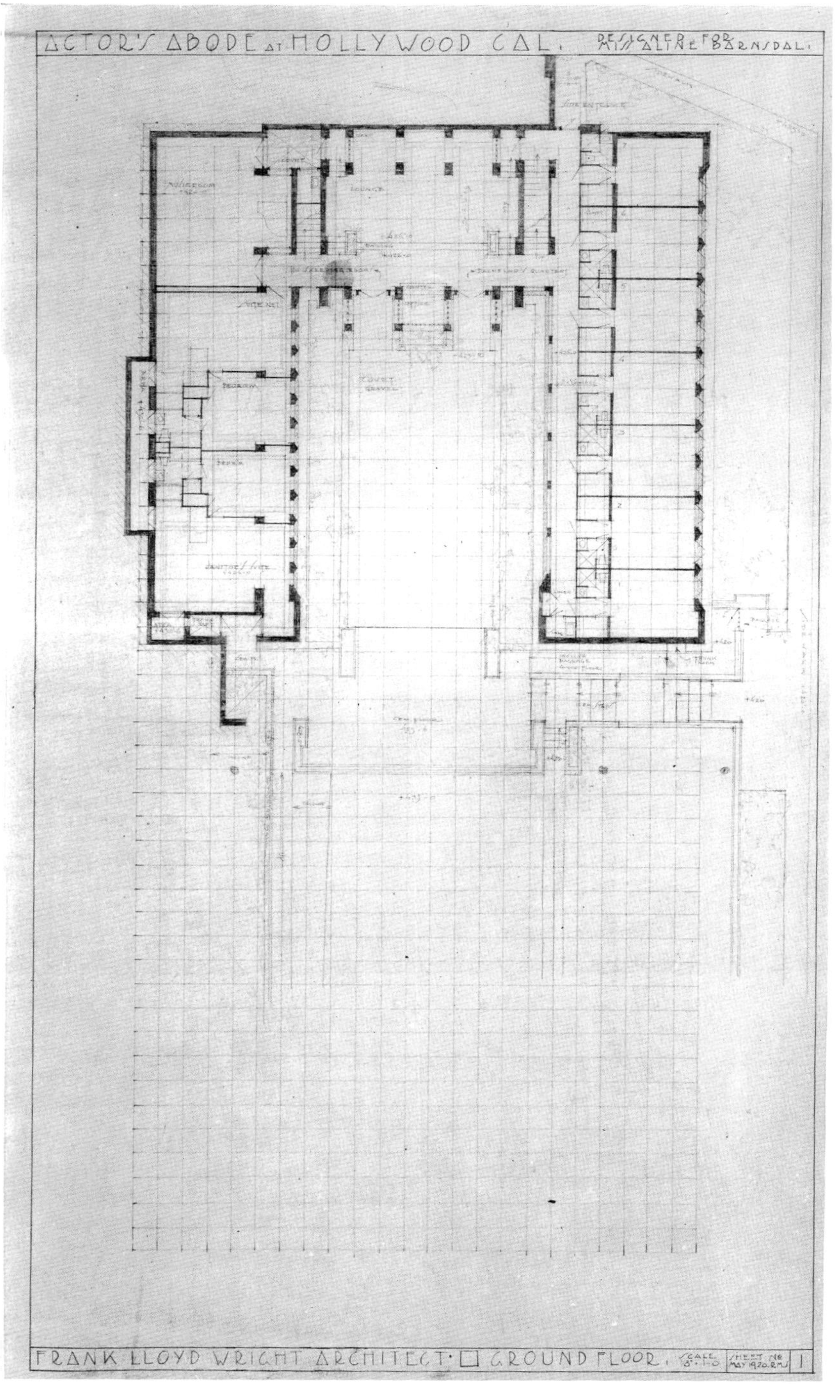

7-2. Actors Abode, ground floor plan, May 1920 (courtesy of the Architectural Drawing Collection, University Art Museum, University of California, Santa Barbara)

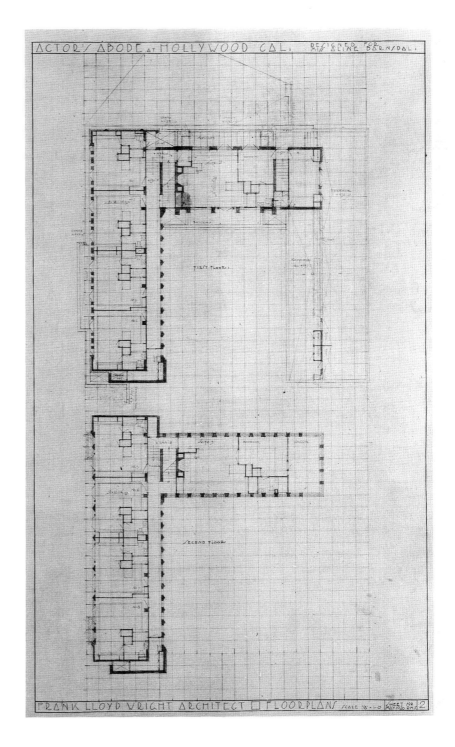

7-3. Actors Abode, floor plans, May 1920 (courtesy of the Architectural Drawing Collection, University Art Museum, University of California, Santa Barbara)

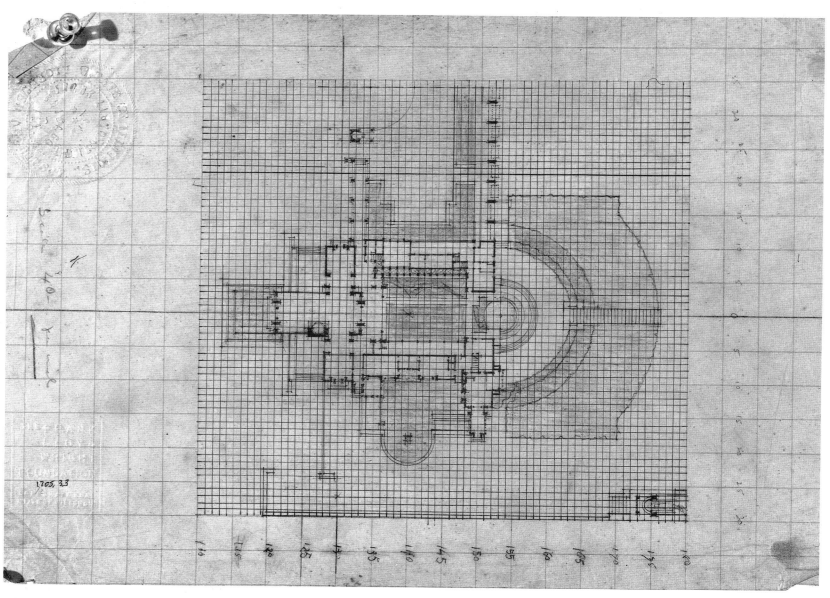

CHAPTER 8

HOLLYHOCK HOUSE/OWNER'S RESIDENCE

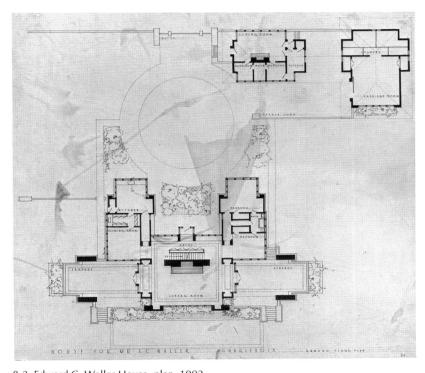

8-2. Edward C. Waller House, plan, 1902 (courtesy of the Frank Lloyd Wright Foundation)

8-1. Hollyhock House, plan, 1919 (courtesy of the Frank Lloyd Wright Foundation). A four-foot grid has been superimposed over the twenty-foot grid of the General Plan.

Despite his earlier warnings to Barnsdall that he would need time to refine his designs, Wright could not abandon his scheme for her house, although he had only two months until his December 1919 departure for Japan. Preoccupied with other matters and under pressure to return to the construction of the Imperial Hotel, Wright was unable to begin again. To satisfy her wishes he placed the building on the crown, and by adding water elements to the master landscape plan, he created a macrocosm of his earlier idea present in the preliminary plans for her house. Unable to address the site first, Wright was at least able to integrate the two thematically. He recalled in his autobiography many years later:

> My client was in a hurry and I was urgently needed in Tokio [*sic*]. If we accomplished more than the preliminary plans themselves in the way of actual building, we would have to amplify the sketches into plans as best we could, making such added notes and details as we went along as would suffice to get the building properly built and turn it over to the help. The manner of work being what it is, this was not unreasonable at the time.[1]

With the exception of the early elevations and renderings and the few plans and perspectives of the general plan, there is only one drawing, the first floor plan, laid out on a four-foot grid, that survived from this period, making it impossible to completely reconstruct the design at this phase. There is enough evidence to suggest, however, that the plans, elevations, and interior spaces were completed; what remained were the detailing and decisions regarding finishing materials.

Because of her dual role as head of a proposed dramatic company and of her own family, Barnsdall's house needed to be theatrical and luxurious. The U-shaped plan (fig. 8-1), which focused on an interior court, was based on a type Wright had used as early as the unveiling of the Prairie house, and was one he returned to over the years for larger houses and (increasingly after 1913) for public buildings. Its first appearance was in 1902 in an unbuilt house for Edward C. Waller in Charlevoix, Michigan (fig. 8-2). The Waller plan was formal, axial, and one of the most completely symmetrical *partis* Wright ever used. The living room was centrally placed, with two perpendicular lateral wings joined diagonally at the corners. This arrangement resulted in clearly defined zones with service (dining and kitchen) separated from the ground floor bedrooms and baths by the public space. The *parti* was expanded in 1908 with great complexity as Harold C. McCormick's summer house in Lake Forest, Illinois (fig. 5-11), a brilliant scheme that went unbuilt. It finally saw construction in a much modified version for the Avery Coonleys in Riverside, Illinois, in 1909. Between 1913 and

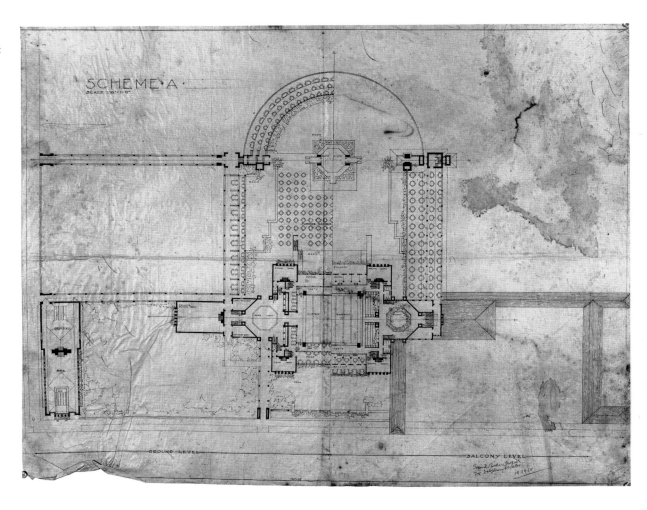

8-3. Vogelsang Dinner Gardens, plan, 1914 (courtesy of the Frank Lloyd Wright Foundation)

1914, Wright used a related U-shaped configuration for a series of public buildings, most notably for the Midway Gardens, the Imperial Hotel, and a little-known project, the Vogelsang Dinner Gardens (fig. 8-3).

For Barnsdall, Wright primarily synthesized elements from two of these unbuilt designs—the 1902 Edward C. Waller House, and the Vogelsang Dinner Gardens, Chicago, 1914. As a result, the design for Barnsdall's house, although domestic in program, had some of the scale and features of a public building. From both earlier projects, Wright used the U-shaped plan organized around an interior courtyard terminating in a semicircle on the major axis. As in the Waller house, the plan created three distinct zones: public (living rooms), private (bedrooms), and service (dining and kitchen). As with the Vogelsang Dinner Gardens, the courtyard became an outdoor amphitheater.

In the Barnsdall plan (compare figs. 8-2 and 8-5) the living room, rotated ninety degrees, was elongated into a rectangle flanked by a music room and a library. The dining room, separated from the kitchen by the pantry, was in one wing, and two bedrooms separated by bathrooms were in the other. The Barnsdall plan was enlarged on the guest bedroom wing with the addition of a breakfast room (conservatory), a child's suite, and a nurse's room. On the kitchen wing it was enlarged with servants' quarters. Unlike the Waller house, the Barnsdall plan was confined to one floor except in the rear wing where Barnsdall's own suite

was over her daughter's. The remainder of the second story was unresolved. Also unlike the Waller house, the flat roofs over the living room and guest bedroom wings were designed as roof terraces with a small stairway providing access from the court. The walls facing onto the court consist of either windows or glazed doors directing the focus toward the garden.

However, Wright articulated the zones in a different manner so that the Barnsdall House far surpassed its precedents in its clarity of zoning. Wright created four areas—the living room group, the dining/service group, the guest bedroom group, and the owner's suite—as independent, free-standing units separated by circulation. Wright had been perfecting this plan-type since its appearance during the Oak Park period. In reference to the typology used in the Coonley House, Wright wrote in 1908, "Each separate function in the house is treated for and by itself, with light and air on three sides, and grouped together as a harmonious whole."[2] In the Barnsdall House, Wright made a clear distinction between the rooms and the circulation. Almost like a Japanese palace, each unit of the house was defined as a self-contained pavilion linked by halls or loggias that opened either directly or visually to the out-of-doors.[3] Although the outside flowed freely around each of the units, which were enclosed either by solid walls as in the guest bedrooms or by doors, the orientation was decidedly private, toward either the center court or the guest bedroom court.

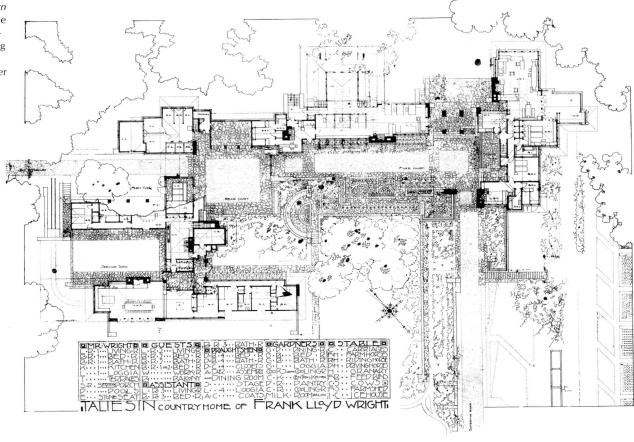

Despite the potential of its location at the summit of a thirty-six-acre estate, and the opportunity for 360-degree views, the visual focus of Barnsdall's house was highly restricted. This orientation can partly be explained by the fact that the house had originally been planned without Olive Hill in mind; however, Wright had increasingly used the U-shaped courtyard scheme after 1913.[4] The plan allowed him to create a transition zone in the living room loggia; bounded by folding glass doors to the court and french doors from the living room, planter boxes on three corners marked the transition between the garden and the house. With the doors pushed aside, the loggia would be simultaneously indoors and outdoors. Although Wright had used the same plan-type for buildings in the Midwest and Japan, in the Barnsdall House, the garden penetrated into the building envelope. The unusual circumstances of the preliminary design prevented Wright from designing the plan with the topography in mind, but the intimate relationship of the indoors and outdoors indicates Wright's response to California's benevolent climate.

While the interior spaces of the Barnsdall house were a refined version of those in the Waller *parti*, the exterior spaces contained ideas that related to both the Vogelsang Dinner Gardens and the Barnsdall Theater. Combined with elements of a water garden reminiscent of the McCormick House, these exterior spaces created an ambitious plan unclear in its intentions and functions. In the Vogelsang Dinner Gardens (fig. 8-3), Wright designed an octagonal bandstand that could be viewed from two directions—from a semicircular amphitheater or from the floor and balconies of the internal courtyard. In Barnsdall's house, this configuration is repeated, with the audience seated either in the exedra around the circular pool or in the courtyard and on the roof terraces of the house.[5] Unlike the Vogelsang project, the second story of the rear wing framed the view, creating a proscenium arch. Yet like the Barnsdall Theater, the audience and performers were still under the same ceiling—the sky. The performers could enter from concealed locations adjacent to either the service or bedroom wings. Although the working drawings do not indicate it, Wright's earlier perspectives (see figs. 4-1, 4-6, 4-7, and 4-8) and an account of the house from the mid-1920s refer to a fountain or jet of water that could serve as a curtain between the stage and the audience.

However, Wright divided the interior court into two sections, with a flagstone walk leading from the living room loggia to the rear pool (fig. 8-5). One side became a grassy lawn and the other a water garden. With the addition of a circular pool, Wright eliminated the most advantageous place for the stage, and performances could take place only on the flat semicircular lawn behind the pool, where sightlines were poor. With one-third of the court devoted to a water garden, he had also restricted the space for the audience. If the arrangement had been flipped, with the audience in the exedra and the performance in the court-yard or on the balcony over the living room loggia, only a small audience could have been accommodated. In designing his own houses, Wright had been intrigued by the idea of a house with its own theater (his 1895 Oak Park Playroom was used as a theater, and the plan for the 1911 Taliesin called for a stage and auditorium in the hilltop wing, fig. 8-4); but with Barnsdall's house, he introduced conflicting elements and diluted his intentions.

After almost a month, Wright was still not ready to review his scheme with Barnsdall. As he had suggested, she arrived in Chicago, once again, on November 16, 1919, to see "dozens of drawings in color," and, once again, she was disappointed. Although Raymond had come from New York, he had not yet begun the renderings. Wright explained that work would continue and that he would bring everything with him to meet her in a few weeks in Los Angeles on his way to Japan.[6]

Wright chose his eldest son, Lloyd Wright, to be his superintendent in Los Angeles. Lloyd Wright had accompanied his father to Europe in 1911 to assist in the preparation of drawings for the Wasmuth portfolio. On his return, between 1912 and 1915, he had worked for Irving Gill in San Diego and Los Angeles. Although his son had no other formal architectural training outside his father's studio, the elder Wright would have had good reason to depend on his son's experience, since he and Gill had known each other in Chicago. Both had apprenticed in the office of Adler and Sullivan, overlapping for the years 1890–1892. Gill then departed for California, where between 1908 and 1909 he had begun to experiment with reinforced concrete. By the time Lloyd Wright left his office, Gill was completing buildings in cast concrete with a new technique for tilt-up walls. Since Lloyd Wright was familiar with construction in Los Angeles, the elder Wright believed he would be able to find a suitable contractor.

Finally, with little over a week before his ship sailed from Seattle on December 16, the elder Wright knew he would never have time to stop in Los Angeles. After toying with the idea of meeting Barnsdall in San Francisco for twelve hours, he realized that he would have to ask her to travel to meet him in Portland. With some premonition of her displeasure, he carefully worded his telegram: "Everything now ready—estimates and landscape—do not let this disconcert our work—all will finally go well. Will keep the drawings with me awaiting your advice."[7]

Lloyd Wright left Chicago on December 7, 1919. On his arrival in Los Angeles he met with Barnsdall, they agreed on his salary, and Barnsdall set an unrecorded financial limit for her house. Lloyd Wright reported to his father:

Miss Barnsdall can not make the trip to Portland or does not want to. It seemed to me best to stay here. Keep on the job and attention riveted to it for moral effect if nothing else. Little we could do together in a day at most.

She feels that you are neglecting her interests shamefully but seems to be pretty game about it, I must confess.

As I look at things developing I do not wonder that you are always in confusion and that you can not accomplish matters in a clean straightforward way. A little rotten luck mixed in with evasion, suspicion and indifference can work "Hell."[8]

Lloyd Wright had already contacted three contractors, but one he had known in San Diego and Los Angeles performing government and general business construction was singled out for special mention. Of the contractor finally selected for the job, S.G.H. Robertson, Lloyd Wright explained:

It seems he is connected with a two million dollar venture here and they are looking for an architect. He asked me if I would have you meet his people. I will do what I can and report. But if you wonder why it is you do not

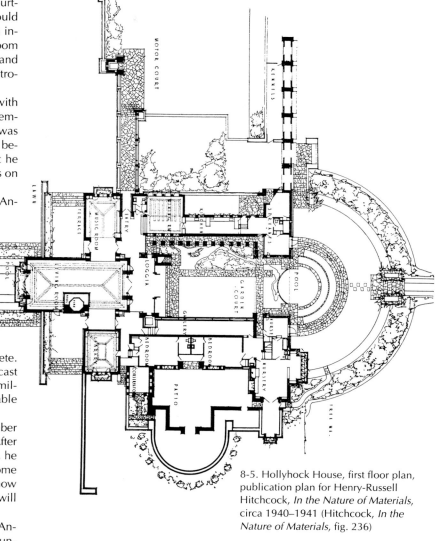

8-5. Hollyhock House, first floor plan, publication plan for Henry-Russell Hitchcock, *In the Nature of Materials*, circa 1940–1941 (Hitchcock, *In the Nature of Materials*, fig. 236)

8-6. Hollyhock House, first floor plan, January 31, 1920 (courtesy of the Frank Lloyd Wright Foundation). In lower margin, "Revised Sept. 10, 1920 O.K.; Revised, Aug. 16, 1920, FLW; Revised, August 10, 1920.

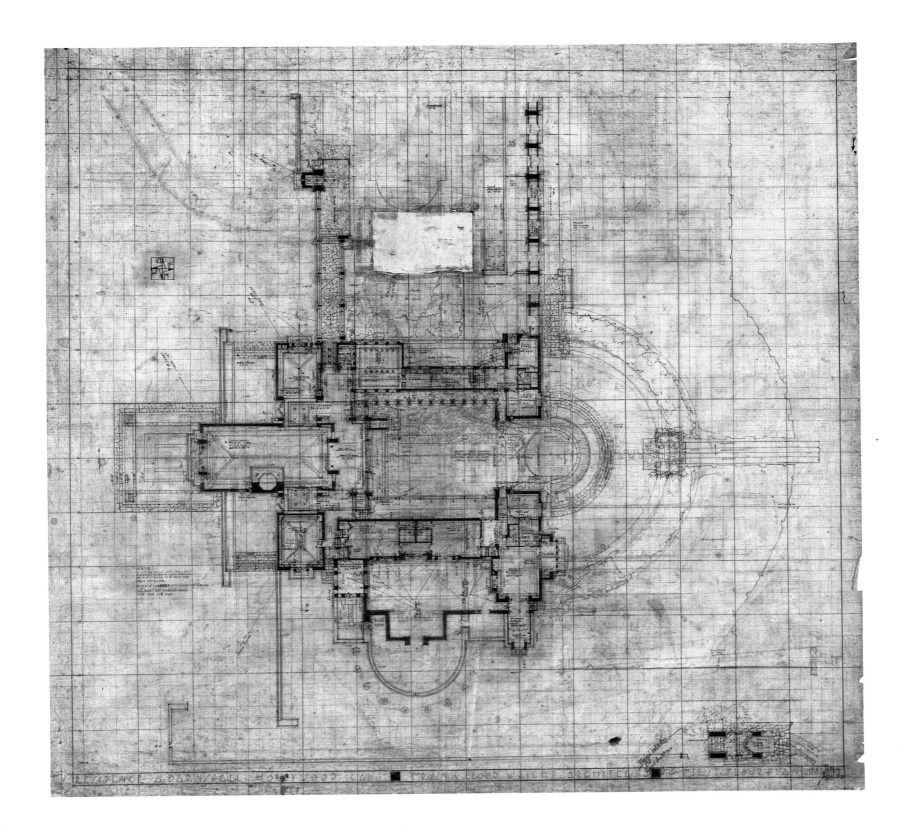

RESIDENCE A BARNSDALL HOLLYWOOD CALIF · FRANK LLOYD WRIGHT ARCHITECT · FIRST FLOOR PLAN

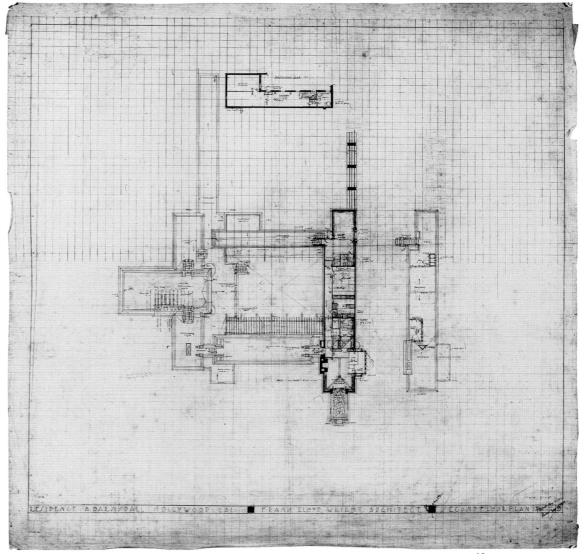

get work in this country, here is the answer, you are not here to get it. But cheer up—we will do the best we can and better than we have ever done before—whether that will be good enough under the circumstances remains to be seen.[9]

Lloyd Wright was worried that Barnsdall had nothing to occupy her mind while her house was under construction. Probably in an effort to protect himself against her anxious inquiries, he urged his father to send some sketches of the theater so a model could be made in his absence, even though another was to be made in Japan. He believed that the house would be well along by Wright's return in May or June 1920. He intended to write or cable if necessary, refer all design decisions either to his father or Schindler back in Chicago, and perhaps hire a draftsman to help prepare drawings for bid.

Lloyd Wright's optimistic tone was encouraging but unrealistic. Yet it would have been difficult for him to predict how the building would proceed because he had probably never worked under such unusual circumstances. Although he was responsible for pushing the job through construction, the architect was thousands of miles away and available only by mail or telegraph. By Lloyd Wright's own account, his telegrams went unanswered. In March the telegraph cable went down and it took two months for an exchange of letters.[10] The client, ready to leave for New York where she was to depart for Europe, was singlehandedly making decisions about various aspects of the building and landscape. The working drawings were being produced by Schindler, working out of the Monroe Building office in Chicago.

After Wright's departure, Barnsdall had not been as calm as Lloyd Wright imagined. Apparently, she had considered going to Japan, but decided against it even before Wright's ship left port.[11] The holidays gave her time to think, and in January 1920 she wrote two letters setting forth her terms and giving him the chance to quit: "The house must be finished,—but if you find it impossible to continue with the theatre in the only way that is safe for me,—we must decide to give it up. Though I earnestly hope this will not be necessary....We won't argue further—only give it up as too gigantic an undertaking."[12]

Her immediate concern was her house, and she expected him to complete colored elevations of the interiors. "Please, please have things visualized for me by spring," she pleaded, "even to rugs and furniture for I want to work like blazes when you return." Her irritation surfaced when she revealed, "I am just restlessly wearing myself out with waiting."[13]

Barnsdall was making decisions in Wright's absence, but the younger Wright viewed these instructions as preliminaries used to obtain bids and get the construction started. He reminded her that his father was designing the interiors in Japan.[14]

However, she had strong ideas about what she wanted. The living room was to contain two Japanese screens on the two largest wall surfaces, with the remaining plaster wall stained a soft purple that she had selected from one of Wright's Japanese prints, with "a touch of gold to link it with the screens," and wood trim in "untouched walnut." The specification notes that probably date from this period call for "selected walnut with white streaks" in the living room, music room, library, and bedrooms.[15] The music room was to be separated from the hall by a low partition with a painting by Monet built into the opposite wall. The dining room was to be finished with mahogany wainscoting (although it was up to Wright's imagination to make it look like something else) to match her existing table, golden rug, and curtains.[16] She had originally placed her bedroom on the second floor at the southeast corner. It was to have a large bay window projecting to the rear, and was to be finished in white hollywood and green-stained plaster. By the end of January 1920, she had instructed Lloyd Wright to convert two bedrooms over the servants' quarters into one large room for herself. "I want to sleep in the centre of the hill," she declared, "away from the outer fringe of noise and next to the Hollywood Hills."[17] To complete her suite she wanted a Pompeian bath. For the furniture he was designing she proposed "a gumwood that has a rosy flush." The specifications called for the floors to be maple throughout, with the exception of the bathrooms, which were to be "small inglazed [sic] square tile." The servants' rooms and the exterior wood trim called for redwood.

It may have been at this time that the hollyhock flower was chosen as the ornamental motif, as Wright recalled much later: "A bit sentimental withal, Miss Barnsdall had pre-named the house for the Hollyhock she loved for many reasons, all of them good ones, and called upon me to render her favorite flower as a feature of Architecture, how I might."[18]

She implored him:

Now please do as wonderful a thing with the inside of my house as [you] have with the outside. The designs Lloyd gave me from your specifications looked as tho [sic] you had thought very little about them—the[y] lacked the ingenuity and care of the outside building. We are going ahead with it but worry because you are not here to decide on the color. I don't want it to *look* green but to *feel* green as a background for the rich hollyhock and rose reds. Its [sic] a pity you are not here.[19]

She believed the house could be finished easily, adding, "It is too large, but necessarily so for it's [sic] position. It is absolutely beautiful in architecture and I feel that you did work with me in spirit in designing it." The theater posed the problem. She explained:

Now, I am willing to wait, but the building cannot start until everything is put into a form that I can visualize and my business man can understand and handle. I require to be shown me, quality of textures, interior drawings and elevations and decorations, quality of furnishings, measurements, and a model that will give the relative value of the seats to the stage. There cannot be less than 1275 seats and 1400 if possible. If you cannot have your Theatre complete,—even as to form of lighting equipment before you start contracting for work, I would rather not begin.

Will you give it up? Take a year or two to complete it in detail? Or have it ready by spring,—beginning everything at once,—after we have had an intelligent, workable understanding?[20]

There is no record of Wright's response, and one can only imagine what he thought when he read Barnsdall's letter, considering his circumstances in Japan.

On his return to Tokyo, he had been informed that the Imperial Hotel Annex had just burned to the ground, that the hotel had a desperate shortage of rooms because of the new building's long delay in construction, and that he needed to design and build a new annex as fast as possible.[21] By the end of January, he had come down with another illness that was so serious that his seventy-eight-year-old mother, Anna, decided to make the long Pacific crossing to be with him. By the time she arrived in Japan on March 2, 1920, the foundations of the hotel had been finished, but with six months remaining until the estimated date of completion, the opening had to be postponed another year.

Barnsdall, who had planned to leave for Europe in February, was still in Los Angeles working with Lloyd Wright. She had decided to begin construction of the Actors Abode immediately on Wright's return because she wanted the income, but as the Director's House could not be completed by then, she had decided to postpone it until the theater was to be built.

On January 27, 1920, Lloyd Wright drew a planting plan for the hill grove, the stand of trees that had appeared consistently in Wright's earlier preliminary renderings.[22] Wright recalled later, "Loving pines because of the mountain carpets they made, she planted pine-groves behind the hill and great masses of the Eucalyptus to enclose the pines."[23] On a motor trip to Arrowhead she sought the name of the pine she desired, writing Lloyd Wright not to plant until she was certain of the type she preferred.[24] In the end, the landscape specifications called for a mass of Italian Stone pines, with two rows of blue gum eucalyptus placed ten feet on center as an outside border.[25] Except for a rectangular area at the north near the garage, reserved for a future swimming pool, the hill grove was completed by early April.[26]

Progress on the Olive Hill moved slowly until Wright's return. Almost a whole month was lost at the beginning while Schindler produced four sheets of plans, elevations, and sections for the Director's House before Barnsdall decided to postpone it. He did not start Barnsdall's house until the last day of January 1920, and it was not until March 27 that he had nine sheets, which included plans, elevations, sections, and details of the principal rooms (figs. 8-6, 8-7, 8-8, 12-5, and 12-9).[27] Lloyd Wright had promised his father that he would have the building far enough along by May so the elder Wright could devote himself to the interior details. Lloyd Wright was forced to put pressure on Schindler by expressing his irritation in a couple of strong letters. "It took the first one," Lloyd Wright explained to his father, "to make him disgorge the plans which I now have in hand. Possibly I have been hyper-critical. I don't enjoy forcing a man's hand, but it seemed in this case...the only way I could get results."[28]

Even before the drawings were begun, it must have been clear that Barnsdall's house was not going to be a reinforced concrete building as the exterior form indicated. Instead, it would combine the region's conventional construction, details Wright had used in his Prairie houses, and finishes and fixtures chosen by the client. The structure consisted of a masonry material, hollow terra cotta tile, surfaced with plaster. Art stone, concrete manufactured to imitate stone, was to be used for the copings, lintels, sills, columns, and ornamental details. All the doors, windows, and skylights, as in the Prairie houses, were to be leaded glass in geometric patterns.

Numerous details from the working drawings Schindler prepared that spring were to be revised repeatedly in the months ahead, but the discrepancy between the interior volumes with their hipped ceilings and the exterior envelope remained apparent. Perhaps no other building in Wright's career more graphically illustrates the transition between the earlier wood frame Prairie houses and the massive enclosures of the textile block houses.

A few days before Barnsdall planned to sail for Europe, her passport was revoked because of her friendship with the political anarchist Emma Goldman. However, she remained in New York where she made plans for extensive dental work.[29] By the first week of April, she wired Lloyd Wright inquiring about the progress of the house and theater model.[30] The younger Wright reported that he was in the process of receiving bids, with the first ones high, but he hoped to obtain a satisfactory figure by April 15. His news about the model was less hopeful—it was only one-fourth completed and was not expected to be ready until May 5. But he reported that Frank Lloyd Wright had cabled his plans to return to the United States in early June.[31]

Remaining optimistic, Lloyd Wright informed his father of the state of the work on March 22, 1920:

> Miss B. is anxious to get the house under way and the walls up ready for your finishing hand in May....Am forwarding photos of the work on the models and the hill planting. Also Schindler's plans for the house as far as he has gone to date....By the time you get this the house foundations will be started and you on your way to L.A. if the schedule you have outlined is to be followed....Am forwarding under separate cover plans, photos, samples, notes, etc. and will send on revised specifications.[32]

The situation became ominous as the date neared for Wright's arrival. First, while still in Japan he had received word that a large group of Japanese woodblock prints he had sold Howard Mansfield, an important New York collector, had been suspected of "revamping." If the accusation were to be proven true, the prints would be virtually worthless, and Wright would be liable to return what could amount to tens of thousands of dollars. To make matters worse, both Mansfield and Wright's most trusted advisor on Japanese prints, Frederick W. Gookin, were away in the country for the summer and not available for meetings.[33]

In addition, Lloyd Wright had not broken ground until April 28, 1920, making it impossible to have half of the building completed by his father's arrival. After revising his schedule, the younger Wright unrealistically informed Barnsdall that the building would be ready by September.[34] He must have been pleased to notify her that "bids on some of the items of the house have been cut for as soon as the plans were filed and the contractors realized that the work was going ahead they flocked in with bona-fide bids and gave their figure. We therefore, will be able to have a working margin, a certain amount of surplus for special finish and safety."[35]

He was also able to give the contractor, Robertson, an enthusiastic endorsement: "Have a practical and efficient builder in charge, a man who has made a record for accurate and economical construction. He is well known and well liked by the labor men and so we will avoid trouble there."[36]

Robertson's contract specified that Hollyhock House was to cost $50,000.[37] Although this figure was twice what Barnsdall had wanted to spend in 1918, it was still substantially less than the $300,000 estimated for the Walker and Eisen design. Many decisions regarding materials and details awaited Wright's arrival. Schindler turned instead to the next building Barnsdall scheduled for construction, the Actors Abode, finishing five sheets by the end of May.

On May 30, 1920, Barnsdall anticipated Wright's return by firing off a letter setting him on notice of her expectations for the coming months:

> Don't you think it is time that we forgot our personal feelings and began to work? The theatre is going to be built—the group not costing over $310,000 as planned, and no work is to begin until it has been so completely finished in drawn plans that complete specifications can be given to contractors—I won't turn one shovelful of earth until I know the cost of the whole—even to equipment. You can see that we have a lot of work before us.
>
> Don't talk about my treating you badly. You know that I like and admire you as an individual almost more than anyone I know—as an architect too

or I wouldn't have chosen you—but—as a *creator* you would spend my whole fortune to create a perfect thing. It is the nature of creation. Why *combat* it and pretend something else—and I as the general director of an enterprise can only spend a certain amount and will [illegible word] your beautiful creation not because I don't understand it but because I don't intend to have it end there or be destroyed like the Midway Gardens—We are going to be enemies on those points, but let's be *reasonable* enemies and good friends between times. Its [sic] one of the human limitations of the work. I think it will be delightful working out this hill with you if we are both perfectly direct and understanding. I have the money for the remainder of the hill—I'm going to invest a part of my theatre fund in it and make it bring the theatre 10% and I want to keep it in my own hands and in yours—if we agree on designs—Now ally yourself with me in this undertaking. I am giving you most—tho [sic] I won't be a slave to anybody's ideas. I am going to be surrounded by too many virile fascinating and gifted personalities for I'm reaching out for "the best" as is "and letting the unknown ones come with the future." If your form is organically right—its [sic] a test of the future—"great things will grow from it without premeditation or constraint." "What man can say that he alone can find the truth!"—I cannot [illegible word] with the belief of the creator but with the belief of the critic. This angers and discourages every artist at first but they remain my friends after it is over because they know it isn't just blind worship that I give—they want this because it tickles their vanity—and more important their nerves—but I should like to see artists of the future a little more friendly and appreciative of each other's output, a little more exacting of themselves than I have found them.[38]

Despite her lecture on their working relationship, Wright was probably both relieved and puzzled to find that Barnsdall was going to spend most of the summer in New York undergoing dental treatment. She was hoping that after he reviewed the interiors of her house they could meet at Taliesin around August 1, and by the end of that month she wanted to sail on her postponed trip to Europe.

Wright was back at Olive Hill by July 1, and surprised to find that the work had proceeded only to the initial foundations. By the time he reached Chicago with the new model of the theater (see Appendix 1, figs. AP-8 and AP-9) he had decided to send Schindler out to Los Angeles to supervise the job. Lloyd Wright was to continue executing drawings and carrying through with the landscape plan.

Finally settled in at Taliesin with Will Smith, Schindler and his new wife, Pauline, Wright left for Chicago to meet with Barnsdall between July 22 and 24, 1920. Barnsdall pronounced the new model of the theater "wonderful," but she repeated that she needed to know the exact cost of construction, and if they decided it could not be built then she had a new idea and wanted to change the general plan.[39] After a short stay in Chicago she was off to Denver, Colorado, on her way to a resort at Estes Park. She wanted to continue their discussions and expected him to join her there, but before this became an issue, her daughter became ill and she left for Los Angeles.[40]

In Los Angeles, Barnsdall became aware that Wright had made changes to the drawings. Eager to see him, she telegraphed, urging him to come to Los Angeles. "Dread another transcontinental trip in heat," Wright cabled on August 6. "Have seen construction myself and as you are to be here September first couldn't we definitely conclude details then."[41] Barnsdall, who apparently canceled her trip to Europe, replied that she believed he was in the United States to work with her and was puzzled at his response.[42] When Wright agreed to come, Barnsdall was pleased. She hoped he would arrive in time to see Irene Franklin at the Orpheum.[43]

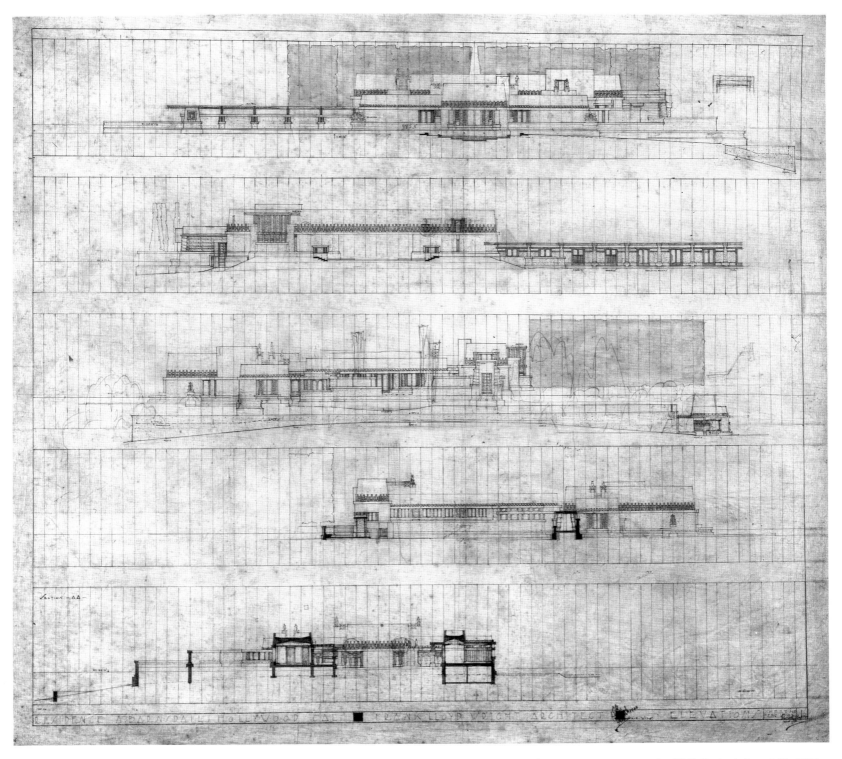

8-8 Hollyhock House, elevations, February 4, 1920 (courtesy of the Frank Lloyd Wright Foundation). In lower margin, "O.K. Revised, August 16, 1920 FLW; Revised, August 20, 1920 FLW."

PART THREE

OLIVE HILL GENERAL PLAN II, 1920

Hollyhock House, perspective, 1921
(courtesy of the Frank Lloyd Wright
Foundation) This ink wash drawing was
executed by Lloyd Wright between
January and June, 1921.

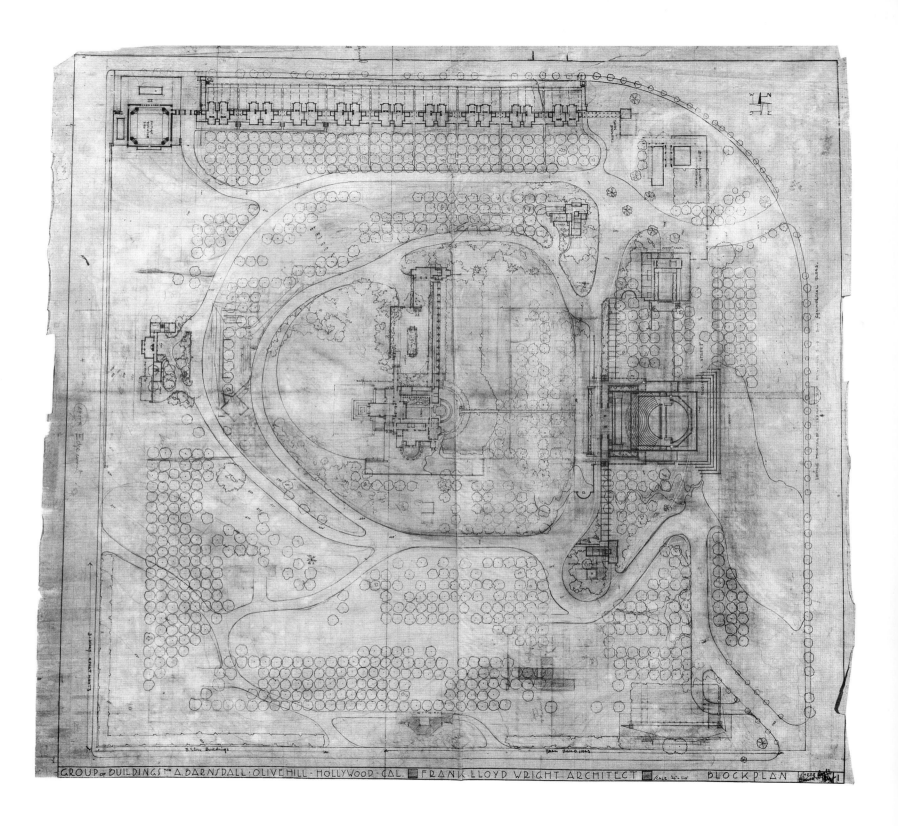

GROUP of BUILDINGS for A. BARNSDALL · OLIVE HILL · HOLLYWOOD · CAL. ☐ FRANK LLOYD WRIGHT ARCHITECT ☐ SCALE 40':1'0" BLOCK PLAN

CHAPTER 9

OLIVE HILL GENERAL PLAN II

9-1. Olive Hill Block Plan, August 4, 1920 (collection of the City of Los Angeles, Departments of Recreation and Parks and Cultural Affairs). Legend reads, in script, "Group of Buildings for A. Barnsdall, Olive Hill, Hollywood, Cal., Frank Lloyd Wright, Architect, Block Plan, Sheet 1, Aug 4th 1920," initialed "RS." At lower right margin, "Revised Aug 20, 1920 FLLW." This linen drawing was extensively worked on over a period of years. The revisions added the commercial zone along Hollywood Boulevard, Residences A and B, and the new watercourse; in 1923, the site plan of the Community Playhouse, the Little Dipper, was added; and, probably in the spring of 1924, when Barnsdall was considering selling the property for development, a commercial and residential subdivision was drawn over it in orange pencil with graphite notations.

By August 12, Wright had stepped off the train in Los Angeles and turned his attention to Olive Hill with little idea that his expected stay of two days would stretch into three weeks. Barnsdall must have felt disappointed that the theater had not progressed to the detailed stage she had demanded; but as she had warned him, she was prepared to change her mind if it was not ready to go into construction. Seeming to vacillate between what she termed, years later, either a "high class real estate developer or patron [of the arts]," she called now for major additions to the general plan.[1]

By August 16, Barnsdall had already brought up the question of new plans for the entire hill.[2] Recalling her Chicago proposal of four years earlier to offset possible losses from the theater with income from rental studios, she focused on the undeveloped frontage along Hollywood Boulevard where she proposed building a commercial zone of stores, duplex houses, and a motion picture theater. According to notes made by Lloyd Wright at this meeting, in addition to the Director's House estimated at $20,000, she added two guest houses, at $15,000 and $30,000 each, to be ready on January 1 and February 1, 1921. The Actors Abode was to be redesigned as an apartment house consisting of one two-bedroom, one-bath apartment, with a combination living/dining room and kitchenette; one one-bedroom apartment with the same additional rooms; eight furnished single rooms with shower baths; and a basement and a storeroom, but no garage. This building was estimated at $100,000 and was to be ready along with the stores and cottages on May 1, 1921. A new completion date of December 1, 1920, was set for Hollyhock House, along with a new budget of $75,000. Finally, the theater group was to begin construction on June 15, 1921, and be completed in October 1922.[3] Wright's reaction to her proposal is unrecorded, but his feelings were probably ambivalent when he thought about time and money. With his next departure for Tokyo imminent, and the restitution of Mansfield's print losses looming in the weeks ahead, he was short of both.

Such a large addition to the general plan necessitated a virtual redesign of the entire scheme. On August 4, 1920, only a week before he left Taliesin, Wright had supervised Schindler's redrawing of the block plan (fig. 9-1). By August 20, when he sat down to revise it, he was faced with an even greater predicament than that of the year before. He had a matter of weeks to design plans and prepare working drawings for larger and more complicated buildings, work out plans for landscaping, furniture, and fixtures, prepare estimates and specifications for bidding, and obtain building permits. In addition, the construction of

9-2. Preliminary sketch of street elevations of Olive Hill, 1920 (collection of the City of Los Angeles, Departments of Recreation and Parks and Cultural Affairs). This drawing by Wright in graphite pencil on butcher paper shows (reading from top to bottom): the Hollywood Boulevard elevation of Terrace Stores and Houses, the Vermont Avenue elevation of the theater flanked by two secondary buildings (Director's House and Entrance Pavilion) and the Sunset Boulevard elevation with Hollyhock House at the crown and the theater at the street. Wright's notes, which read "Tanyderi" and "Taliesin," reveal that he made a connection between Olive Hill and his own community of buildings in Wisconsin.

9-3. Vermont Street elevation, perspective, 1921 (courtesy of the Frank Lloyd Wright Foundation). This ink wash drawing was executed by Lloyd Wright between January and June 1921.

9-4. Hollywood Boulevard elevation, perspective, 1921 (courtesy of the Frank Lloyd Wright Foundation). This ink wash drawing was executed by Lloyd Wright between January and June, 1921.

OLIVE HILL · HOLLYWOOD · CALIFORNIA · FRANK LLOYD WRIGHT · ARCHITECT

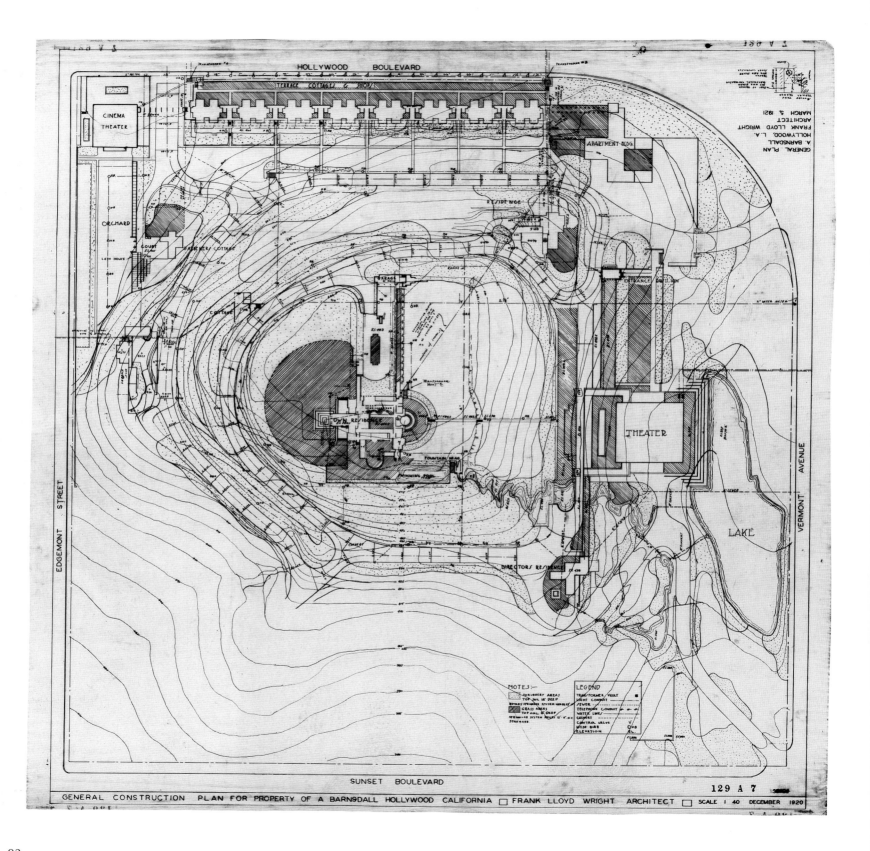

GENERAL CONSTRUCTION PLAN FOR PROPERTY OF A BARNSDALL HOLLYWOOD CALIFORNIA □ FRANK LLOYD WRIGHT ARCHITECT □ SCALE 1 40 DECEMBER 1920

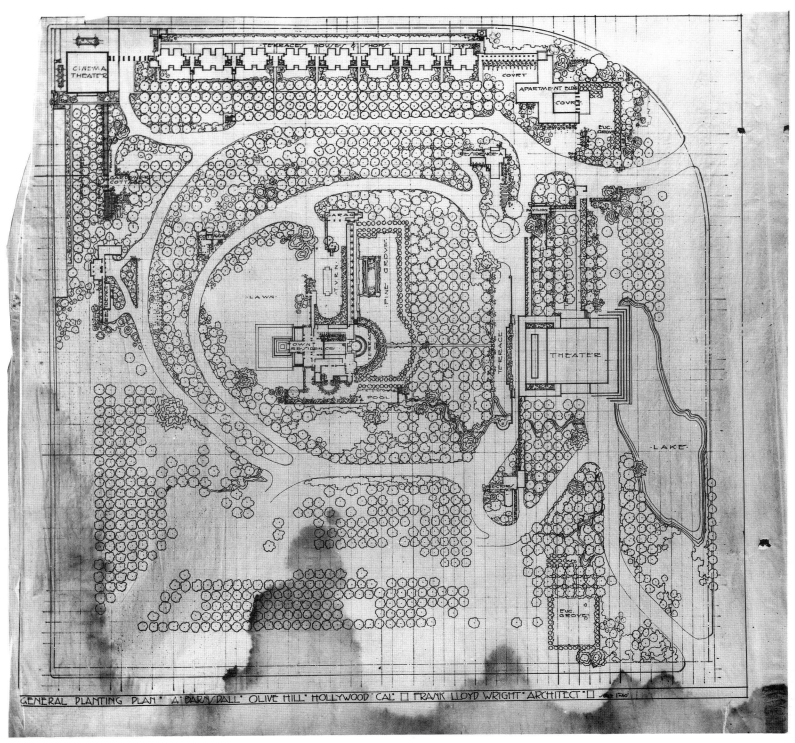

GENERAL PLANTING PLAN · A BARNSDALL · OLIVE HILL · HOLLYWOOD CAL · □ FRANK LLOYD WRIGHT · ARCHITECT · □

9-5. Olive Hill General Plan II, December 1920 (collection of the City of Los Angeles, Departments of Recreation and Parks and Cultural Affairs). This ink-on-linen drawing was executed before Wright's departure for Japan but was revised March 5, 1921.

9-6. General Planting Plan for Olive Hill, 1920, blueprint (courtesy of the Frank Lloyd Wright Foundation). The partition does not appear between the library and living room providing a clear visual axis through the public rooms.

Barnsdall's house was moving slowly, and it was becoming evident that Robertson, the contractor, was not sympathetic to the work.

Barnsdall had focused her attention on a gradual slope fronting Hollywood Boulevard, the main street that connected Olive Hill with the business district of Hollywood to the west. Wright's plan (fig. 9-1) called for building ground level stores and terracing a row of houses over them, hence the title Terrace Stores and Houses. A motion picture theater terminated the row at the west corner. All the small houses were designated with letters of the alphabet. Wright sited Residence A (on the northeast slope above Hollywood Boulevard) on axis with New Hampshire Street to the north. He saved some time in design by adapting the plans for the Director's House for this building. On September 1, 1920, he made preliminary drawings for the second guest house, Residence B, sited on the west slope facing Edgemont Street, and on September 2, Wright drew a preliminary plan for the Terrace Houses, which ultimately became Residences D, E, and F. No evidence has survived documenting Residence C; however, the general plan did call for a house for the director in its former location, which would account for its existence. When Wright left for Taliesin on September 5, Barnsdall indicated that she would be in Chicago in a few weeks on her way back to New York. Wright promised that he would have the drawings well along and would show her "pictures" of the hill.

The addition of new buildings to Olive Hill required adjustments and refinements to the plan (fig. 9-5), which Wright worked on until his departure for Japan in December. He relocated the Actors Abode, which simply became the apartment building, extending the Hollywood Boulevard frontage (fig. 9-4) to the east and closing off the automobile entrance to the hill. A row of ground level stores now opened directly on Hollywood Boulevard, but the theater (fig. 9-3) was rotated 180 degrees, turning its back to the street. The theater entrance became more intimate and private, and the plan was modified to provide a formal path leading to a pavilion in the former position of the Actors Abode. From the pavilion, guests were directed along a pergola to a side entrance of the theater.

With the entrance to the theater now facing inward toward the hill, Wright was faced with the problem of providing a connection between this major public building and the street. His solution was to redesign the watercourse. Moving the symbolic and visual emphasis from the Director's House to the theater, he shifted both the course of the stream and the reflecting pond to the latter building (fig. 9-6). Although he abandoned the powerful double waterfall entrance to the Director's House, he created a clearer hierarchy with a logical termination at the most important building. Visual focus was drawn to the theater by its mirror reflection on the surface of the man-made lake. The watercourse now recalled the unity of the McCormick scheme, but Wright retained the steep waterfall at the southeast corner. In its isolated position, it was the only remnant of the original concept.[4]

The Director's House and the former Actors Abode, now the Apartment Building, both initially designed in 1919, were redesigned. Unfortunately, the new footprints that appear in the general plan dated December 1920 are the only surviving evidence (fig. 9-5).[5] They show a remarkable progression from the strongly axial ordering systems of the Prairie house to a free and daring asymmetrical pinwheel configuration that anticipates Mies van der Rohe's Concrete Country House of 1923 by three years. One can only speculate about Schindler's participation in their design, since nothing quite like them appeared in Wright's work in the following years, and they most closely resemble the footprint of Schindler's own studio-residence of late 1921 (fig. 9-7).

Barnsdall had definitely made Wright's life more difficult, but she had also provided him with a program that anticipated issues he explored over a decade later in Broadacre City. Olive Hill was more than a private estate, even more than a cultural community—it now was divided into three distinct zones: com-

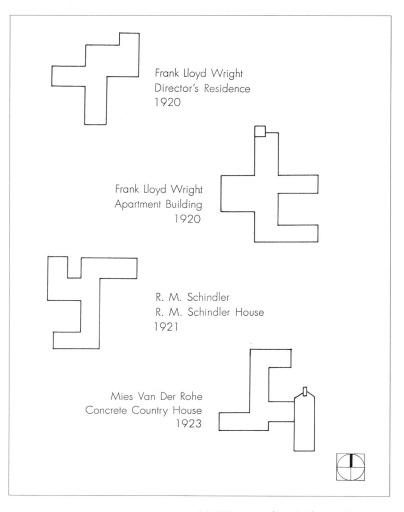

9-7. Diagrams of *partis* (drawing by Eulogio Guzman)

mercial, cultural, and residential. The new plan called for a clear distinction in use among Hollywood Boulevard, Vermont Avenue, and the crown and adjoining slopes of the hill. Broadacre City, with its more complex functions of government, industry, and farming, represented the self-sufficient community. Its similarities to Olive Hill reflect Wright's inherent concerns, and its differences point out Olive Hill's deficiencies.

Like Olive Hill, Broadacre City is square, but larger in scale—four square miles compared to thirty-six acres. The former was organized along axial planning principles, while the latter was divided into four different but equal quadrants. Both were planned for low density dispersion over countryside tamed to an agrarian ideal. A unifying visual and symbolic element in both is a watercourse: a stream and a lake. The greatest difference between the two is glaring: by 1932, Wright had incorporated the automobile into the plan as the dominant factor, but at Olive Hill, parking is virtually unrecognized. For Barnsdall's entire site, Wright provided only twenty-two parking spaces: sixteen for the commercial zone, one for the director in the theater zone, and five among the three houses circling the hill.

Although the Olive Hill plan does not reflect it, Wright was profoundly influenced by the use of the automobile in Los Angeles, where the Schindlers noted he went everywhere in a chauffeur-driven car. "Modern transportation may scatter the city," he observed only three years later, "open breathing spaces in it, green it and beautify it, making it fit for a superior order of human beings."[6] Expressing an aversion to New York similar to Barnsdall's, Wright wrote of bringing the country to the city and the city to the country, which is precisely what the Olive Hill plan did; it was not an urban scheme in any conventional sense. Despite their temperamental differences, Wright and Barnsdall shared certain fundamental beliefs; perhaps this kindred spirit kept them working together over the years and provided the basis for their lifelong friendship in spite of their heated clashes.

Producing the working drawings before Wright's departure required a frantic burst of activity, not only to meet the pace of construction on Barnsdall's house but to have enough drawings ready to obtain bids on the other buildings. Barnsdall arrived from California around September 20 to approve the revised drawings for Residence A and a preliminary sketch for a typical store. The Residence A plan remained essentially the same with a few exceptions because of its relocation away from the theater (figs. 9-8 through 9-12). The entrance was widened with the elimination of the waterfalls (fig. 9-9), the garage was flipped to the opposite side, and the roof terrace was reduced to a pair of doors that opened onto a small area of composition roofing (fig. 9-10). In conformance with Barnsdall's own house, Residence A was to have reinforced concrete foundations, wood and terra-cotta hollow-tile walls with sand-finished plaster, and a composition roof. The interiors were to be stained plaster with a wood trim of white-streaked red gum.[7]

Pressure began to mount with each day as the prospect of Barnsdall's return to the Midwest grew closer. Before she left for New York she promised to be back in ten days to review the progress. Wright made an effort to have the drawings for Residence B ready for approval on her return.

9-8. Residence A, perspective, 1921 (H.Th. Wijdeveld, ed., *The Life-Work of Frank Lloyd Wright*, 1925). Drawing by Lloyd Wright.

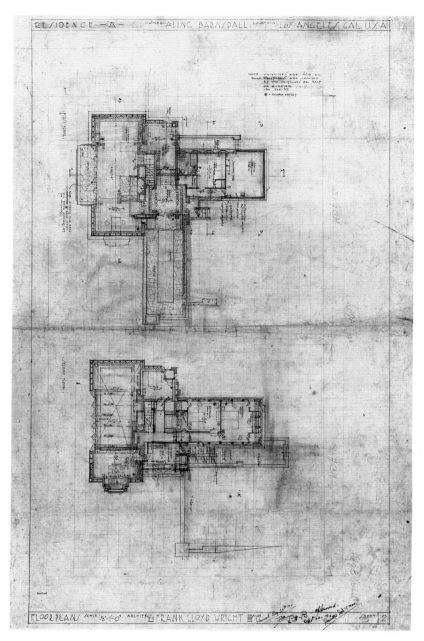

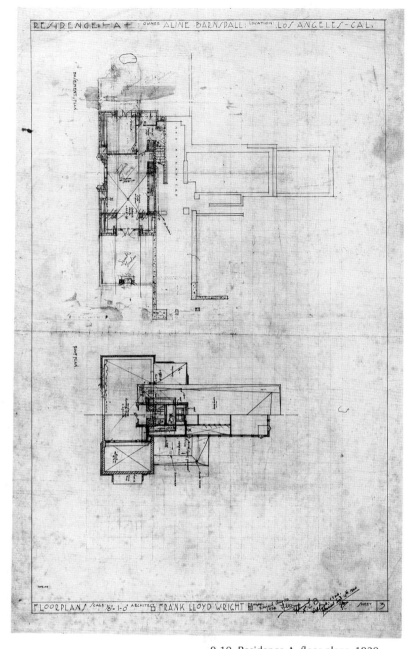

9-9. Residence A, floor plans, 1920 (courtesy of the Frank Lloyd Wright Foundation). The marginal notations read, "Revised Aug 25th 1920, FLW; LAB Approved, Sept. 20, 1920; Revised Sept. 15th, 1920; Oct 2 Rec'd." LAB are initials for Louise Aline Barnsdall. Compare with fig. 6-6.

9-10. Residence A, floor plans, 1920 (courtesy of the Frank Lloyd Wright Foundation). The marginal notations read, "Revised Aug 20, 1920, FLW; Approved LAB, Sept. 20, 1920; Revised Sept. 15th, 1920 FLW." Revisions in pencil indicate a remodeling on the basement level to include the conversion of the garage to a studio bedroom flanked by an enclosed and sunken garden. Compare with fig. 6-7.

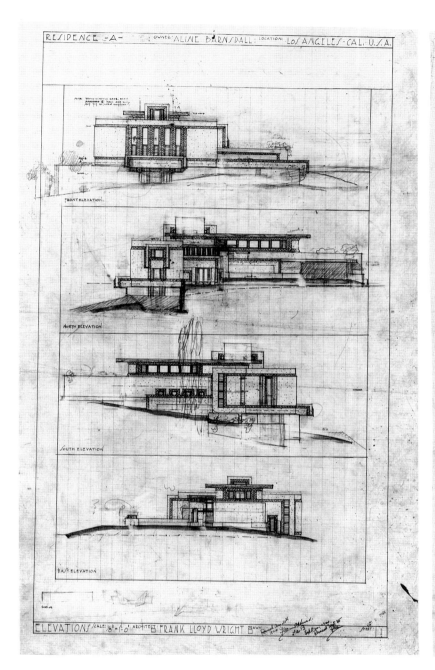

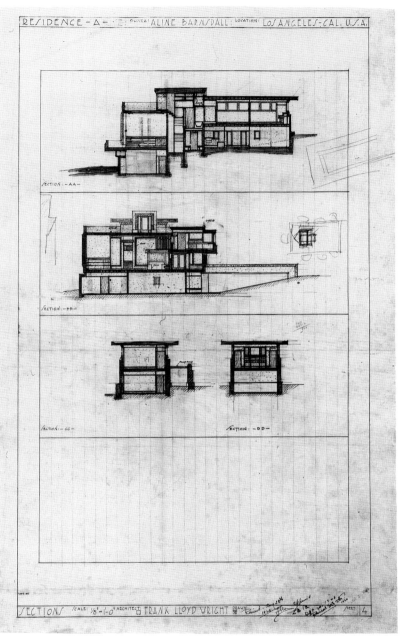

9-11. Residence A, elevations, 1920
(courtesy of the Frank Lloyd Wright
Foundation). The marginal notations read,
"Revised August 25th, 1920, FLW;
Approved, LAB, Sept 20, 1920; Revised
Sept 15, FLW; Oct 2 Recd." Pencil
sketches over the ink-on-linen drawing
indicate that additional changes were
made at a later date, probably in 1923.
They include the addition of windows on
what was now the east wall of the living
room (read: south elevation). Compare
with fig. 6-8.

9-12. Residence A, sections, 1920 (cour-
tesy of the Frank Lloyd Wright
Foundation). The marginal notations read,
"Revised Aug 25th 1920, FLW;
Approved, LAB, Sept. 20, 1920; Revised
Sept. 15th 1920; Oct 2 Recd." Compare
with fig. 6-9.

97

RESIDENCE "B" OLIVE HILL

CHAPTER 10

RESIDENCE B

10-1. Residence B, perspective, 1921 (collection of the City of Los Angeles, Departments of Recreation and Parks and Cultural Affairs). This ink wash drawing was executed by Lloyd Wright, January to June 1921.

From the first sketch through four sheets of working drawings, Residence B was produced in one month. This haste did not allow for prolonged study of the site, which resulted in a problem later on; however, the zoned plan provides an interesting transition between the larger Prairie houses and the more compact Usonian houses.

Entry was from the rear where five doors opened to the motor court (fig. 10-5). The three zones—living, bedroom, and service—were condensed into distinct units connected by an elongated circulation spine. The living room was centrally placed behind the wide, stone-floored loggia, with the bedroom wing perpendicular to it at one end, and the service wing on line at the opposite end. The living room (measuring thirty-nine by eighteen feet) was designed for private and public entertainment and included areas for a library and dining room. Wright defined these by manipulating the vertical space; a double-height living area rose to a skylight over the free standing fireplace, flanked on either side by two one-story enclosed alcoves (fig. 10-7). On the west side of the living room, three doors leading onto a roofed balcony opened to views of the Pacific Ocean. The bedroom wing contained three bedrooms, two-and-a-half baths, and a covered sleeping porch; two servant rooms were located behind the kitchen. The main stairhall led up through the sleeping porch, a regional feature, to a narrow passage that opened to a balcony overlooking the living room. From the balcony, the opposite door led to a sod-covered terrace over the garage.

Although Residence B recalled some elements of the larger Barnsdall House—a zoned plan wrapped around an interior courtyard—its organization was based on an elongated spine rather than axial symmetry. Residence B anticipated buildings such as the Ennis House, the larger House on the Mesa, and the later Usonians such as the Theodore Baird House of 1940.

From the exterior (figs. 10-1 and 10-6), Residence B appeared unrelated to the theater and Barnsdall's house. The flat, unadorned surfaces contrasted with strong, horizontal details; the lapped boards (outlining the upper stories, the cornice, and the major openings) were laid horizontally rather than vertically, creating a corbeled appearance. The steep slope required more extensive foundations of concrete retaining walls and footings than the other two houses, but the structure also was of wood frame and hollow tile. The specifications called for exterior and interior surfaces of tinted, sand-finished plaster, with interior birch trim.

Just as progress was being made on the new buildings, Barnsdall received news in New York that construction on her house had slowed down, awaiting

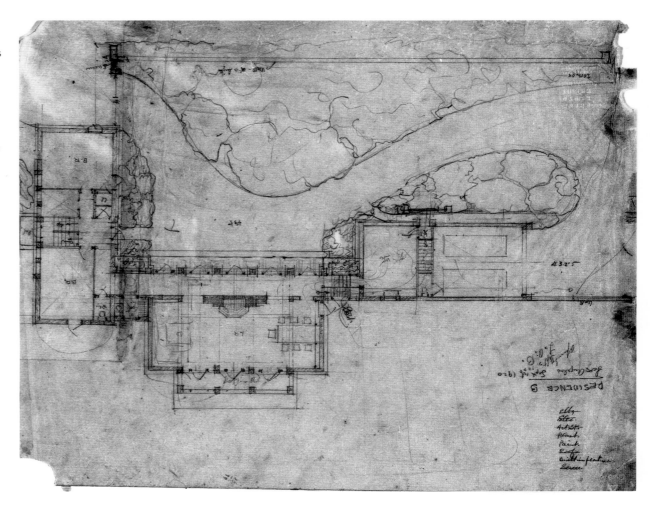

10-2. Residence B, preliminary plan, 1920 (courtesy of the Frank Lloyd Wright Foundation). In margin, "Residence B, Los Angeles, Sept. 1st, 1920; Approved, Sept. 2, 1920, LAB." (This drawing is shown upside down to correspond with fig. 10-5.)

drawings. On September 24, 1920, she cabled Wright about the problems and inquired whether everything would be ready for her to see by October 1. He cabled back immediately:

> Impossible to get help. We have been working day and night since I got home—nearly worn out. If you can delay until October 10th to 15th much better. All details for Own House and Residence A in Los Angeles. Stores and Small Dwellings and Residence B nearing completion. Rug designs and Furniture designs ready—but no perspective drawings yet—experts promised to come to work Monday.[1]

On September 29, she cabled that she would wait until October 10, but because of the lack of drawings, bids were being held up on Residence A, and delays on her house were becoming expensive. Wright shot back that the drawings had been sent to Los Angeles. "Shall I get estimates on Living Room rug and Furniture here," he inquired, "or await your approval and send to Los Angeles."[2] By October 1, Schindler had finished four sheets on Residence B— the plans, elevations, sections, and details—but working drawings for the largest and most complicated new building, the Terrace Stores and Houses, had not been started.

10-3. Residence B, east and north elevations, 1920 (courtesy of the Frank Lloyd
Wright Foundation). The north elevation
has been pasted on the lower left corner
of the larger drawing.

10-4. Residence B, west elevation, 1920
(courtesy of the Frank Lloyd Wright
Foundation). At upper left, "FLW, Sept 4th
[*sic*], 1920."

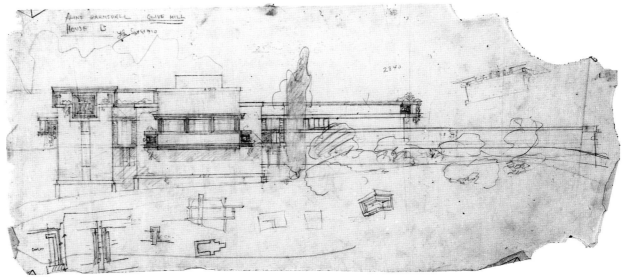

10-5. Residence B, floor plans, September 28, 1920, blueprint (courtesy of the Architectural Drawing Collection, University Art Museum, University of California, Santa Barbara). At the lower margin, signed "Frank Lloyd Wright" and noted "Approved November 10, 1920, Aline Barnsdall."

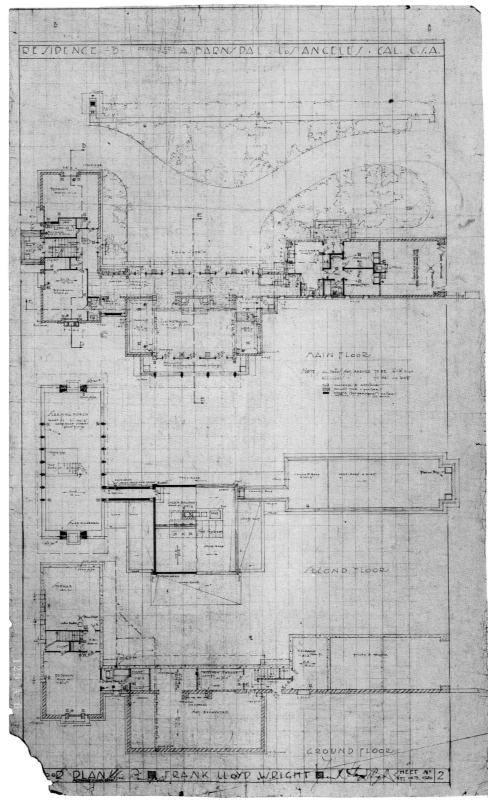

10-6. Residence B, elevations, September 28, 1920, blueprint (courtesy of the Architectural Drawing Collection, University Art Museum, University of California, Santa Barbara). At the lower margin, signed "Frank Lloyd Wright" and noted "Approved November 10, 1920, Aline Barnsdall."

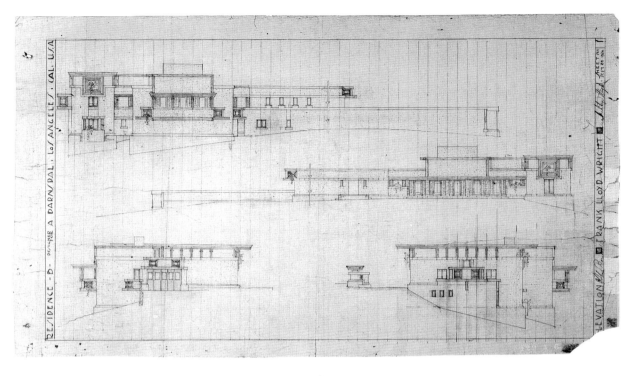

10-7. Residence B, sections, September 28, 1920, blueprint (courtesy of the Architectural Drawing Collection, University Art Museum, University of California, Santa Barbara). At the lower margin, signed "Frank Lloyd Wright" and noted "Approved November 10, 1920, Aline Barnsdall."

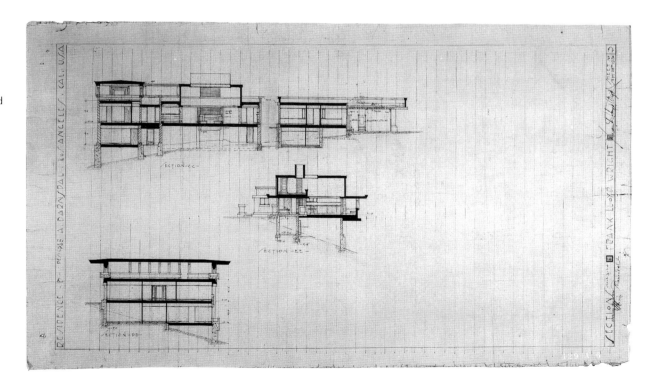

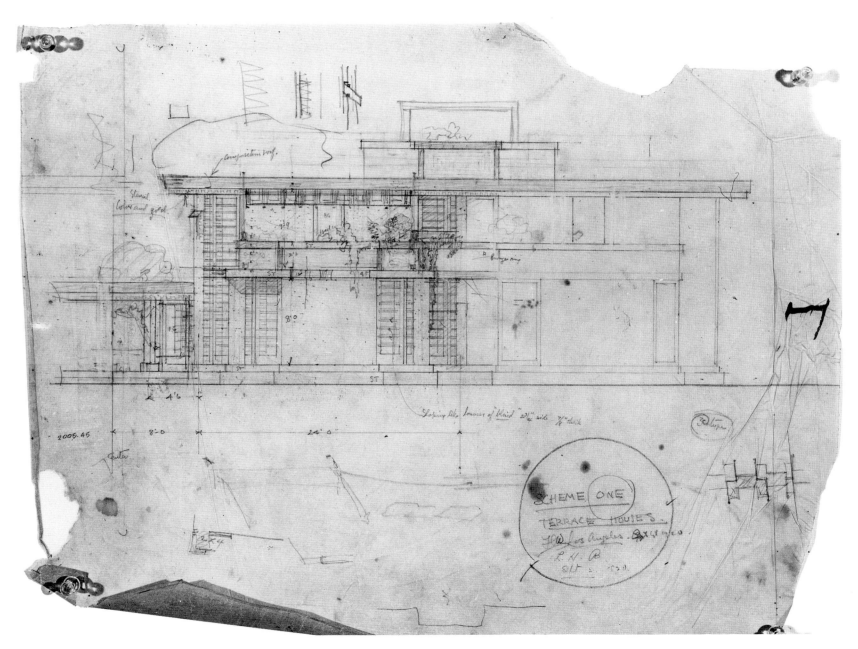

CHAPTER 11

TERRACE STORES AND HOUSES

11-1. Terrace Houses, preliminary elevation, 1920 (courtesy of the Frank Lloyd Wright Foundation). In the lower right corner, "Scheme One, Terrace Houses, FLW, Los Angeles, Sept. 1st, 1920; LAB, Sept. 2, 1920."

Wright got word that Howard Mansfield would be arriving at Taliesin in mid-October 1920 to settle the dispute over the suspected "revamped" Japanese prints. If Wright was called upon to refund Mansfield's money, he would lose whatever gains he had made on the dwindling Imperial Hotel commission. When Barnsdall's September 29 telegram came, Wright was making preparations for Mansfield's arrival. Pauline Schindler reported to her parents on September 29, "For two weeks on end Mr. Wright has been playing around with his print-room,— manipulating light-effects; arranging screens and rugs and lacquer cabinets and Chinese vases dating a hundred years before Christ,—all with relation to their modification of the prints....The folk who come...from New York, will really make or unmake Mr. Wright's finances."

By October 5, Pauline Schindler revealed, "Mr. Wright and Smith are still mounting and arranging Japanese prints,—and meanwhile there have been several 'dress rehearsals'...placing and arranging them for view before us,—and a critical noting of the effects of lighting, sequence, etc."[1] Wright wrote, much later, "[W]e held...what was known as 'The Print Party.' I threw open the vault... with its collections to Howard and his friends. They were free to choose what they would in exchange for the restored prints....That party cost me about thirty thousand dollars."[2]

Mansfield's visit came in the middle of work on the Terrace Stores and Houses, the most ambitious building project Barnsdall had proposed except for the theater. Perhaps Wright's preoccupation with his print dealings, among other things, partly explains the uncharacteristic process of design development. Anticipating aspects of his urban projects of the 1930s, such as Monona Terrace in Madison, Wisconsin, and Crystal Heights in Washington, D.C., Wright conceived of a two-story building (ultimately 688 feet long) that was the architectural equivalent of a landscaped, terraced hillside (fig. 9-4). Using a sixteen-foot grid, he proposed an arcade of long, narrow stores that backed up against the hill facing Hollywood Boulevard, with a row of duplex houses set back from the street forming a second story (fig. 11-2). The floor-to-ceiling plate glass bays of the sixteen- by seventy-foot stores (figs. 11-2, 11-4, and 11-5) were recessed under a canopy supported by twin asymmetrical columns, or stanchions, that met a square flower box at the street. The canopy and the major portion of the stores' roof were laid out as a landscaped "street in the sky" with a curbed and guttered sidewalk bordering lawns and walks leading to the houses (fig. 11-4). Access to the terrace was provided by staircases at the east and west ends (fig. 11-7). The building terminated at the west in a garage for sixteen cars with offices above (fig. 11-4). Although the program called for the street to be lined with a wall of buildings, Wright's scheme still integrated nature into an urban setting. The theme of the building, a terraced hillside, held great potential, but the details are surprisingly clumsy for Wright. It is conceivable that they were brought on by pressure of time or client or both.

The site itself had two inherent problems. First, facing north, the Hollywood Boulevard location received only indirect natural light. Second, the site, including the existing public sidewalk, sloped nine feet from east to west. In addition to all glass facades, Wright added a band of transom windows and tilted the canopy at a thirty-degree angle in an effort to maximize the light. To maintain the continuous horizontal line of the roof, however, all the vertical elements in the stores—the columns, walls, and transom windows—were graduated in height from east to west. The difference was so great that mezzanines were added to six stores on the west that were one floor higher than those on the east (fig. 11-5).

The stores and houses did not create an integrated architectural solution; the houses simply rested on the roof of the stores below. After choosing a solution that did not respond to the slope, Wright compounded the problem by introducing elements, such as transom windows and columns, that called attention to the glaring difference between one side of the building and the other.

As the months passed, he was to face still another problem. His preliminary drawing called for forty-three stores and nine duplex houses, but in the working drawings the number of stores was reduced to thirty-nine. Either before or after Wright's departure for Japan in December 1920, additional changes were made and the drawings were revised again, further reducing the number of stores to thirty-five and the duplexes to eight (figs. 11-4 and 11-5). The last major adjustment shortened the row by sixty-four feet.

Unlike the other buildings on Olive Hill that had reached the development phase, the Terrace Stores called for an extensive use of concrete for both structure and ornament. Behind the glass curtain wall of the commercial facades, mushroom columns supported the roof slab; but in other areas brick was used for party walls, wood frame and hollow tile were used for interior partitions, and the floors were finished cement.

The preliminary sketch (figs. 11-8 and 11-9) of a single house plan was redesigned on a two-foot square grid creating three variations of the same *parti* called Residences D, E, and F (figs. 11-10, 11-11, and 11-12). Presumably under time pressure, Wright based his scheme on an earlier project, the Monolith Home for Thomas P. Hardy (fig. 11-14), designed by Schindler during Wright's absence in Japan in 1919. About ten years later, Wright explained that he believed Schindler's design "gave my own stuff in my own style....If drawing ideas and schemes of the Masters can make them the draughtsman's it is only necessary for the Master to turn his back and his help can steal him blind. They do."[3]

Hardy, a former Prairie house client, proposed to build eighteen houses on a site bordering the Root River in Racine, Wisconsin. In July 1919, Schindler had drawn a preliminary first and second floor plan and a perspective that he labeled the Worker's House. These drawings were followed in the same month by five sheets of working drawings, a site plan, and a perspective of the overall development (figs. 11-13 and 11-15), which could be compared successfully to Le Corbusier's Quartier Moderne at Pessac for Henri Fruges, 1924–1926.

The Monolith Home, as it was now called, was based on the theme of one material—cast concrete—used throughout the exterior and interior for floors, walls, and roof. The drawings show a building on a two-foot square grid, wholly comprised of solid and transparent planes. With one exception in the storage room, no two planes joined at right angles to enclose a corner. In the slots between the wall slabs, bands of transparent glass extended from floor to ceiling—and, in some areas, the full two stories—in an unbroken rhythm of units,

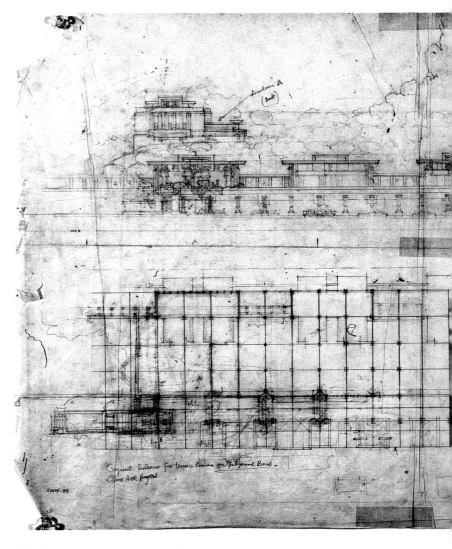

11-2. Terrace Stores, preliminary plan and elevations, 1920 (courtesy of the Frank Lloyd Wright Foundation). Note that the elevation drawing includes Residence A at upper left and Hollyhock House at upper center.

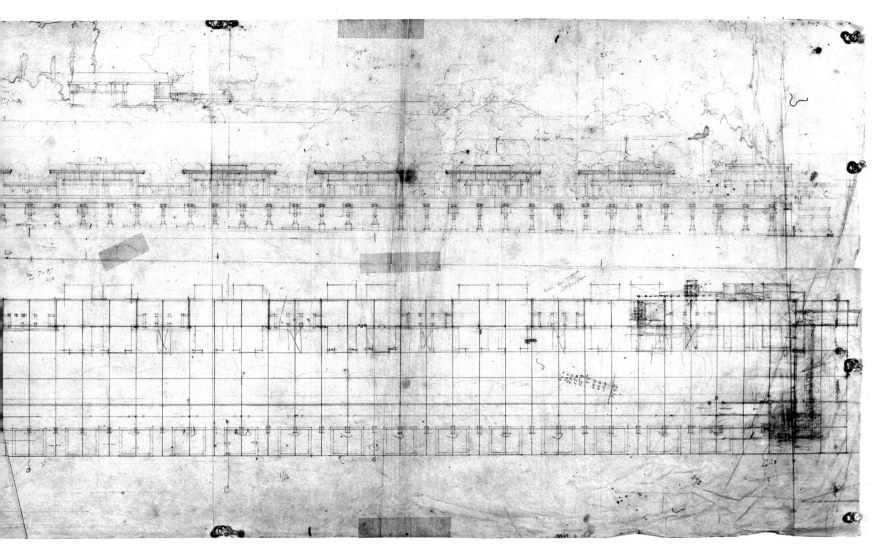

11-3. Terrace Stores, preliminary drawing
of a typical store, 1920 (courtesy of the
Frank Lloyd Wright Foundation). Note
that on the lower half of the drawing
Wright has sketched the connection
between the east end of the Terrace
Stores and the relocated apartment building in plan and elevation. Below this
sketch in pencil, "Sept 20, 1920, LAB."

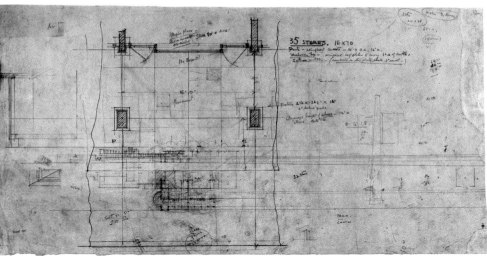

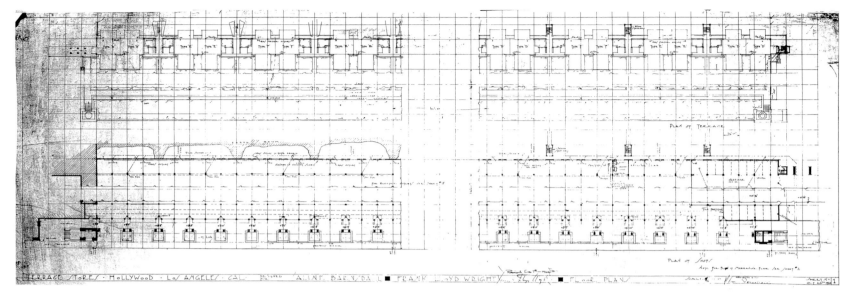

11-4. Terrace Stores, floor plans, October 26, 1920, blueprint (courtesy of the Architectural Drawing Collection, University Art Museum, University of California, Santa Barbara). In the lower margin, "Revised Dec 7th 1920 FLW; Approved November 10, 1920, Aline Barnsdall."

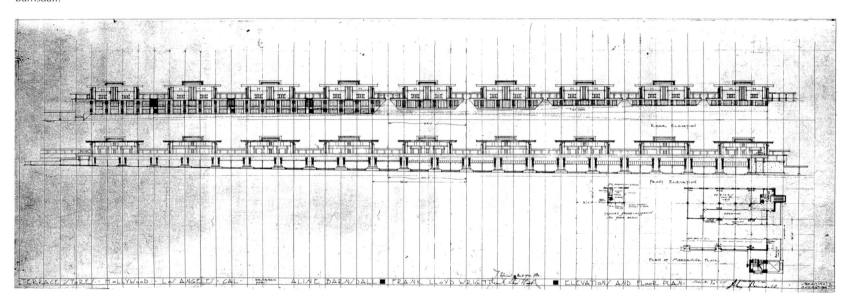

11-5. Terrace Stores, elevations and floor plan, October 26, 1920, blueprint (courtesy of the Architectural Drawing Collection, University Art Museum, University of California, Santa Barbara). In the lower margin, "Revised Dec 7th 1920 FLW; Approved November 10, 1920, Aline Barnsdall."

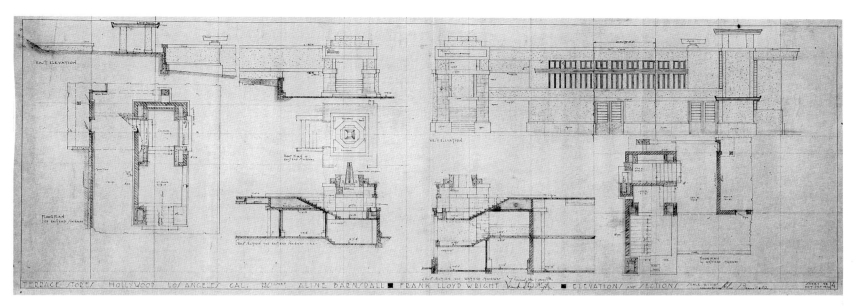

11-6. Terrace Stores, elevations and
sections, October 23, 1920, blueprint
(courtesy of the Architectural Drawing
Collection, University Art Museum,
University of California, Santa Barbara).
In lower margin, "Revised Dec 7th, 1920
FLW; Approved November 10th, 1920
Aline Barnsdall."

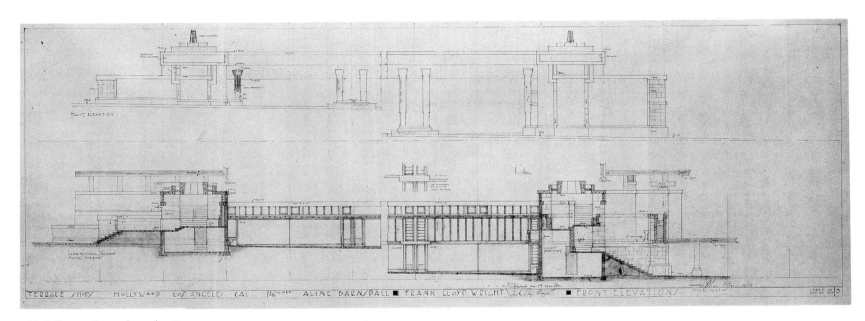

11-7. Terrace Stores, front elevations,
October 25, 1920, blueprint (courtesy of
the Architectural Drawing Collection,
University Art Museum, University of
California, Santa Barbara). In the
lower margin, "Revised Dec 7th, 1920
FLW; Approved, Nov. 10, 1920
Aline Barnsdall."

virtually erasing the distinction between doors and windows.[4] Schindler opened the living room on the diagonal by butting two vertical bands of glass together to create an inverted corner window.

Although inspired by Wright's earlier work both stylistically and structurally, Schindler's scheme went a significant step further in its degree of abstraction and its uncompromising use of unfinished concrete. The consequences were three-fold: structurally, the materials and method declared their industrial origins; socially, the low-cost, minimal dwelling was directed at the worker; spatially, outside and inside interpenetrated fluidly through the vertical slots of glass, although the interior was compartmentalized to accommodate the program. In September 1919, Wright had revised the scheme's details without changing either the form or the plan; but by the time new drawings were made in April 1920, perhaps at the client's suggestion, the title had been changed to Residences and the materials to concrete foundations, wood frame, and stucco.[5]

For the Terrace Houses, Wright repeated the geometry of the Monolith Home project in plan—two overlapping, perpendicular rectangles divided by a primary and secondary axis, creating four zones, or rooms (figs. 11-10, 11-11, and 11-12). As in the earlier project, the living room, dining room, kitchen, and storage were on the ground floor with two bedrooms, a bath, sleeping porch, and roof garden on the second floor. Although his preliminary sketches (figs. 11-8 and 11-9) made in Los Angeles recall the Monolith Home almost exactly, on his return to Taliesin, Wright had more time to review the scheme and make changes. His critique of Schindler's scheme was directed primarily at the plan. Schindler sacrificed efficiency and spaciousness for a strict adherence to geometric rigor; to maintain the symmetry of the room arrangement, he devoted excessive space to circulation, storage, and open porches in a harsh climate. Although Wright retained the second floor plan (which was more suitable in southern California) with some minor adjustments, he opened up the first floor living areas dramatically. His fluid and asymmetrical space planning was in direct contrast to Schindler's arbitrary composition. His focus was on the living room which, with the addition of a masonry fireplace replacing Schindler's built-in stove, was enlarged considerably by incorporating the dining area and, in Residences D and F, condensing the kitchen and the storage room.

On the exterior, Wright made alterations that added decorative detail and richness to Schindler's abstract composition of solids and voids (fig. 11-1): a band of ornament, repeating forms from Residence A, outlined the walls, pattern mullions were added to the vertical window bands, and the roof cornice was stenciled in color and gold. The structure was to be hollow terra-cotta tile and wood, with stained plaster and wood trim inside and out.

Wright grouped two houses together, flanked on each side by a separate entry, to create a duplex. On the exterior, he joined the two separate units with a double chimney. Each duplex used the same plan, and the nine pairs were arranged in the following order: D-E-F-E-F-D-F-E-D. Some months later, the fifth unit was eliminated to shorten the row.

Although Wright probably used Schindler's scheme because of the tremendous time pressure he felt in the fall of 1920, the Terrace Houses provide a clear illustration of Wright's confrontation with the European modernism of a younger generation. Schindler was the first of a group of architects, including Richard Neutra, Walter Gropius, and Mies van der Rohe, who left Europe for America. He was also the first and only one of this group whose synthesis of European modernism and the lessons of the Oak Park studio was carried out *in* the Oak Park studio. Just as Wright was delving deeper into the mysteries of nature, Schindler was turning to industrial methods and materials to create spatial solutions for a new social order. The formal means that he chose was to carry Wright's geometric abstraction to its logical conclusions. Like Mies after him he converted

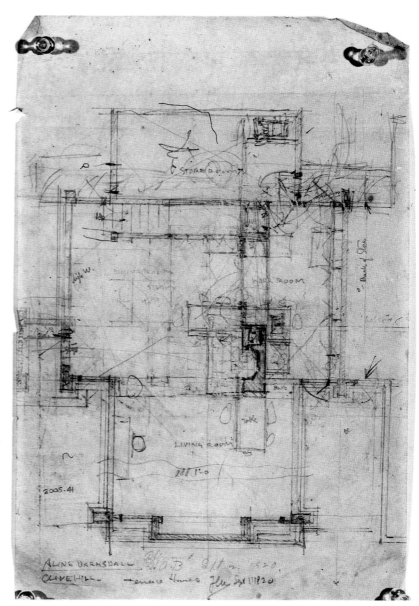

11-8. Terrace Houses, preliminary first floor plan (courtesy of the Frank Lloyd Wright Foundation) At the lower margin, "Approved LAB, Sept. 2, 1920; Terrace Houses, FLW, Sept. 2, 1920."

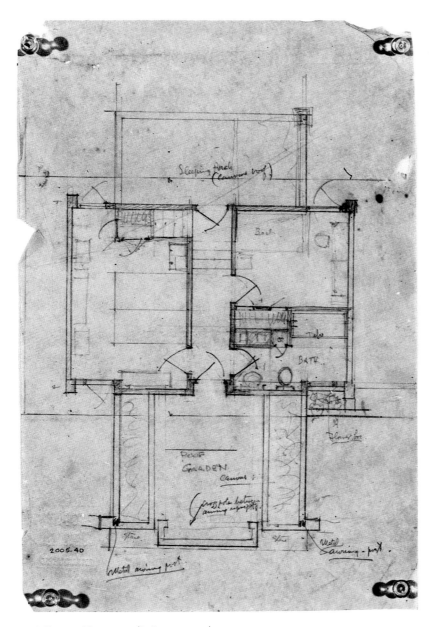

11-9. Terrace Houses, preliminary second floor plan (courtesy of the Frank Lloyd Wright Foundation).

Wright's abstractions of architectural elements—walls, windows, doors, roof—into pure geometric objects. The result of this abstraction was the elimination of human scale and references to nature that Wright could not tolerate then any more than he could a decade later, when he could no longer avoid acknowledging its importance.

However, there was no immediate sign of the deeper impact of Schindler's Monolith Home on Wright. It was not until the completion of the Imperial Hotel and his return to Los Angeles in 1923 that Wright began in the textile block houses to synthesize the reawakening of his own modernism with his search for an integration with nature. When the synthesis was complete at Fallingwater in 1936, Wright finally provided Schindler with his best answer to the Monolith Home.

But during the first weeks of October 1920, Wright was anticipating the arrival of both Barnsdall and Mansfield within days of each other. The pace picked up in the drafting room, and although a new draftsman arrived around October 5, even Pauline Schindler was drawn into the work, tracing and inking detail drawings.[6] On October 6, Barnsdall cabled that she would stop by Chicago on her way back to California from New York.[7] There is no record of whether this meeting took place, but by October 10, only the drawings for Residence B were ready. Work on the Terrace Stores and Houses did not pick up until after Mansfield departed on October 16.[8] On October 22, just as Pauline Schindler was reporting that "everybody [is] very busy in the studio, until late each evening," Barnsdall cabled from Los Angeles that work on her house had stopped for lack of drawings.[9] With his attention directed at designing her new buildings, Wright could not keep up with the detailed drawings for masonry, millwork, sheet metal work, and electrical plans that were required on the construction site. Not quite two months after his last trip to Los Angeles—having postponed his trip to Japan until December at Barnsdall's request—Wright gathered up the last drawing for the Terrace Stores and caught a train for California. As the train pulled across country, perhaps his spirits began to revive when he thought about his new property connecting Taliesin with his aunts' Hillside Home School (fig. 5-14). Apparently Mansfield's visit had turned out better than he had expected, and he was now thinking about the landscaping his new purchase would make possible.[10]

However, in the fall of 1920, a number of factors were conspiring to create dissension on the Olive Hill site—the original overly optimistic prediction that the building would almost be finished by the end of the year, Wright's absence in Japan and distraction with the new building plans, Barnsdall's constant travels, Lloyd Wright's inexperience, and the inability of Robertson and the subcontractors to adapt to Wright's method of building. Cost was becoming a formidable factor. Even with a new budget, it was evident that Barnsdall's insistence on a fixed limit not to exceed $75,000 was no longer realistic. At least two subcontractors either canceled their contracts or demanded a higher price.

Barnsdall was unhappy about the construction problems and distressed that Wright was not helping her get the details she wanted in her house. Wright later recalled that Barnsdall "had by now been angered by certain failings of her architect. They got tangled up with his virtues, among them one difficult to untangle and that one, most offensive at this time, was a distinct failure to regard the mere owner of a work of art in hand like the romanza, as of ultimate importance in the *execution* of the design."[11] Wright began to persuade Barnsdall to see it his way on certain finish details, such as changing most of the interior wood to white oak, but in resolving the problems on the site they were at a deadlock. Wright wanted to remove Robertson, who he believed was not compatible with his way of working. Barnsdall wanted to hold Wright to his original choice, but replace Lloyd Wright with a clerk of the works at Wright's expense. Barnsdall won out, and Wright informed Schindler that he should prepare to depart for

California. In turn, Wright pressed his case and demanded that all subcontractors deal directly with his office. He explained later that "all too often the Owner at first sign of trouble with the Architect takes refuge in the Contractor. And this is what now happened. She did."[12]

Wright managed to find some time to produce a few sketches for the one remaining building, the motion picture theater (figs. 11-16, 11-17, and 11-19). The sketches reveal a design that is almost identical to a theater he had designed in Tokyo (fig. 11-18).[13] As in the Tokyo project, Wright used the idea of one square rotated forty-five degrees over another square. This overriding geometry determined all aspects of the plan—circulation, seating, sightlines, and position of the screen. The auditorium could seat 926 on the ground floor and in an upper and lower balcony parallel and at right angles to the screen. Wright's insistence on the idealization of a pure geometric idea compromised the function of the motion picture theater; although the space was dynamic with strong diagonal axes, most of the audience, especially in the upper and lower balconies, could not see the screen. It was one of Wright's most daring designs for Barnsdall, but he probably knew it was unlikely ever to be built.

On November 10, Barnsdall reviewed and signed the drawings for Residence B and the Terrace Stores and Houses and decided that these buildings and Residence A would be the next group to go into construction. With little more than a month until his ship sailed for Japan, Wright demanded an open bid to sidestep Robertson.

Work continued night and day at 522 Homer Laughlin Building, Wright's Los Angeles office. Barnsdall was keeping up the pressure, even if it was from long distance. From San Francisco, she wrote on November 12, enclosing specifications for wood trim and utilities that she wanted incorporated into the plans for the Terrace Stores and Houses. She reminded him that she was still awaiting the perspective drawings of Olive Hill.[14]

As Wright's ship sailed on December 16, 1920, the future of the next phase of construction was still in doubt. "At present, RMS [Schindler], Lloyd Wright (who is at least six feet tall), two draftsmen and an office boy are all crowded into two small office rooms, which are otherwise already overflowing with huge drafting tables and desks," Pauline Schindler observed, "and on TOP of them, various stenographers coming in to bring rush copy of contracts, while burly contractors stand about looking crafty and expensive."[15] Bids on the two small houses had come in over estimates, and the Terrace Stores and Houses were awaiting engineering drawings and special approvals from the building department to build into the public sidewalk.[16]

Presumably in an effort to distance herself from the conflict on the site, Barnsdall informed Wright's office that she would be represented by the new Olive Hill Construction Company. By this time, C.D. Goldthwaite had been successful in his bids for Residences A and B and the Terrace Stores and Houses, but the contracts could not be signed. As Barnsdall's business manager, Clarence Thomas would approve everything for the new company, but Lloyd Wright noted that Goldthwaite investigated and determined that the company did not legally exist. Goldthwaite demanded that the company incorporate before he would do business with them.[17]

With Wright out of the country and Barnsdall replaced by a corporation, Schindler and Lloyd Wright were forced to deal with Thomas and Robertson. Since her purchase of Olive Hill, Barnsdall had seen Wright only sporadically, and she was angered by his lack of attention. She, on the other hand, was becoming what Wright would later consider "his most difficult client."[18]

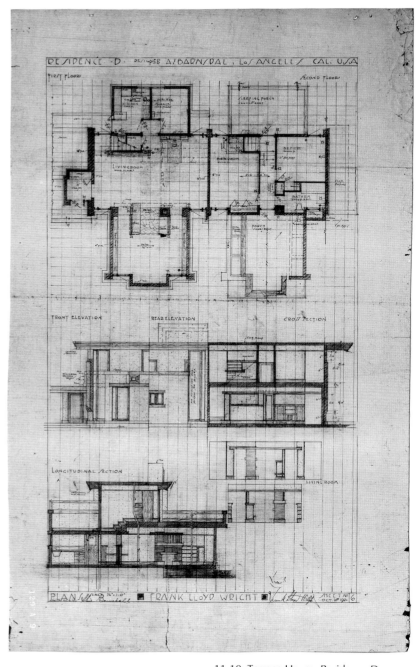

11-10. Terrace House, Residence D, October 10, 1920, blueprint (courtesy of the Architectural Drawing Collection, University Art Museum, University of California, Santa Barbara). In the lower margin, "Approved Nov. 10, 1920, Aline Barnsdall; signed Frank Lloyd Wright."

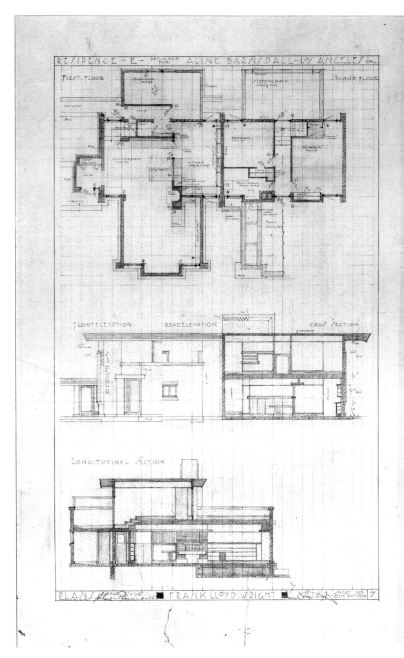

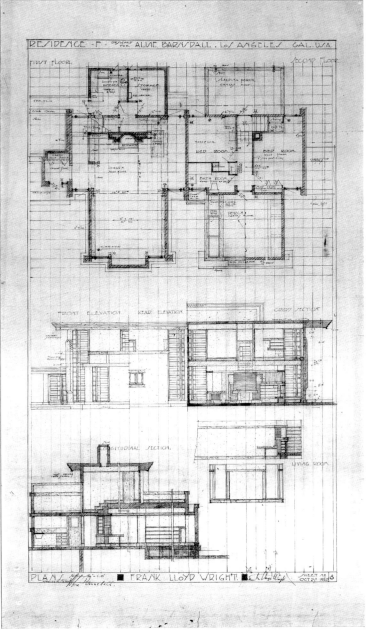

11-11. Terrace Houses, Residence E,
October 24, 1920, blueprint (courtesy of
the Architectural Drawing Collection,
University Art Museum, University of
California, Santa Barbara). In the lower
margin, "Approved Nov. 10, 1920, Aline
Barnsdall; signed Frank Lloyd Wright."

11-12. Terrace House, Residence F,
October 23, 1920, blueprint (courtesy of
the Architectural Drawing Collection,
University Art Museum, University of
California, Santa Barbara). In the lower
margin, "Approved Nov. 10, 1920, Aline
Barnsdall; signed Frank Lloyd Wright."

113

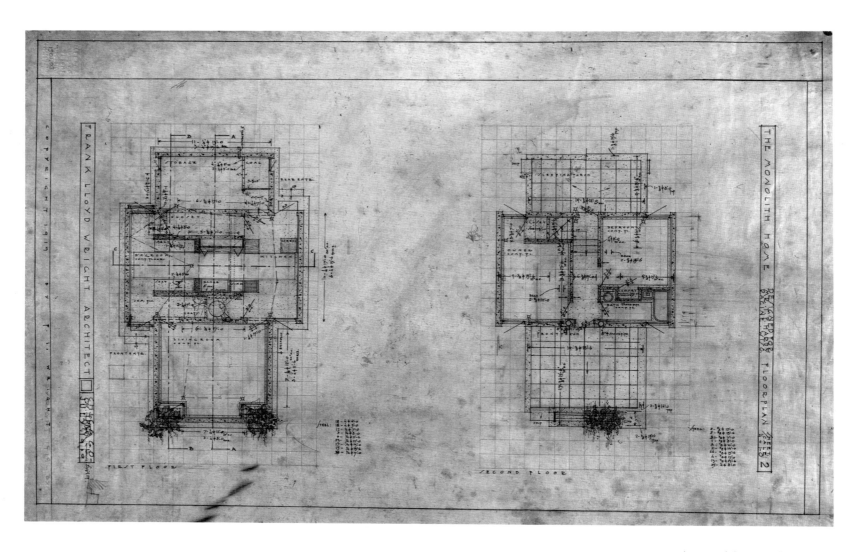

11-13. The Monolith Home, floor plan, July 1919 (courtesy of the Frank Lloyd Wright Foundation). In the lower right corner, "O.K. F.L. Wright, Revised Sept. 18."

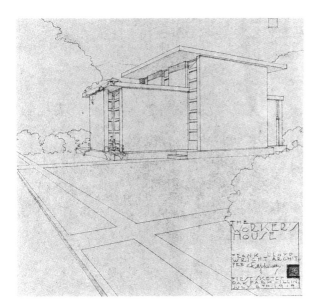

11-14. R.M. Schindler for Frank Lloyd Wright, The Worker's House, 1919, blueprint (courtesy of the Architectural Drawing Collection, University Art Museum, University of California, Santa Barbara). This drawing is dated July 6, 1919.

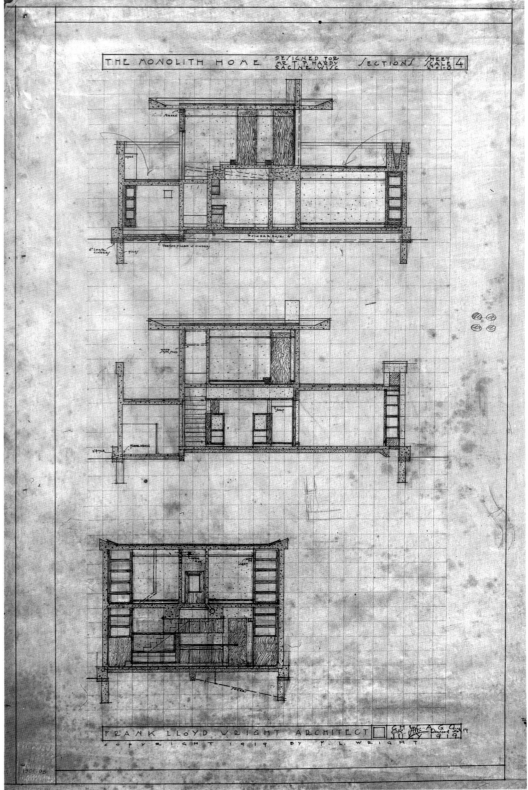

11-15. The Monolith Home, sections, July 1919 (courtesy of the Frank Lloyd Wright Foundation). In the lower right corner, "O.K. F.L.W, Revised Sept. 18."

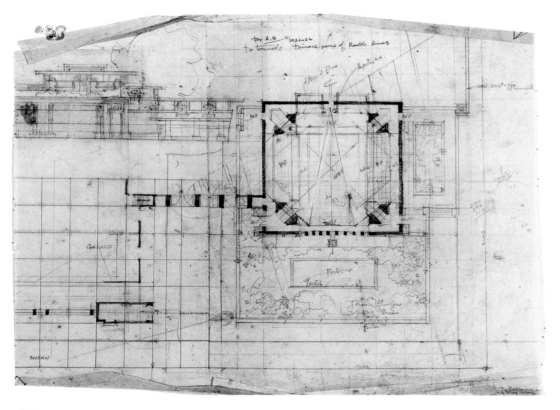

11-16. Barnsdall Motion Picture Theater, plan and elevation, 1920 (courtesy of the Frank Lloyd Wright Foundation)

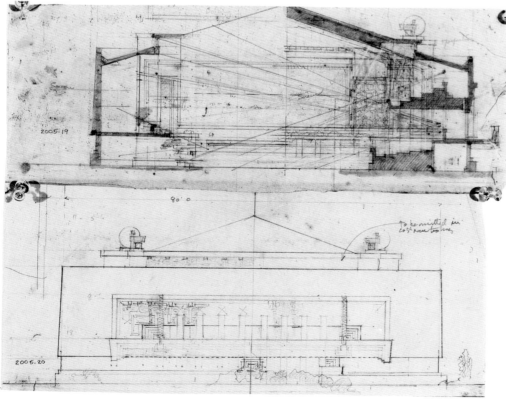

11-17. Barnsdall Motion Picture Theater, section and elevation, 1920 (courtesy of the Frank Lloyd Wright Foundation). Note that the section has been pasted to the elevation drawing.

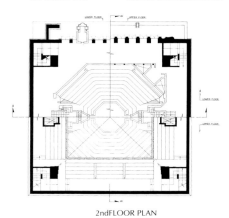

2ndFLOOR PLAN

11-18. Ginza Motion Picture Theater, circa 1918 (Masimo Tanigawa, *Measured Drawing: Frank Lloyd Wright in Japan*). This building is documented by a plaster model that Wright gave to Professor Takeda, who donated it to Nihon University. At an early date it acquired its attribution as a movie theater, although there is no other evidence to substandiate this claim. It is more likely that it was a proposal for a theater-in-the-round.

11-19. Barnsdall Motion Picture Theater, plan and section, 1920 (courtesy of the Frank Lloyd Wright Foundation). Note that the section has been pasted onto the plan.

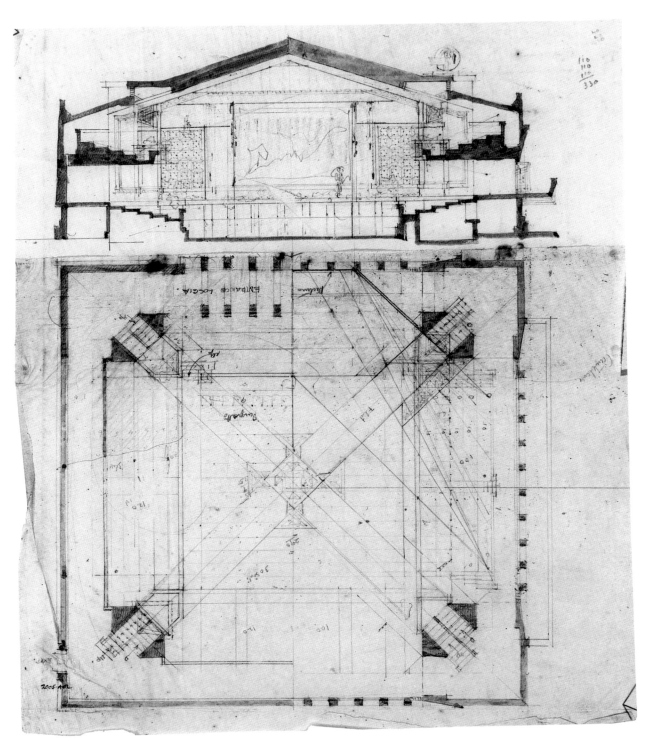

117

CHAPTER 12

CONSTRUCTION OF HOLLYHOCK HOUSE

12-1. Hollyhock House, living room,
circa 1926 (courtesy of Michael Devine)

The structure was going up on the foundations of Barnsdall's house by the time Schindler took over supervision in earnest just after the New Year, 1921. He began by dealing directly with the subcontractors, as he continued to provide sheets of construction details to keep pace with the work. It is uncertain how many drawings were made for Hollyhock House. According to the numbering system, there may have been at least twenty-three sheets of plans, elevations, sections, and details of each room, although some have been lost. There were, without doubt, dozens of full-size details of stone, woodwork, and sheet metal that have not been preserved. Unfortunately, except for some furniture studies and a sketch of the fireplace mantel, there are no surviving preliminary drawings to provide insight into the development of the ideas. The best evidence of Wright's intentions, made with Barnsdall's participation, is the set of drawings originally executed for bid by Schindler between late January and March.[1] These drawings were extensively revised by Wright, sometimes at least three times on one sheet (on August 10, 16, and 20, and September 10, 1920). Details were erased and redrawn numerous times, obliterating the information beneath. In addition, before Wright's December 1920 departure, sheets were made for woodwork, leaded glass details, furniture, rugs, and an electrical plan.

Undoubtedly Barnsdall's insistence on a tight budget dictated the use of hollow terra-cotta tile as the major structural material. It was a material that Wright had never used before, but it was widely employed, especially in residential construction in Los Angeles. It is unlikely that Wright would have chosen such a structural system if there had been other choices. Years later, Wright admitted, "Conscience troubled me a little. That 'voice within' said, 'What about the machine crying for recognition as the tool of your age?' Well, my critics, one does weary of duty. Even of privilege—while young, I again told the voice to 'go to' for a time. Hollyhock House was to be another holiday for me."[2]

The walls, which were consistent in material on the exterior and interior, were built on brick and concrete foundations and surfaced with lath and sand-finished plaster.[3] The contrasting element was art stone, concrete manufactured to imitate stone, perhaps the greatest anomaly. In addition to its use for applied ornament such as the hollyhock motif around the edge of the roof, it was molded for columns, lintels, sills, and copings.

Of the major industrial materials of the twentieth century, steel and concrete, Wright had chosen the latter for architectural innovation as early as 1904 in the Unity Temple. It continued to interest him until the end of his life, and he used it to great effect in many of his most important buildings such as the frame of the

Imperial Hotel, the textile block houses, Fallingwater, and the Guggenheim Museum. Seven years after the construction of Hollyhock House, he wrote, "I should say that in this plasticity of concrete lies its aesthetic value. As an artificial stone, concrete has no great, certainly no independent aesthetic value whatever. As a plastic material—eventually becoming stone-like in character—there lives in it a great aesthetic property, as yet inadequately expressed."[4]

Unlike the houses that he would design two years later using a sixteen-inch square concrete block module, the art stone details of Hollyhock House conformed to the use of cut stone. The molded blocks, traditional in shape, were joined with mortar in imitation of stone construction. Although a machine process was employed instead of handicraft, it was not used to construct the building in a new way, nor did it affect the traditional form of architectural elements: base and wall, columns and lintels, sills and copings.

In contrast, the interior (figs. 12-13 and 12-14) was more in keeping with the Prairie house type, with stained plaster walls, wood trim, and leaded-glass windows, doors, and ceiling grilles over recessed light fixtures and skylights. Barnsdall had made it clear in their 1919 contract that she wanted to choose the colors and finishes to suit her preferences and existing furniture. Wright's absences

12-2. Hollyhock House, front elevation, circa 1923 (courtesy of the Frank Lloyd Wright Foundation)

12-3. Hollyhock House, front elevation, circa 1923 (courtesy of the Frank Lloyd Wright Foundation). Early photographs indicate that a sunken garden once outlined the square pool.

not only gave her more freedom to carry out her ideas, but limited his use of personal persuasion, which he had exercised so successfully with many of his clients. Indeed, on May 3, 1920, when Lloyd Wright had reported the room sizes that were incorporated into the bid documents, he had reassured her that "all the other details of the house remain as you had planned before you left, with no cuts or omissions...in fact all the details are as originally included."[5] She repeatedly expressed frustration at Wright's absence during this phase of design, yet several years later, at the height of his anger toward her, Wright threatened to sue her "for damages for interference with work which resulted in injury to interests of architect."[6] He explained to her then, "[I have] had so much serious effort aborted by your interference and arbitrary ignorance in depriving me of all responsibility for my own work thereby aborting so much really great effort on my part in your behalf...."[7]

The revised drawings indicate that the result of this constant tug-of-war was often a compromise. In some cases she won, in others he did. For instance, her original preference called for a variety of woods in different wings or rooms: white-streaked walnut in the living room, music room, and study; mahogany in the dining room; and white holly in her bedroom.[8] Wright preferred quarter-sawn white oak. The result was a compromise, with the millwork schedule calling for white oak in the public rooms and genezero, an exotic mahogany, in the dining room. Ultimately, although white holly was specified on the millwork schedule, Barnsdall's room was left unfinished, as the budget became exhausted.[9]

Schindler had to work hard that winter of 1921 to solve problems caused by the six-month delay and still keep the construction costs close to the budget. The masonry subcontractor, Robert Preston, submitted a claim for additional money based on the argument that Lloyd Wright had misrepresented the work, which proved more complicated and costly than he indicated.[10] Preston continued to press his claim and labored slowly through February and March, holding up the plaster work.

Schindler immediately ran into trouble with the manufacturer of the art stone, George Taylor of William Smith Architectural Concrete Stone. Schindler was pushing the pace of work, insisting that columns, lintels, sills, copings, and ornament were behind schedule and holding up other work. An exchange of letters continued for several months as Taylor argued that the drawings were insufficient or that significant errors existed between the drawings and the measurements on the site, both resulting in higher cost. Citing a specific case, Taylor argued, "this is another example of what you refer to as delay, it is about time we referred to it by another name, that is an expense that must be paid as an extra."[11] Taylor took special exception to Wright's use of a grid to determine measurements.

> We do not find any attention has been given to the fact that a great deal of stone work must be made to fit *the building*, the unit system of estimating measurements employed by you on this work has proven very costly to us from the start of this contract and in order to expedite the work, we delegated one draftsman to devote all of his time to this work.[12]

This friction and confusion may explain the appearance of a pair of columns at the west and east ends of the living room (fig. 12-9) and at the north and south ends of the music room and library. Although earlier drawings, such as the first electrical plan, dated June 15, 1920, and surviving blueprints of the detailed plans of the rooms before the late August revisions did not indicate it, the revised detail sheet for the living room and the music room (a mirror version of the library) shows an art stone column set directly in front of a leaded glass window outside the wall plane. A note on this drawing, sheet #6, refers to the dimensions of the lintels with the note, "No span greater than 5'6"." According to the drawing of the living room, the distance between the inset columns is greater than 5'6", necessitating another structural member. Although the same condition did

12-4. Hollyhock House, porte cochere, circa 1920s (courtesy Lloyd Wright Studio)

not apply to the music room and library, the columns may have been added at those two points to maintain a consistent rhythm. There is no surviving evidence to indicate whether this change was made by Wright or by Schindler after Wright's departure.

Schindler kept up a steady correspondence with Taylor, answering questions and pressing to keep the job moving. At one point the strain caused him to reply, "We decline to receive any further opinions as to our theories and drawings, what we want is *Stone* and not idle words."[13] When he did receive stone, Schindler often questioned the quality on the basis of size, color, or surface texture when it did not match existing work, but eventually both Preston and William Smith Architectural Stone received payment above their initial contract price.

Meanwhile, C.D. Goldthwaite began construction on Residences A and B, which had been issued building permits on December 29, 1920. The drawings had been turned over to a draftsman, whose name was not recorded, who was responsible for obtaining the building permit. Lloyd Wright noted:

> He had considerable difficulty with the building dept [sic] and discovered to his chagrin that the plans he drew up were very sketchy and incomplete. It angers me to see how glibly he places the responsibility for there [sic] incompleteness on your shoulders. However he has had to do the work of bringing them up to snuf [sic] at least sufficiently to pass the building dept. [sic][14]

The contract was signed on January 14, 1921, with a price of $18,000 for the former building and $21,000 for the latter.[15] Although work proceeded more smoothly with these two houses than with Hollyhock House, Goldthwaite did run into a problem almost immediately on Residence B. Before pouring the concrete foundations, it was determined that the existing grade did not correspond to the working drawings, necessitating much higher foundations than those drawn. Rather than pay the extra charge, Schindler ordered Goldthwaite to lower the whole building three feet six inches.[16]

Barnsdall was unhappy with the way construction was proceeding. By January 24, 1921, she was in New York preparing to sail for Europe, but before she left she sent Wright a letter with her final instructions:

> Tomorrow I am sailing for Europe to stay until my house is completely finished. This will probably be a satisfaction to you because it leaves you the choice of a number [of things] that I would have attended to myself. I have sent Mr. Thomas $5000.00 to cover the cost of furniture for living room, dining room, servants [sic] rooms and laundry: and curtains for living room, loggias, halls, breakfast room, servants [sic] rooms, guest rooms and Sugar Tops [sic] entire suite. I have curtains for my bedroom, library and dining room and music room. Susan [her secretary] will have charge and knowledge of where each piece of my furniture will be placed.
>
> Everything is now arranged so that the two houses can be built, a certain part of the landscape finished and the roads finished. I can take no further responsibility until my house is *completely* ready to live in according to present specifications.
> ...it grows too confusing.[17]

One of the details she was able to carry out before her departure was to instruct Lloyd Wright on the landscape plan, especially concerning the gardens around Hollyhock House. She had left the choice of the specific plant material to the younger Wright, but had created a scheme of graduated colors that determined his choice of flowering plants. Although a variety of plants in many colors from perennials to vines were specified, a palette of warm colors (reds, pinks, and yellows) predominated.[18] On February 10, Barnsdall's house was ready for roofing.[19] Schindler wanted the lathing and plastering to begin almost immediately, but by March 29 he had to release the subcontractor E.O. Ward from his deadline. The delivery of the art stone was behind schedule, so plastering continued throughout April, two months late. Although the plumbing seemed to proceed smoothly, Schindler had to deal with three electricians before he found one who would finish the job. In December 1920, after some initial installation, the first subcontractor, H.G. Stone, had canceled his contract (signed on June 17, 1920) because of the six-month delay. Schindler spent four weeks interviewing and then rejecting a second contractor, Elliott Lee Ellingwood, and settling Stone's claim through his lawyer before he hired the final electrician, H.H. Walker. During their negotiations, Ellingwood was forced to execute a new electrical plan based on Stone's initial work. Although Ellingwood was never hired, Walker must have faced the same conditions. His electrical plan has not survived, but certain features—the most important of which was a double row of six indirect lighting fixtures with perforated wood grilles in the dining room, that are not visible in archival photographs (fig. 12-6) but appear on the blueprints documenting details before August 16, 1920—do not appear to have been executed.

While Schindler was in charge of overseeing the buildings, Lloyd Wright was supervising the landscaping of the entire hill. The property had been divided into terraced sections: Hollyhock House; an area including Residences A and B; the site of the Terrace Stores and Houses; and the site of the theater and its auxiliary buildings. All but the last section were planned for extensive work throughout 1921. Lloyd Wright was directing the grading of the building sites, the construction of roads, and laying out water and electrical lines, and irrigation systems. He was also overseeing the planting of trees, shrubs, flower beds, and ground cover, and supervising the construction of the man-made water gardens in the Hollyhock House courtyard (figs. 12-7, 12-11, and 12-12) as well as the main stream with its seven check dams. There is some evidence that Barnsdall had instructed Lloyd Wright to supervise farming of the olive orchard and harvesting of the crop.[20]

Lloyd Wright was also executing the promised, but extremely late, perspectives. Separated from his wife, Elaine Hyman, and in the process of a divorce, he rented an apartment in Hollywood to be close to the site and sent periodic reports to his father in Japan. Sometime in January, he had written:

> Fortunately and strangely enough Thomas has allowed me to proceed full speed ahead with the landscape work without question and has signed up contracts in Aline's name. And I am pushing it while I may.
> Rudolph [Schindler] has caught Robertson in a proposition whereby Robertson was going to put over a deal with a plaster contractor. He nipped [it] in the bud and Robertson swore at him and said he'd get him. I really didn't think Robertson would give way that easily. But he has [illegible word] badly in the job and it is dragging as badly as before. There [sic] all jumping in on Rudolph but from all indications he is well able to hold his own.
> Smith still kicking and Preston too, of course [art stone and masonry subs] with Robertson openly telling Rudolph that you had double crossed him in letting the contracts for the cottages on the Hill [Residences A and B] and threatening him for insisting that Robertson take no part in the

12-5. Hollyhock House, sections, February 5, 1920 (courtesy of the Frank Lloyd Wright Foundation). In lower margin, "Revised Aug. 20, 1920, FLW." In August 1920, Wright erased portions of the drawing and made his revisions in ink. The changes made in pencil to Section E-E over the rear pool were for a proposed art gallery addition for the California Art Club in 1932 (see figs. 16-9 and 16-10).

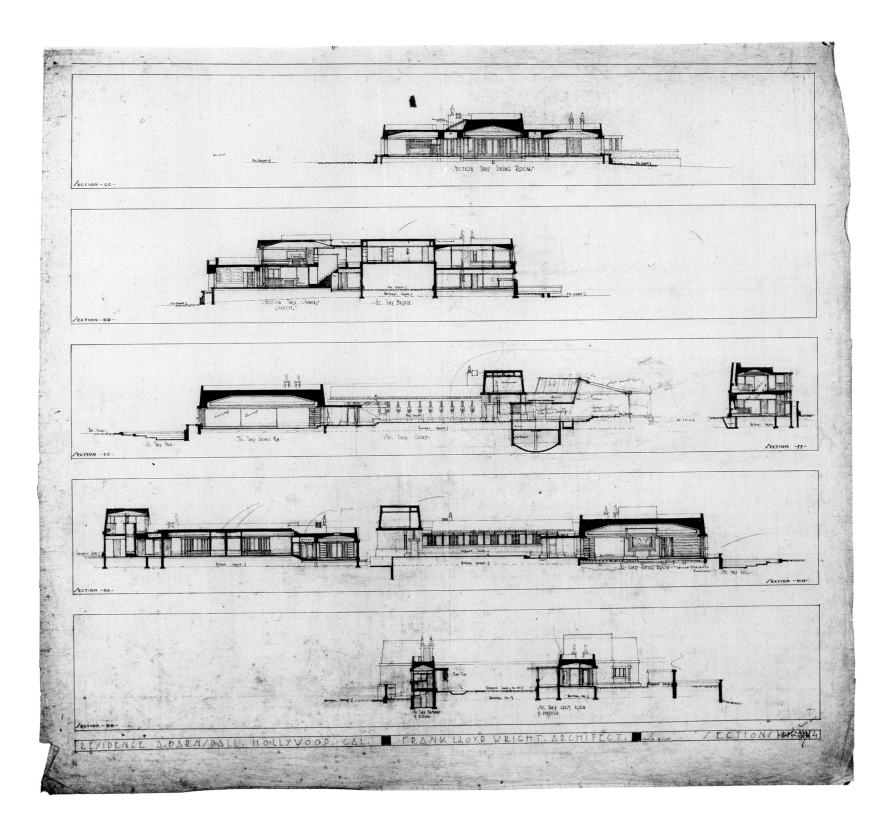

SECTION -CC-

·SECTION THRU LIVING ROOM·

SECTION -DD-

·SECTION THRU OWNERS QUARTERS·   ·SEC THRU BRIDGE·

SECTION -EE-   ·SEC THRU POOL·   ·SEC THRU LIVING RM·   ·SEC THRU COURT·   SECTION -FF-

SECTION -GG-   ·SEC THRU LIVING ROOM·   ·SEC THRU ECC·   SECTION -HH-

SECTION -DD-   ·SEC THRU BASEMENT & KITCHEN·   ·SEC THRU GUEST ROOM & PERGOLA·

RESIDENCE A. BARNSDALL, HOLLYWOOD, CAL.   ■   FRANK LLOYD WRIGHT, ARCHITECT,   ■   SECTIONS

bidding and that all work and propositions come thru [sic] this office first. Of course it stands to reason that he, Robertson, is agitating the sub contractors on the job also to make as much trouble for the architect as possible. The condition is an intolerable one and must end soon.[21]

Meanwhile, both Lloyd Wright and Schindler optimistically awaited the commencement of construction of the estimated $400,000 Terrace Stores and Houses.[22] Again in January, Lloyd Wright had written his father, "The shops and cottages are being thrashed out with the building commissioner....He is attempting to make them tenements and increase the cost some $40,000 or more. But we will, I believe, be able to work out of that."[23] Almost a month later, on February 20, 1921, Pauline Schindler noted that "the terrace stores and apartments [are] about to be 'put' through the City Hall, prepatory [sic] to the signing of the contracts."[24] However, six weeks passed and on April 15, Lloyd Wright complained in a letter to Barnsdall, "Nothing yet has been started on the Terrace Shops or Residences, and this in spite of the fact that the work has been in every detail ready for actual construction since March 4th. The Olive Hill Construction Company has persistently refused to sign contracts or allow us to proceed with this work."[25]

Although there is no recorded explanation for the delay, a nasty conflict flared up between Thomas and Schindler at precisely that time. Apparently in a move to make Goldthwaite the contractor for all the building projects on the hill, Schindler and Lloyd Wright suggested to Thomas that Robertson be replaced. Thomas replied that Robertson was not their contractor but was acting as the superintendent for the Olive Hill Construction Company, and he rejected their suggestion. He wrote to Schindler on March 10, 1921:

> We will proceed with the building of the dwelling, as we have in the past— I am not accepting the suggestion emenating [sic] from your office that we turn over the finishing of the building to Mr. Goldthwaite or any other contractor.
>
> I was answering your rather insinuating letter—I am about tired of your camouflage. You must think that you are damn wise or I am a damn fool. Try for a time to play with the truth—
>
> There is [sic] no politics. That's your excuse. And the hedge behind which you wish to hide—when you are confronted with your own plottings. Enough of this! Do the work, you are being paid to do—and the work will proceed as it should. And there will be no reason for such letters as you have written.[26]

Schindler shot off a reply the next day:

> We have received two letters from the office of Aline Barnsdall signed Mr. Thomas, accusing this office and our representative of the following unethical deeds and intentions:
>
> First: The letter of March 8th, 1921 insinuates that Mr. Goldthwaite's bid for the finishing of the Main Residence was based on an improper understanding of [sic] our part with this contractor as to the amount.
>
> Second: That we are camouflaging our actions and have reason to do so.
>
> Third: That we are plotting secretly against the interests of our clients.
>
> Fourth: That Mr. Schindler has been lying.
>
> We give herewith Mr. Thomas a period of four days in which to retract these statements and to send us his written, thorough and complete apology.
>
> Should this not be forthcoming we shall take the necessary legal steps to procure it.[27]

The relationships between Schindler and Lloyd Wright, on the one hand, and Thomas and Robertson, on the other, were at their lowest point at this time. Schindler's letters were addressed to Aline Barnsdall with a salutation of "Dear Sir" and signed "Frank Lloyd Wright per R.M. Schindler." Both Barnsdall and Wright were out of the country, and this deteriorating situation may have been all that was needed to stall the Terrace Stores and Houses indefinitely.

12-6. Hollyhock House, dining room, circa 1925–1927 (photo by Viroque Baker; collection of the author). The carpet extended only up the steps to the dining room. The dining table and chairs are by Wright, but the fixture over the table apparently was added by Barnsdall. The six wood ceiling grilles that appeared in the dining room detail drawing dated March 25, 1920, were never installed, the victims of budget overruns and the confusion caused by having three successive electricians. An Oriental carpet is laid on the floor.

In the meantime, Schindler pushed Barnsdall's house on day by day. "The difference between working with a contractor on the job and doing the work oneself," Lloyd Wright observed, "is indeed considerably different. No worry or drag or real pressure in the work."[28] Even with Robertson out of the picture, Schindler was having enough trouble with the subcontractors. The plaster work was held up by the delay in finishing the art stone, and when it commenced months behind schedule, there was trouble with the quality. On April 27, 1921, the plaster contractor, E.O. Ward, served notice that he would not apply the finish coat. Noting that a high quality finish was not in his specifications, Ward refused to do the work for any price. Instead, he offered men and materials and suggested Wright's staff supervise the work themselves.[29] As the job turned out, the exterior plaster was not uniform in color, and in September it was painted at extra cost.[30]

Problems arose at just about every step of the building process as Wright's arrival date in the spring neared. The glazed openings were probably the most difficult items in the entire building. Wright had decided to use leaded glass in every window, door, and skylight, and the frames were of a variety of wood

12-7. Hollyhock House, courtyard, circa 1925–1927 (photo by Viroque Baker; collection of the author). View from the loggia through the folding glass doors; the stream is to the left. The walk that was to lead from the terrace to the circular pool was never installed. A sculpture was placed in the center of the pool instead of to the left and overlooking the pool as indicated in Wright's plan (see fig. 8-6).

veneers to match the rooms. The measurements on the drawings did not match the sizes of the openings on the building. Schindler instructed the subcontractor Weldon and Glasson Planing Mill, San Diego, to take the measurements from the building. Weldon and Glasson then shipped the frames to Judson Glass Studio in Pasadena where they were fitted with the glass.

Schindler was trying to keep pace with the plaster work. From March until even beyond Wright's return in May, he found that he was either ahead or behind. If the frames arrived too early, they had to be stored and protected from moisture, and if they arrived late, it put the building behind schedule. Matters did not improve toward the end of the job. Sashes and flyscreens were urgently awaited on July 8, 1921, when the factory burned to the ground with all the paperwork. Within two weeks, Weldon and Glasson started up operation again, but requested that all items go first to the job site to be fitted and corrected for size before being sent to Pasadena for installation of the glass, because too many changes had been made during the job.

As the buildings on Olive Hill neared completion, Wright prepared for his trip to the United States, although only five months remained until the scheduled opening of the Imperial Hotel on November 3, 1921, and his presence in Japan was urgently needed. Some parts of the hotel were in a more advanced stage of completion than others, and Wright's builder, Paul Mueller, predicted that "unless unforeseen difficulties arise we will be able to turn over the main building and the north wing for the formal opening on scheduled time."[31]

By the time Wright arrived in Los Angeles in late May or early June, Barnsdall's house was ready for interior finishing and corrections, one year later than the original estimate. Wright was convinced, as he told Schindler, "that the waste of money and time on [the] work [was] no less than criminal. Chargeable, they [Thomas and Robertson] will try to show to the impotence of the architect."[32] After a week or so in Los Angeles, Wright left for Taliesin with plans to return in July on his way back to Japan. Goldthwaite, who had finally been awarded the contract for the Terrace Stores and Houses the week of May 14, 1921, promised Residences A and B would be completed by the middle of July.[33]

Although Wright wrote extensively about Hollyhock House in his autobiography, his account deals primarily with the friction on the construction site, with few references to the creative process or the specifics of his design. He recalled:

Nevertheless from out of this confusion, from this welter of misunderstanding and misapplied heat and fury—enough to have consumed the work out of hand and finally resulting in brutal violence—a shape appeared, inviolate. A strangely beautiful "form" crept inexorably into view. Even the quarreling pack began to see and be impressed by it. Something had held all this shifty diversity of administration together enough to enable a new significance to come out and adorn that hill crown. Was it the marks on the paper that this quarreling was all about, these traces of a design that, no matter how abused, *would* show itself in spite of friction, waste and slip? Of course.[34]

"It was a transition building," Wright told Barnsdall ten years later, "and deserved a better fate."[35] Perhaps there is no greater illustration of this transition in Wright's work than the distinction between the interior and exterior of Hollyhock House. Although the inside represented Wright's last major statement of the arts and crafts vocabulary of the Prairie house, the exterior introduced, for the first time in a residence, Wright's interest in primitivism as a universal rather than regional expression. So great is the difference between the inside and outside of this house that it almost appears to be two different buildings.

The most commonly known aspect of Barnsdall's house—the use of the stylized hollyhock flower as the building's ornamental motif—represented the culmination of a period of Wright's philosophy that had begun as early as 1901 with his famous speech, "The Art and Craft of the Machine."

12-8. Hollyhock House, courtyard, circa 1923 (courtesy of the Frank Lloyd Wright Foundation). View through the window next to the entrance hall overlooking the stream and the courtyard colonnade.

12-9. Hollyhock House, living room detail, March 12, 1920 (courtesy of the Frank Lloyd Wright Foundation). In the lower margin, "O.K. Revised Aug. 16th 1920 FLW; Revised Sept. 10, 1920; Revised Aug. 20, 1920 FLW." The major changes that appear on this drawing are structural. A blueprint of the drawing before the revisions (in the collection of the City of Los Angeles, Departments of Recreation and Parks and Cultural Affairs) indicates that the large columns were originally hollow tile with hollow centers. They were paired with smaller concrete columns where wood posts are now drawn. The concrete columns in between, which are in front of the window, were added in pencil. By the time the revisions were made to the drawing the foundations had been built, and some of the structure was being manufactured and constructed.

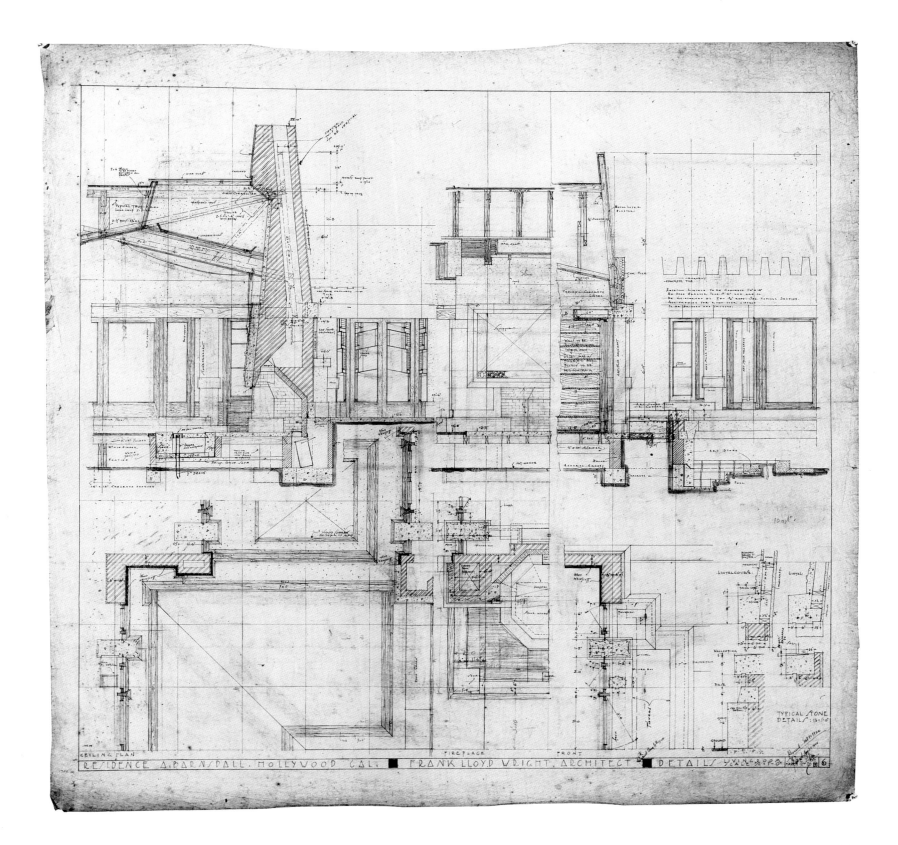

CEILING PLAN · RESIDENCE A. BARNSDALL. HOLLYWOOD CAL. ■ FRANK LLOYD WRIGHT ARCHITECT ■ DETAILS ¼"=1'-0"

TYPICAL STONE
DETAILS ¾"=1'-0"

To get from some native plant an expression of its native character in terms of imperishable stone to be fitted perfectly to its place in structure, and without loss of vital significance, is one great phase of great Art. It means that Greek or Egyptian found a revelation of the inmost life and character of the Lotus and Acanthus in terms of Lotus and Acanthus Life. That was what happened when the Art of these people had done with the plants they most loved. This imaginative process is known only to the creative Artist. Conventionalization, it is called. Really it is the dramatizing of an object—truest "drama."[36]

In Hollyhock House, Wright used several forms of abstraction that marked different stages in his career: the stylization of the hollyhock flower in the capitals of the columns (fig. 12-11), reminiscent of his use of the sumac leaf as the motif for the Dana House; the geometric, decorative patterns in the leaded glass (see color plates) that he had used in numerous houses as early as the Bradley House; and the monumental geometric abstraction over the fireplace (see color plates) that recalled murals in the Midway Gardens and the Imperial Hotel.

Although Wright left no record of the meaning of the mechanistic mantel relief, over fifty years later Lloyd Wright explained that it depicted Aline Barnsdall, on the left, as an Indian princess seated on her throne, surveying her lands—the desert mesas.[37] Even if this interpretation was accurate, the mantelpiece must inevitably be compared with the polychromatic mural in the Midway Gardens, titled *City by the Sea*, and the two polychromatic and oya (native Japanese volcanic stone) stone mantelpieces in the Imperial Hotel. Like its precedents, the Hollyhock House mantelpiece represents Wright's progression from narration—depicting a theme through metaphor—to nonobjective art. The subject matter of the Hollyhock House mantelpiece is geometry and space: a bas-relief of circles, squares, and diamonds in an asymmetrical composition that creates spatial relationships on a two-dimensional surface by juxtaposing receding and projecting geometric figures. The geometric abstractions Wright designed from 1914 onward regenerated his architecture and bore fruit in the next decade when he introduced these new geometric relationships into his planning.

Until 1907, the fireplace which formed the spiritual center of Wright's Prairie houses usually occupied the center of the plan.[38] Although the fireplace in Hollyhock House was no longer on axis, it was given added significance not only by the abstract relief but also by the unprecedented introduction of a half-octagonal pool directly in front of it. By combining fire and water, Wright made a direct reference to the cosmic elements; above the pool he placed a skylight that directed the eye heavenward. With these gestures, he transcended the secure center of the domestic environment and created an altar to the mysteries of nature.

The most obvious departure from his earlier work, the undisguised reference to the form of a Mayan temple, would reappear in the years ahead as Wright began to synthesize pre-Columbian forms into his own vocabulary.[39] The silhouette of Hollyhock House appeared again for Barnsdall only two years later when she commissioned a second house in Beverly Hills (fig. 13-3). It had appeared earlier in the 1918 Yamamura House in Japan, in a more abstract form in House C of the Doheny Ranch project of 1923, in the Ennis House in Hollywood in 1924–1925, and again in the Phi Gamma Delta Fraternity for Madison, Wisconsin, in 1925. But the elements of Hollyhock House did not appear fully distilled until Wright built his own quarters, Taliesin West (fig. 12-10), in the Arizona desert in 1938. In the masonry walls of the original guest bedroom wing to the east of the drafting room, the Mayan profile was condensed into an abstraction. At once the wall of a desert canyon and the earth architecture of a primitive people, the form Wright created condensed and transcended both metaphors.

In 1908, Wright had boldly concluded the most cogent statement of his philosophy of architecture with a prediction for the years ahead.

12-10. Taliesin West, bedroom wing, circa 1940s (courtesy of the Frank Lloyd Wright Foundation)

As for the future—the work shall grow more truly simple; more expressive with fewer lines, fewer forms; more articulate with less labor; more plastic; more fluent, although more coherent; more organic. It shall grow not only to fit more perfectly the methods and processes that are called upon to produce it, but shall further find whatever is lovely or of good repute in method or process, and idealize it with the cleanest, most virile stroke I can imagine.[40]

This startling declaration of a man of forty-one was to guide Wright into his sixties and seventies, but in designing Hollyhock House he had sacrificed coherence for expression.

In 1921, as the job neared completion, even the last remaining details, the furniture and furnishings, had become an issue of contention. Although Barnsdall was willing to accept only living room, dining room, and servants' rooms furniture, Wright's office went ahead with furniture for the music room, study, and two bedrooms, as well.[41] The entry, living room, and steps into the courtyard loggia were to be covered in a specially designed carpet, unifying the space.

Wright had designed the furniture and carpet before his departure for Japan the previous fall. The living room was organized around two sofas set on

12-11. Hollyhock House, courtyard, looking east, circa 1923 (courtesy of the Frank Lloyd Wright Foundation). The stream and the pool are visible at the left and center, respectively. The sculptural figure has not yet been added.

12-12. Hollyhock House, courtyard, circa 1923 (courtesy of the Frank Lloyd Wright Foundation). The pool and the stream are visible at the bottom of the photo. The landscape specifications called for the pool to be planted with water plants.

12-13. Hollyhock House, living room, circa 1926 (courtesy of Michael Devine)

a diagonal to the fireplace, repeating the half-octagonal shape. All other furniture in the room—either desks, chairs, or indirect lighting—was built or arranged in relation to the sofas (figs. 12-13 and 12-14). The upholstery was a golden tan velour, and the cushions were decorated with a patterned square in gold thread.

In the rush of Wright's December 1920 departure for Japan, Barnsdall had approved the carpet design and requested that the colors and texture match a rug she already owned. W. & J. Sloane in New York was chosen as the manufacturer, and Wright's drawings and Barnsdall's rug had been shipped to New York in November 1920 with a request for an estimate and a sample.[42] After Wright had sailed, Barnsdall visited W. & J. Sloane on her way to Europe in January 1921. She approved the samples and colors and informed them that the architect was out of the country and would not be available to answer questions.[43]

Luckily, Wright's office heard from W. & J. Sloane almost by accident in February 1921. Unable to proceed without further clarification as to color, Sloane had written to Wright's office in Los Angeles hoping that someone would answer. Schindler requested yarn samples and repeatedly corrected the color until he was satisfied. Although archival photographs do not document the color, an observer from the early twenties described the background as an unusual

mauve with details that Schindler noted as blue, golden brown, and a "mulberry that is more like beny [Chinese pigment of red] of Chinese rugs."[44]

As the last item in the building, the furniture became a heated issue when Thomas declared that the building was over budget. Wright's office had proceeded with Barker Brothers, who were well along with the execution of the furniture when Thomas, unaware of Barker Brothers's progress with the work, informed Wright the cost was too high. Thomas wanted to get bids from other manufacturers, and he requested that Wright turn over the drawings, specifications, and samples so that he could proceed.[45] "Am calling his bluff," Wright cabled Schindler on June 15, 1921, "accept no order for A, B. Either he runs it or we do all or nothing."[46]

Thomas wrote Wright outlining his position, with a copy to Barnsdall in Europe. Wright directed the full force of his fury at Thomas in a cable:

Your letter a malicious misrepresentation intended for Miss Barnsdall's consumption not mine, am calling your petty bluff, Schindler will turn over furniture details schedules and quality samples to you, get busy with your little monkey-wrench, again your stupid egotism and envious insolence interferes with my work to the loss of both work and owner, your statement

12-14. Hollyhock House, living room, circa 1926 (courtesy of Michael Devine)

concerning the Terraces is a lie on it's [*sic*] face, you will go ahead with nothing, I withdraw my propositions wholly, now damn you, make good.[47]

From Taliesin, Wright was forced to send instructions to Schindler by telegram. Undoubtedly, Wright's accumulated anger toward Thomas came to the surface, as he explained to Schindler on June 16:

He accused me of delaying the Barker bids purposely until the eve of my departure and suggests that my approved contract with them was a bait to string Miss B...refers to *"the month"* I spent on the building in a casual way—all written to deliberately disaffect Miss B...[Wright's ellipsis] in every possible way that would occur to a coyote like him—his eyes were not set close together and crossed—for nothing.[48]

Wright's outrage seemed to grow as the days passed. By June 20, 1921, he cabled Schindler to hire an accountant to audit Thomas's books. "[Take] legal steps if necessary," Wright ordered, "claiming conspiracy to injure architect by intent to defraud commission also misrepresentation [of] facts to owner [with intent] to injure architect."[49] Finding his hands tied with Barnsdall out of the country and without her address, Wright resorted to asking Thomas to relay a message to her: "Absolute minimum appropriate furnishings [for] three houses eleven thousand. Thomas appropriation ninety three hundred. Am I authorized to abandon work or faithfully execute as far as money goes. Financially responsible all respects to you. Pay nothing until present and satisfied."[50]

Meanwhile, on June 16, Barnsdall had cabled Wright on Olive Hill, assuming he was there, that she was sending an additional $20,000 and no more; anything above that would have to be deducted from his fee.[51] Schindler repeated Barnsdall's message in a telegram to Wright, but it arrived in an unintelligible form. Unaware of Barnsdall's offer, Wright kept up the pressure. He urged Schindler to investigate lowering the costs by deducting the music room, study, dining room, and bedroom furniture.[52] While Wright kept pressuring Thomas for an account, Schindler repeated Barnsdall's telegram, but added that Thomas claimed the $20,000 had been used up in "extras."

By June 24, more than ten days after the crisis had started, Wright was exploding with fury. Thomas refused to forward Wright's message to Barnsdall or to provide a detailed account of expenditures, and with Wright's next departure for Japan only a little over a month away, every day was crucial. Wright's irritation with Schindler began to grow when Schindler could not find either a set of drawings that had been left behind in Los Angeles or the whereabouts of a

131

12-15. Hollyhock House, aerial view, circa 1923–1924 (courtesy of Security Pacific Photograph Collection/Los Angeles Public Library). The pile of debris to the right of the house between the library and breakfast room may indicate that repairs were undertaken because of water damage. The pile of debris at the lower left margin is next to the site of the Little Dipper.

Stair leading from chamber to roof terrace over bedroom bridge. The motif for the house was based on the hollyhock, Barnsdall's favorite flower, and Wright used a variation of it to create these finials.

Front (west) elevation looking into the living room, with the music room on the left and the library on the right. The gradual slope of the hill is just visible at the extreme right.

Front (west) elevation with entrance, music room and living room (right to left). Stairs, marked by hollyhock finials, to the terraces over the bedroom bridge and the living room are visible from left to right, respectively. A view southeast to downtown Los Angeles is visible at the extreme right. In Wright's first plan of 1919, he placed the entrance drive in this position, so this photograph represents what would have been the first view of the house from the approach.

Interior courtyard and stairs to the roof terrace. The living room loggia is to the left; the colonnade borders the service wing (dining room and kitchen). In recent years the canopy extending from the loggia has been used as a stage, with an audience seated on the lawn.

Interior courtyard looking toward the exedra (east). The bridge, like a proscenium, frames the area, which may have been intended as a stage. Under the bridge, to the left and right, respectively, are doors leading to the service wing and the guest bedroom wing (which could have served as actors' entrances). This view from the glass doors that enclose the living room loggia directs the focus of the house inward rather than to the views of the city or to the Pacific Ocean (to the west of the living room).

Interior courtyard looking toward the living room (west) with the service wing at right and the guest bedroom wing at left. The corridor outside the guest bedrooms is enclosed by a glazed pergola. The visual axis lies on the major east-west axis of Olive Hill, which continues through the center of the circular bowl of the Little Dipper site (to the west of Hollyhock House). If the courtyard and the exedra had been intended as a theater, this view shows the position of the actors in relation to the audience.

Terrace to the south of living room. The side door to the living room (west of the fireplace) is at right. The hollyhock motif was paired as a support for the planters.

Entrance seen from the rear (west). The rear view of the sculptural niche behind the porte cochere is visible at left. In Wright's 1919 plan, the niche was rotated 180 degrees and the drive passed between it and the porte cochere.

View toward entry and music room with service wing to the right. Wright provided numerous entrys to the courtyard from all wings of the house.

Living room roof terrace looking to the northeast across courtyard. The stairs lead to the roof terrace above the chamber. The finials feature the hollyhock motif on one side and a stylized human face on the other. Hill Grove, of stone pines, is visible in the background.

ABOVE View from roof terrace looking down to side door on south side of living room. The "Hollywood sign" on the Hollywood Hills (to the northwest) is just visible above the edge of the roof.

RIGHT View into the living room with downtown Los Angeles to the right. The transparency of the house and its relation to the gardens are evident, especially when the doors to the living room balcony are open to the pool. The juxtaposition of earth, water, fire, and sky exemplify Wright's statement about the power of cosmic elements. The sculptural figure, formerly placed at the porte cochere, has in recent years been moved indoors near the entry.

View from the courtyard into the loggia and living room. The three layers of space—exterior, intermediate, and interior—are evident. The loggia acts as a circulation zone between the courtyard and the living room, which can be closed off with its own french doors.

LEFT Living room looking west toward Pacific Ocean. With the exception of several upholstered chairs, all furniture is built into the two furniture pieces set on a diagonal with the fireplace. The early 1920s ambience of the living room was recreated through a reproduction of the color scheme described in documents of the period and verified by microscopic examination. The original Oriental screens were removed before 1925–1926; they may have been damaged when the roof leaked extensively in 1922.

ABOVE Fireplace with partition separating the living room and library at left and the side door to the living room terrace at right, behind drapery. This is one of the last major extant works of Wright's executed abstractions of the 1910s. The other examples (the Midway Gardens and the Imperial Hotel) have either been destroyed or removed from their original contexts. This is the first instance where Wright placed water directly in front of a fireplace. He later made a similar juxtaposition of fire and water at Taliesin West. With the introduction of the skylight, Wright converts the solidity of the roof into a translucent opening to the sky. The fireplace becomes an altar to both art and nature.

ABOVE Living room looking toward
courtyard through loggia (extreme left)
and hall to guest bedrooms (left of
fireplace). The reconstruction of the
original sofa, table, lamp units, and
footstools was based on photographs
taken while Aline Barnsdall was in
residence.

LEFT Living room looking through
entrance hall to dining room. Diagonal
axes open the spatial enclosure of various
rooms to provide a feeling of
expansiveness. The entry into the living
room has a low ceiling that dramatically
expands in height upon entry. The pool
in front of the fireplace hearth is visible
at right.

Dining room with original table and chairs (note the hollyhock motif). French doors open to the courtyard beyond the colonnade, although early working drawings (before revisions) indicate casement windows like those on the opposite wall. The diagonal axis leads to the living room, with the music room behind the slatted screen at right. The ceiling fixture was a much later addition.

View of dining room, which is raised
above the entry for privacy.

TOP Entry with music room behind screen at left. Concrete doors give the entry a massive and monumental appearance. The handles and lock cover were designed and added by Schindler in 1925.

ABOVE View from Betty (Sugar Top) Barnsdall's room toward her glass enclosed play porch at left and access to the south terrace at right. Wright used leaded glass extensively in this area of the house. The wall that screens the garden from the semi-circular terrace is pierced by an opening just at child's height (visible at right).

RIGHT The living room loggia, both a circulation spine and indoor-outdoor area. Planter boxes at each corner reinforce the idea of a transitional garden zone. The complex spatial relationships and the contrasts between light and dark, openness and enclosure are most evident as the visitor enters the house.

Northwest corner of the living room. The relationships between the two columns, with the smaller one outside of the wall plane and directly in front of the leaded glass window, is evident at left. This is surely one of the errors Wright observed on his return to the construction site in summer 1921.

12-16. Hollyhock House, living room,
circa 1926 (courtesy of the Frank Lloyd
Wright Foundation)

devoted primarily to the sale of Japanese prints and to Barnsdall's projects. In the back of his mind, he undoubtedly knew that without Barnsdall, he had no work. With the majority of the Olive Hill general plan unexecuted, Wright had good reason to explain to Barnsdall why, from his point of view, the first phase of construction had progressed so unsatisfactorily.

Knowing that he would not see her before he sailed on July 30, Wright wrote her two letters in two days, on June 26 and 27. The first letter has been lost, but in the second he gave a lengthy explanation for the various problems and provided a detailed explication of his method of work (see Appendix 2 for the full text). Although he admitted his major mistake was in choosing Robertson as the contractor, he blamed Barnsdall for not allowing him to correct his mistake when it proved fatal.

> I needed a veteran builder familiar with this original type of building. I needed him because the whole is an invention, the details to the smallest, all inventions. Imagination and enthusiasm and experience and loyalty should meet in the builder at my back, or the difficulties of my work be turned against me as sins of omissions or evasion or incompetence. You were led by peripatetic amateurs' advice to assume that what amateurs could see and understand of the usual thing in the *usual* way was what should apply to me and my way of work. The superiority and distinction you sought when you came to me was to "happen" somehow, as a gift to you, no matter how you tied me up.[56]

He also believed that her fear of exceeding financial limits, which led to her reliance on strict rules of business conduct and ultimately to turning her authority over to Thomas and Robertson, was of even greater consequence and unlike anything he had experienced "in building 176 unique buildings."

> The financial cost to you and to me and to everybody else has been greater because of this senseless friction and confusion. Perfunctory "rules of business" could no more gauge the *personal* equation of execution necessary to such creative work than it [sic] could gauge the nature of the conception itself. The arbitrary requisitions made by them, like passing the "Terraces" through the Department before letting the general contract were mere obstructions—as I can prove—of no possible benefit nor even protection to you. They have only abused the successful issue of a terrible struggle for that success.
>
> It is no more possible to tell me how I shall get my work done than it is to tell me how I shall conceive it, nor is it any more reasonable,—Because the personal equation is present from first to last or else the result is as dead as what you see around you everywhere.
>
> I know it is hard to understand this.
>
> It does seem as though the one, execution of the design, was business and the conception of it art. But in my experience both are allied and both in a sense art.[57]

He continued passionately:

> COST!—EXTRAS! They loomed over your horizon like some terrible spectre of defeat. You took every measure to defend yourself, but threw away the only one that could have protected you—that one was the cooperation of your architect.
>
> Do you now remember waving me aside when I pleaded with you for your confidence? You said, that you had no confidence in any "Artist." And you told me in no uncertain terms to get what I could for my work, and you would take care of yourself? You gave me then and there to understand that it was each one for himself or herself and a sporting chance for either to win through. And in so many words.[58]

In spite of his observation of her "disinclination...to stand the discipline of steady sustained endeavor," Wright, looking ahead to the future, set out the terms

Cadillac that had been shipped to Japan in December 1920. His frustration was evident when he cabled to Schindler, "Force immediate accounting [with Thomas] or stop work and come home."[53]

The next day, June 25, Wright received a letter from Barnsdall written in England on May 25, addressed to Olive Hill and then forwarded to Taliesin. He was encouraged to learn that she still wanted to build the theater, although she also indicated that she wanted him to find the capital to build the Terrace Stores and Houses, the apartment building, and the motion picture theater. Believing that possible, he vowed to "keep faith on the Hill by building it all as she discussed it and more besides—in time—in spite of hell and the fumes of 'clerks.'"[54]

Wright was preparing to leave for New York and arrive in Los Angeles a few days later, between July 14 and July 30, to supervise the final details on Olive Hill before sailing for Japan.[55] With the Imperial Hotel nearing completion, he planned to return to the United States for good soon. In the three years since his initial departure for Japan in the fall of 1918, he had made only brief visits home,

157

12-17. Residence A, west elevation, circa 1923 (courtesy of the Frank Lloyd Wright Foundation)

12-18. Residence A, entrance, circa 1923 (courtesy of the Frank Lloyd Wright Foundation)

under which he would agree to work. He demanded a trustworthy businessman, a reliable, competent, sympathetic builder, and carefully worked out but general plans, with the freedom to make changes as construction progressed.

The work I do is not drawing-board Architecture. I must have my own privileges in the field where my battle is inevitably fought on and eventually won or lost. This attempt to nail me fast to my drawing-board, on suspicion, is unwise. Even were it possible, and it is not possible.

For this margin in the field I should have a competent fund, which experience has taught me should be between fifteen and twenty percent on work like yours. This fund should be provided in some sensible way, fair to all concerned.[59]

Finally, he wanted to lay to rest future recriminations about her house, which he felt did not express his intentions successfully.

Well—the building stands. Your home.

It is yours for what it has cost you. It is mine for what it has cost me.

And it is for all mankind according to its cost in all its bearings.

Can we not pronounce benediction upon it, now, absolving the building itself at least from rancour and false witness?

Whatever its birth pangs it will take its place as your contribution and mine to the vexed life of our time. What future it will have—maimed as it is—who can say?[60]

In the meantime, Schindler, still following orders, reported on June 28, 1921, that a lawsuit to secure the audit of Thomas's books would take months.[61] "Man, wake up," Wright cabled Schindler, "Barnsdall letter makes all the difference."[62] Schindler still did not understand and continued to cable Wright about the lawsuit. "In touch with owner," Wright repeated, "concentrate on finishing building, drop Thomas." Revealing his exasperation, he added, "Raise no question, nor be caught napping, hell is no place for somnambulists."[63]

In Wright's absence, Schindler had been responsible for interpreting the drawings and seeing that Wright's design intentions were faithfully executed despite obstructions from Thomas and Robertson. When Lloyd Wright questioned Schindler's usefulness, Wright responded:

I know R.M.S.' faults—He is doing his best—but his attitude has always been what it is. He means neither harm nor disrespect really—It is not that he respects Wright less but values his hope of Schindler rather more in the secret recesses of his soul. It is the artist in him characteristically seducing

12-19. Residence B, west elevation, 1923 (photo by Kameki Tsuchiura; courtesy Mr. and Mrs. Kameki Tsuchiura)

12-20. Residence B, west elevation, circa 1921–1922 (courtesy of the Frank Lloyd Wright Foundation)

12-21. Residence B, east elevation, circa 1921–1922 (courtesy of the Frank Lloyd Wright Foundation)

12-22. Olive Hill, aerial construction photo, April 7, 1921 (courtesy Aerial Photo Archives, Department of Geography, University of California, Los Angeles). The superstructure of Hollyhock House is visible in the center. Residences A and B, at the upper right and lower left, respectively, are rising from their foundations.

and soothing his innermost Ego....It is not really a question however of what his limitations are. It is a question of whether he is trustworthy on the whole—and in any situation like the present he would wear slim. I ought probably not to depend upon him—but I will put you together to see what the mix is like for the next three weeks. I need the son's loyalty and help as far as he can go.[64]

Before Wright sailed on July 30, he was in Los Angeles supervising changes and corrections to the interior and exterior plaster color.[65] In August, Schindler began the painstaking job of supervising omissions, corrections, and repairs on Hollyhock House and Residences A and B (figs. 12-17 through 12-21). He was having difficulty with Goldthwaite, whose work had deteriorated in both quality and speed. Presumably aware that the much more lucrative job for the Terrace Stores and Houses had been canceled, Goldthwaite lost his incentive to perform. At one point, Schindler was even forced to threaten to have his work completed by the bonding company.

The poor workmanship that had plagued the construction process continued to affect the building in the finishing stages and after; "patches, leaks, and contracts" preoccupied Schindler in the last weeks of the job. "You very well know how it is," he confided to Louis Sullivan on September 13, 1921, "just the many little adjustments at the end of [the] job which take time and nerves. Especially since people here do not seem to know what a promise means, and time seems to affect them less than the farmer."[66] Except for the swimming pool and the second floor bedroom wing in the Hollyhock House which were left unfinished undoubtedly for financial reasons, Schindler, anxious to depart for a vacation with his wife by late September 1921, considered the work substantially complete.

With the first group of buildings in the finishing stages (fig. 12-23) and the remainder of the general plan postponed, Wright turned his attention to the collection of his fees. On September 12, 1921, he cabled Barnsdall from Tokyo: "In trouble. Kindly settle with Schindler. Humiliating reprisals unnecessary. Concessions will be reciprocated."[67]

From the date of their initial contract, September 15, 1919, until the end of 1921, the total sum of improvements to Olive Hill had increased from $375,000 to $990,000, including architect's fees.[68] Barnsdall had negotiated the payments so that Wright was to be paid 2½ percent for preliminary drawings, 5 percent for working drawings, and a remaining 2½ percent for supervision until the buildings were ready for occupancy. The best available evidence indicates that Wright had been paid between $36,000 and $38,000 by the end of 1921.[69] With the construction costs of the buildings calculated at approximately $71,703 for Hollyhock House, $18,000 for Residence A, and $21,000 for Residence B—resulting in fees to Wright of $11,070—the remaining $24,930 to $26,930 would have been paid against preliminary plans and working drawings for the unbuilt buildings, landscaping, and models.[70]

Wright's finances were as desperate as usual, with his commission on the Imperial Hotel being eaten away by the prolonged construction, and his profits on sales of Japanese prints jeopardized by restitutions. By November it was certain that the hotel was not going to be ready on time. Schindler, whose anticipated trip to Tokyo was canceled, noted that Wright was not "willing to start much other work in Japan after the hotel. The climate makes him sick and conditions are not particularly favorable."[71] With Barnsdall's contract in hand, Wright's plans for the future seemed inevitable.

Predictions of Barnsdall's arrival from Europe in July 1921 were greeted with apprehension. She was on Olive Hill by August, staying in Residence A (figs. 12-17 and 12-18) while her house neared completion.[72] There is no record of her first impression of Hollyhock House or even of whether she occupied it

12-23. Olive Hill, aerial construction photo looking west, November 9, 1921 (courtesy Aerial Photo Archives, Department of Geography, University of California, Los Angeles). From top to bottom: Residence B; Hollyhock House; hill grove of pines and eucalyptus; space for the unexecuted first swimming pool (behind the pergola connecting Hollyhock House to the garage); and, at lower right, Residence A.

before Wright's return to the United States the following summer. In March 1922, returning from another extended trip to Europe, Barnsdall discovered that her house had suffered badly during the winter. Lloyd Wright reported, "We have had three times as much [rain] this year as last—some twenty inches."[73] The building had leaked so extensively that damage was not confined to a small area. By July 24, 1922, Lloyd Wright was preparing a contract for repairs and additions to correct drainage; to repair, replace, and vent the foundations; to waterproof all exterior plaster and replace or refinish buckled wood floors in all rooms except the kitchen and service wing; and to repair and repaint damaged exterior and interior plaster, and replace warped sashes and doors. "Yes, build a Frank Lloyd Wright house," Barnsdall chided her architect many years later, "if you don't mind camping in the front yard when it rains."[74]

The most serious problem was the roof. Wright admitted in later years that "the worst feature of the house was always [the] lack of the intended roof. The roof was only temporary waiting for the tile pavement that made the roof surfaces into terraces."[75] He maintained that Barnsdall refused to carry through with the original intention when the additional cost exceeded the budget. The schedule for repairs and additions called for all roofs, except those over the garage, pergola, entrance, and dining room, to be tiled. "I spent almost twenty thousand dollars trying to make the roof stop leaking after your contractor gave up," Barnsdall reminded him. "I insisted upon starting the tiled roof...and I was told that the leakage was caused by the two materials, the side wall and concrete frieze...[that] shrank in a different way under dampness."[76]

The inferior construction was one of Barnsdall's principal criticisms in later years. "It was a great design badly executed," she declared to Wright. Wright agreed, adding, "We all did our dam'd'est and it was damn poor—except the motive."[77]

Her main objections, however, appeared to be more personal than practical. She remarked to a friend that her suspicion of Wright had stemmed from the fact that he had misled her about the size of Hollyhock House.[78] Declaring that she preferred Residence B (figs. 12-19, 12-20, and 12-21), although even it seemed too massive for a house, she admitted about Hollyhock House, "Its more ornate beauty never satisfied me."[79] But Barnsdall's fundamental dissatisfaction was more elusive. "My heart was not in it," she confessed. "I never felt well on Olive Hill and I was still on my quest for Arcadia in the U.S.A."[80]

Olive Hill, aerial photo looking northeast,
1922 (courtesy of Bruce Torrence
Historical Collection, First Federal of
Hollywood). Top: Residence A. Middle:
Hollyhock House and the Spring House.
Bottom: Residence B. Lloyd Wright supervised the completion of the roads and
landscaping in the first six months of
1922.

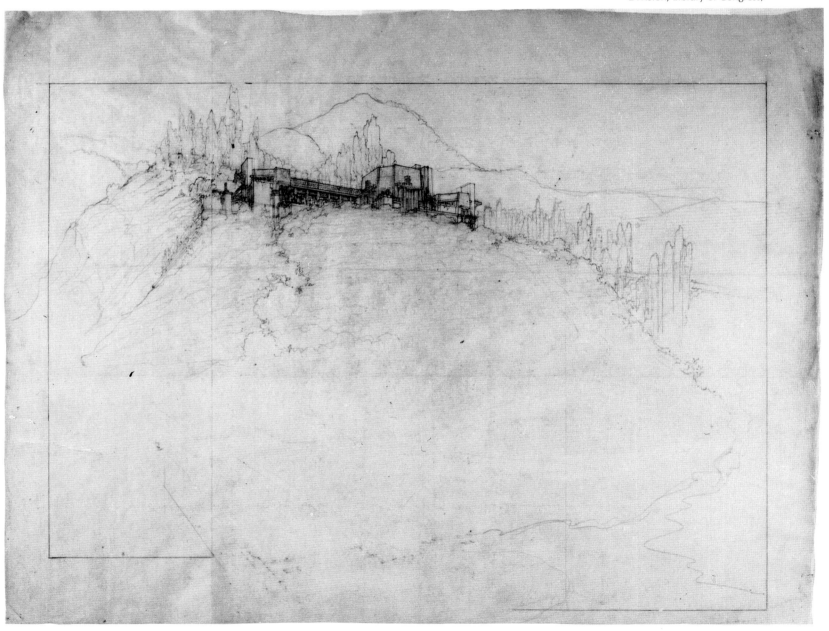

13-1. Beverly Hills House, perspective, 1923 (courtesy of Prints and Photographs Division, Library of Congress)

CHAPTER 13

BEVERLY HILLS HOUSE

13-2. Harper Avenue studio, 1923 (photo by Kameki Tsuchiura; courtesy of Mr. and Mrs. Kameki Tsuchiura). From left to right: Harry (office boy), Nobuko Tsuchiura, and William E. Smith. Samples of textile block are visible at the upper right.

By the time of Wright's permanent return from Japan in August 1922, Barnsdall had made up her mind not to build the Olive Hill plan.[1] In the six years that her house had been in planning and construction, her life had changed. Her daughter was now five years old, and it had been exactly that long since she had worked in the theater. In the interim, she had tried to be both a patron of the arts and a "high class real estate developer" without success. With the exception of the restricted period of World War I, the one constant in Barnsdall's life had been travel. Ownership of three houses and acres of undeveloped land had not brought the fulfillment she sought. Indeed, it had become a burden. "The question is do I want the management of a theatre, cafe, and several charming houses," Barnsdall queried Bel Geddes some months later. "I do know that I want a year to read and travel before I can do it. Mr. Wright said, 'Wait, you know you haven't had your head above water for so long.' He is right I have been under a tremendous strain for the past six or seven years. I am coming out of it and I want a kind of spiritual rest....I can't quite give up the theatre and I can't quite grip it."[2]

She struggled over the next six months with the future of Olive Hill. She was guided by what she said Wright "called [her] weakness, which [she] called her strength that [she] hated to part with money as long as it [was] not balanced by money coming in—[and] that [she would] not borrow [from] or jeopardize [her] father's fortune."[3] She considered selling all or part of the land, donating part as a park and selling the rest, or donating part and building the theater as planned. The enormous profits to be gained by buying and selling land in southern California became hard for Barnsdall to ignore. By June 1923 she was willing to consider selling the entire thirty-six-acre site for $1,800,000, netting her a profit of well over a million dollars in four years.[4] Ultimately, she could not "bear to think of selling her home to the hotel syndicate and have it turned into a jazz parlour where smokers would congregate."[5] She also considered donating the crown of the hill with Hollyhock House to the City of Los Angeles for use as a library and public park. Although she vacillated between speculation and philanthropy, she was sure she wanted to leave Hollyhock House.

Wright referred indirectly to the loss of the second phase of construction on Olive Hill when he confided to Louis Sullivan, on November 30, 1922, "I am going to tell you a secret which I hope you will keep. I am extremely hard up—and not a job in sight in the world."[6]

His prolonged absences in Japan and California had created a void both in his practice and in his professional standing. During those six years, his reputations in Europe and America had evolved independently of each other and of his own making. Although known more at home for the notoriety of his personal life, critical attention from Europe (primarily Holland) focused directly on his theory and practice. His absence from the United States deprived him of the opportunity to influence opinion at home. Between the years 1918 and 1922, seven of the nine articles published on his architecture were by Europeans—J.J.P. Oud, Robert Van't Hoff, Jan Wils, and H.P. Berlage.[7] With little knowledge of his recent activity, the Dutch focused attention on Wright's career up to 1910, reserving particular praise for the Larkin Building, Unity Temple, and the Dana, Martin, Robie, and Coonley houses, underscoring points Wright made in his 1908 essay, "In the Cause of Architecture." With no commissions and few prospects, Wright was confronted in November 1922 with two articles that reviewed his more current work: one, a scathing attack by the San Francisco architect Louis Christian Mullgardt in the November issue of *Architect and Engineer*; the other, primarily favorable, by Berlage in a 1921 issue of *Wendingen*.

Mullgardt, on a tour of the Orient, reviewed the Imperial Hotel only four months after Wright's departure. Although he reserved his strongest criticism for its style and ornament, Mullgardt also attacked the structure, materials, plan, function, safety, and cost of the building. In unusually vituperative language, Mullgardt concluded that "the errors are so numerous and flagrant that it may be said this structure should never have been built."[8]

Berlage, on the other hand, continued his interest, first expressed in a series of lectures delivered in Holland, Germany, and Switzerland in 1912. While he acknowledged Wright's genius, Berlage questioned his ultimate importance to modern architecture. Debating whether his "work represents a general rather than a particular value," Berlage concluded, "I believe I must regard...[it] as typical of the latter." He explained, "I find it difficult to see Wright otherwise than as a romanticist and [I find it difficult] to see him as his very anti-pode, that is, as an 'industrial architect', as many like to see him—as he likes to see himself."[9] Although he found admirable qualities in his country houses, Berlage singled out Unity Temple and the Larkin Building as Wright's best work. Of the Larkin Building, he noted, "the character of this building...is more consistent than any other with that which Wright developed in his 'programme of principles'."[10] Despite direct and indirect references to Wright's theory and practice before 1910, Berlage's article was illustrated with photographs of Taliesin II, Midway Gardens, and Lloyd Wright's 1921 perspective drawings of Olive Hill. Nevertheless his comments concerning the recent work were brief and included references only to the Imperial Hotel and the Barnsdall Theater and House, of which he remarked, "Fantastic pales rise up, angularly grooved, and similar beams and chassis project, everything for the sake of effect that is certainly Japanese in character."[11]

Although Wright was troubled by Mullgardt's criticism and reacted defensively by writing rebuttals, expressing outrage to Louis Sullivan, and lobbying to place favorable reviews in the architectural press, Berlage's more trenchant assessment struck a deeper chord. "Yes, you are right. I have been romancing—," he wrote Berlage on November 30, 1922, "engaged upon a great Oriental Symphony—when my own people should have kept me at home busy with their own characteristic industrial problems—work which I would really prefer to do and I have done."[12]

Berlage's article was not the only indication Wright had that he was moving away from the progressive movement in architecture. He had returned to Los Angeles to find that Schindler, continuing the development begun with the Monolith Home, had used a modular tilt-slab method of concrete construction to build his own studio-residence. In 1921 Schindler had confided to his friend Richard Neutra that "Wright is a complete and perfect master of any material—and modern machine techniques are at the base of his form-making."[13] However, many years later he recalled that "[the Barnsdall buildings] clung to the classical Greek vocabulary (base, shaft, cornice)."[14]

Between November 1922 and February 1923 Wright made the biggest changes in his life and practice since his departure for Europe in 1909. His first step was a decision to move to Los Angeles to open a practice with his son Lloyd as a landscape architect, designing "foothill properties between Hollywood and the sea."[15] They discussed plans to build a new studio in Beverly Hills, but temporarily rented a house a few miles to the east at 1284 Harper Avenue. Wright and Miriam Noel lived a few miles away. Wright cabled his former Japanese draftsman Kameki Tsuchiura in Tokyo, who arrived with his wife, Nobuko, in April 1923, to reside at the Harper Avenue studio (fig. 13-2) with Will Smith.[16] In the meantime, Schindler walked over from his studio-residence a few blocks away to work on drawings in the evening during February and March.[17]

Wright's move to Los Angeles also coincided with his rededication to the principles Berlage and the younger Dutch architects admired in his 1908 manifesto. As if orchestrating another stage of European recognition similar to the Wasmuth episode of 1910, by February 1923 Wright had announced his intention to go to Europe, had written the next installment for *Wendingen* of "In the Cause of Architecture," entitled "The Third Dimension," and had begun work on a new structural system using square concrete blocks.

Wright's essay, which set the theoretical context for his invention of the textile block system of concrete construction, was primarily a reiteration of points he had made earlier in either the 1908 essay or his introduction to the 1910 Wasmuth portfolio. Speaking with the voice of an industrial architect, Wright advocated the use of the machine, both as a tool and as a principle in the form of "standardization and repetition." He championed the use of industrial materials such as steel framing and reinforced concrete, and expressed his opposition to the use of historical styles, reserving special approbation for Renaissance classicism. He singled out what he termed the third dimension, or depth, as the essential ingredient of all great architecture, apparently using the term both literally and figuratively, and reminded his readers of his use of these principles in the Larkin Building, Unity Temple, and the Coonley House.

The essay is conspicuous in its omission of Wright's work during the previous fifteen years, with the exception of an oblique allusion to the Barnsdall House. "I feel in the silhouette of the Olive Hill house," Wright wrote, "a sense of the breadth of the romance of the region and in the type as a whole something adaptable to conditions." He then went on to introduce his innovative structural idea:

> This type is made from the gravel of decayed granite of the hills easily obtained there and mixed with cement and sand in molds or forms to make a fairly solid mass either used in small units or monolithic in construction, or in combination. This is the beginning of a constructive effort to produce a type that would fully utilize standardization and the repetition of appropriate units. This standardization and repetition are essential values in the service rendered by the Machine. They should be employed as elements in any architecture modeled by the "third dimension". I am still engaged in this effort to produce an integral Architecture suited to the climatic needs of California.[18]

Barnsdall was one of Wright's first clients for his experimental system. She buoyed him against the loss of the Olive Hill jobs by offering him the commission to design a house for her on a spectacular sloping ridge in Beverly Hills to the north of Pickfair, the estate of the silent screen stars Douglas Fairbanks and Mary Pickford. Without a commission for an industrial building, Wright dedicated Barnsdall's new house to the principles of standardization and repetition in a structural experiment with concrete blocks. He proposed to use two concrete shells, for the exterior and interior walls, that would be laid up block by block, row upon row, with mortar, without reinforcement, similar to brick construction.[19] Along with the design for a new house for Alice Millard in Pasadena

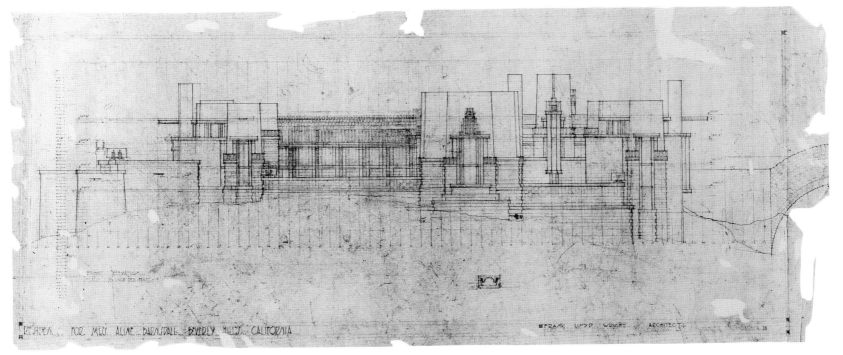

13-3. Beverly Hills House, front elevation, 1923, blueprint (collection of the City of Los Angeles, Departments of Parks and Recreation and Cultural Affairs)

and the rebuilding of his 1895 house for Nathan Moore in Oak Park, Wright's practice remained residential in scope.

Although it bears decided similarities to Hollyhock House, Barnsdall's Beverly Hills House is even more revealing of Wright's struggle to bridge the gap between his Prairie house vocabulary and his new experiments in structure and space. Barnsdall later explained that it was the size of Hollyhock House that dissatisfied her, but the new program that she presented to Wright necessitated a house that was equal to or larger than the one she already owned.[20] As with Hollyhock House, Wright designed a zoned plan, but one that was based on his earlier scheme for the Coonley House. In the manuscript for "In the Cause of Architecture: The Third Dimension," he had written of the scheme he intended to use:

> The Coonley house at Riverside is of a type employing simple individual buildings adapted each to its separate purpose, finally grouped together in a harmonious whole—simple materials revealed in construction, the style of the Coonley home, is due to this simple use of materials, with the sense of the human figure in scale, the Prairie as an influence, and a sense of the horizontal line as the line of domesticity: this home and all its relatives, grow up as a part of the site, incorporating with it, not planted *on* it, and this sense of the indigenous thing, as a successful treatment, of any problem in modern sense—as it was intuitively the secret of success in all great old work wherever it may be found.[21]

As he did for the Coonley House and Hollyhock House, Wright proposed a U-shaped plan, systematizing Barnsdall's program into four zones, each in a separate wing: the social group, the service group, the owner's apartments, and the guest house (figs. 13-4 and 13-5). Unlike the Coonley House and more reminiscent of Hollyhock House, the walls were terminated by a sloping attic story that gave the elevations a strong vertical emphasis (fig. 13-3).

Over the next four months, Wright took the scheme from early sketches to nine sheets of working drawings. Barnsdall's site, which she had not yet purchased, comprised twenty-four acres of mountainous terrain along Summit Ridge Drive, a serpentine road rising steeply behind Pickfair.[22] Wright's first idea for the Beverly Hills house may be a marginal sketch that appeared on the early preliminary plan (figs. 13-7 and 13-8). He chose to push the house forward to the edge of the hill, where it was flanked on one side by a steep ravine approximately 100 feet deep and on the other by Peavine Canyon, later Coldwater Canyon (fig. 13-6). Rather than providing an entrance from the road directly behind the site, Wright directed visitors over a bridge spanning the ravine and down a long driveway to the side of the living room. The thumbnail sketch (fig. 13-6) of the house indicates that he intended the large, square living room to form a pivot for two lateral independent units connected by a circulation spine. The S-configuration of Summit Ridge Drive and the contours of the site were echoed in the hemicycle of the entrance and its reverse curve in the garden in front of the living room.

As the plan developed, a service wing housing the kitchen, pantry, and a small dining room, probably for Sugar Top, was added parallel to the driveway (figs. 13-5 and 13-6). Along with the bedroom wing on the east, the plan now formed a U around a terraced courtyard that rose in tiers with the hillside to the rear. The dining room section in the preliminary drawing was torn away (fig. 13-8) because Barnsdall objected to it; she thought it was too far away from the kitchen. The ceremonial driveway, just over 240 feet long, terminated in a three-car garage and a room that probably served as a chauffeur's quarters or storage. A section in the lower left margin of the drawing (fig. 13-8) indicates that the two-story living room was to rise dramatically to a domed ceiling crowned with an oculus.

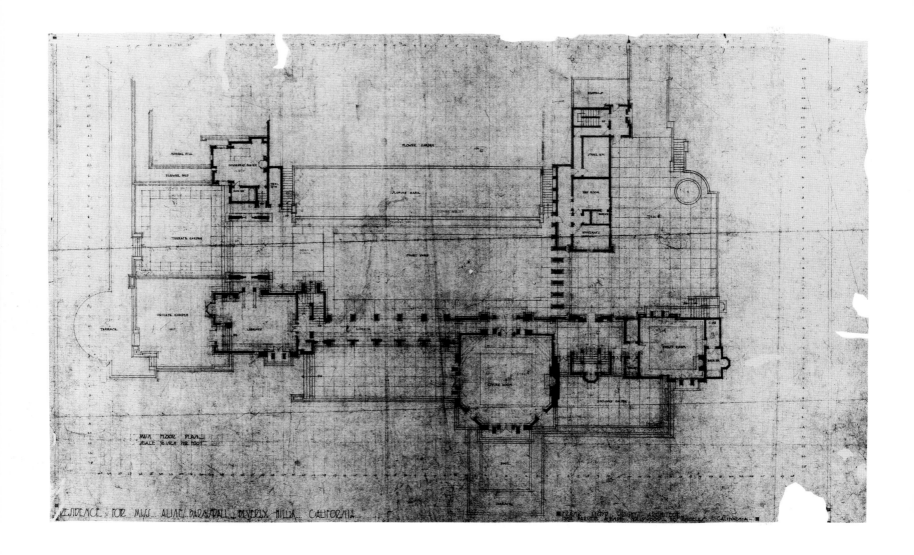

13-4. Beverly Hills House, main floor plan, 1923, blueprint (collection of the City of Los Angeles, Departments of Parks and Recreation and Cultural Affairs)

The main or south elevation shows that Wright placed the house straddling the hill, with the crown directly opposite the terrace off the living room and in front of the open loggia, where dramatic views of the entire Los Angeles basin and the Pacific Ocean would be visible (figs. 13-3 and 13-6). The strong horizontal line of the Coonley House, echoing the Midwest prairie, was replaced by a canted roofline emphasizing the strong verticality of the hillside site (fig. 13-3).

In the Coonley House, all the public and private rooms were on one floor set upon a raised basement containing the entry and playroom. The Summit Ridge site necessitated two floors with a gymnasium, a room for an extra bedroom, playroom or small theater, and a terrace below.[23] The double-height living room, with a ceiling thirty-six feet in diameter, rose off a square base as an octagonal drum. A gallery, with loggia below, extending 124 feet behind the living room, terminated on the west with the owner's apartments, which contained the library and governess's room on the main floor and bedrooms, baths, terraces, and sleeping and play porches for Barnsdall, her daughter, and the governess above. On the east, the dining room and guest bedroom below formed an independent unit separated from the living room by a formal entrance hall. The kitchen and extensive servants' quarters made up the largest wing to the north.

The preliminary drawings and studies for perspectives indicate that Wright was experimenting with the basic orthogonal geometry of the Coonley plan by inserting circular and diagonal forms (figs. 13-4 and 13-5). The principal changes were in the living room, Barnsdall's suite, and the dining room unit. After establishing the strong geometry of the domed ceiling rising within an octagon, Wright struggled with the circular and octagonal shapes of the terraces and small balconies. However, the most dramatic change was the use of a virtual diagonal axis as the orientation for Barnsdall's bedroom and the dining room (fig. 13-5). Both rooms were created by superimposing a square with diagonal corners cut at a 45-degree angle over a rectangle. Although Wright would experiment with the integration of orthogonal, diagonal, and circular geometries throughout the twenties, in the Beverly Hills House they remained unresolved.

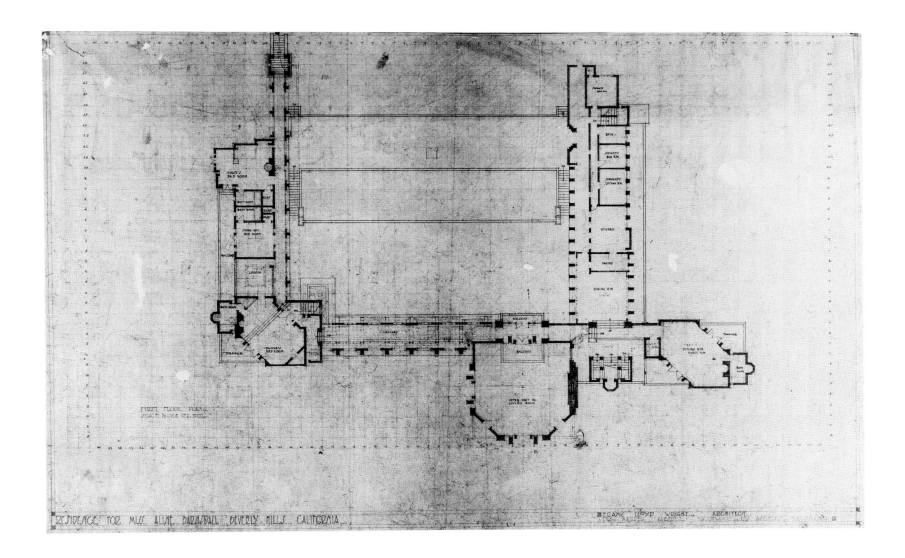

Probably by either April or May 1923, Wright had completed plans of the three floor levels, elevations, and sections. The local newspaper, *Holly Leaves*, reported on May 18 that Barnsdall had purchased "24 acres...at a cost of about $60,000 and will erect a residence to cost $150,000."[24] The negotiations must have fallen through before the sale became legally binding, however, because by June 9, when Barnsdall sent Wright a check for $6,250 for his work to date, she informed him that the plans had to be redrawn to fit a new site, which was not specified. She also wanted the house, which she set at $125,000, to be scaled down in size.[25]

Despite past disappointments and tensions, Wright and Barnsdall were more cordial than at any other time in their relationship. "Let's be friends," she wrote, "and get something done that can be a complete expression—even tho [*sic*] it is smaller in scope than you [have] drawn and done a little at a time. California is full of waste places...."[26]

13-5. Beverly Hills House, first floor plan, 1923, blueprint (collection of the City of Los Angeles, Departments of Parks and Recreation and Cultural Affairs)

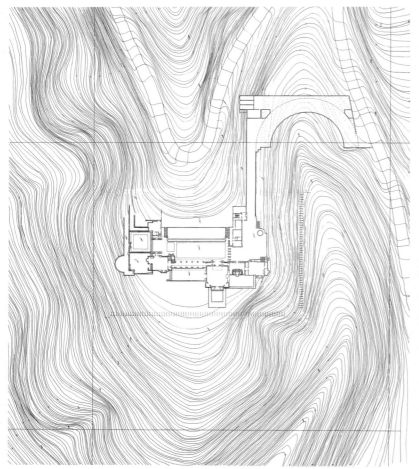

13-6. Beverly Hills House, site plan (drawing by Jason Shirriff). This conjectural drawing was based on Wright's preliminary plan, ground floor plan, and a 1923 topographical map of the site. Conjectural decisions were made to adjust the driveway and garage to accommodate the topography.

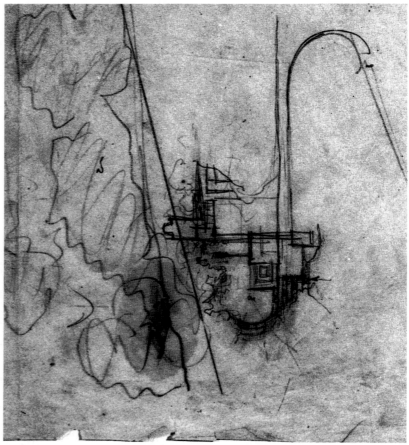

13-7. Beverly Hills House, detail of preliminary plan, 1923 (courtesy of the Frank Lloyd Wright Foundation). Wright's marginal sketch indicates that the living room acted as a hinge with the dining room and bedroom wings as appendages, and the S-curve of the driveway and semicircular front garden echoed the S-curve of Summit Ridge Drive.

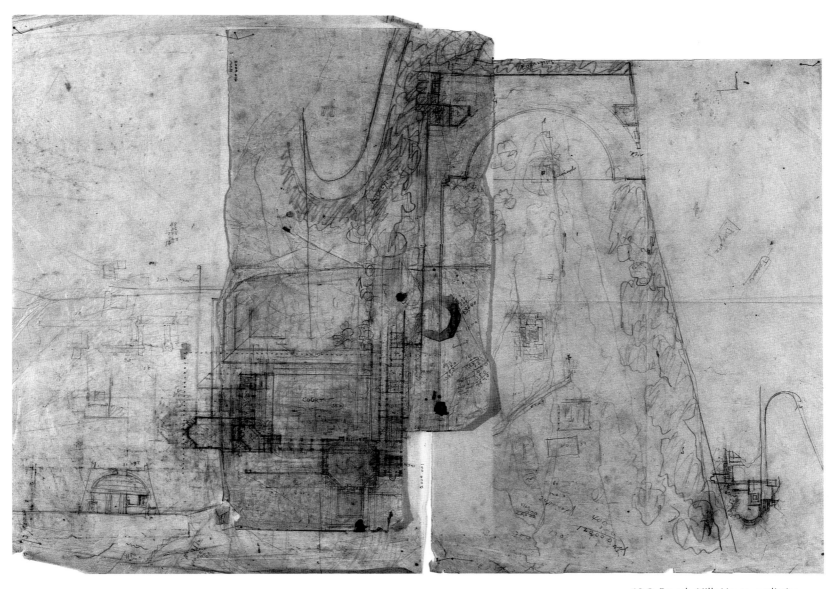

13-8. Beverly Hills House, preliminary plan, 1923 (courtesy of the Frank Lloyd Wright Foundation). This is the only extant drawing that shows the building and the site. Summit Ridge Drive is on the right adjacent to the entrance over the ravine. The section of the drawing containing the dining room has been torn away. Barnsdall had pointed out that the dining room was too far from the kitchen.

14-1. Studio Residence B, Edgemont Street elevation, 1923–1928 (courtesy of the Frank Lloyd Wright Foundation). Although the corbeled posts supporting the balcony canopy and the attic story over the living room are visible, the proposed studio addition clearly was not executed (see fig. 14-4).

14-2. Studio Residence B, dining alcove of the living room, 1930 (collection of the author)

CHAPTER 14

STUDIO RESIDENCE B

During the summer of 1923, Barnsdall was considering the future of Olive Hill. In a letter to Wright, she revealed her struggle over selling the property:

> ...Please don't argue it with me. I can take advice from nobody. I've been at it so long that I am temporarily tired and would prefer a few months in Europe—I am only continuing for your sake because I know that it is the best time for you to build for me. You can't imagine how weary I am of the fruitless discussion. Why should I live in this haggling atmosphere, or give away gold under my feet![1]

Finally, by July, she discovered a solution that would preserve both her house and her fortune and would allow her the option of either building the theater or selling portions of her land in the future.[2] She decided to give Hollyhock House and the crown of the hill to the City of Los Angeles as a public library and park. She would be free then of the constant burden of maintenance and taxes, and the buildings and gardens would be preserved intact.[3]

With the decision made, Barnsdall commenced plans both to outfit Hollyhock House for its new function as a library and to make a major addition to Olive Hill that would be included in her gift. In July 1923 she commissioned Wright to design both additional furniture for her house and a community playhouse to house her own private school for children between the ages of five and fifteen, including her daughter—now often called Betty—who was about to turn six years old. Located on the slope directly west of Hollyhock House, it was to be surrounded by terraced gardens that would ultimately comprise part of the Theodore Barnsdall Memorial Park. Despite past difficulties, by the summer of 1923 Barnsdall and Wright had reached an understanding and she agreed to rent him Residence B. Wright proposed to remodel it substantially by adding a studio below the living room and a second story over the garage, along with other changes.

His first ideas appear to have been sketched in pencil directly over the original ink-on-linen set of plans, elevations, sections, and details (figs. 14-3 and 14-4). As a record of the design process, the conflicting details in the drawings undoubtedly reflect concessions to either as-built conditions discovered in design or ideas that simply were changed.

Following the precedents of both Oak Park and Taliesin, Wright combined a drafting room and offices with living quarters, presumably for himself and his draftsmen.[4] Locating the studio on the ground floor directly beneath the living room provided an opportunity to create a separate entrance that led from Edgemont Street to a two-level terrace (figs. 14-3 and 14-5). In the spacious

173

workroom (eighteen by forty feet), Wright brought light in through three bays of west-facing, floor-to-ceiling louvered windows opposite a fireplace. In the north wing, he pushed a new bedroom forward, converted an original bedroom to an office, and appears to have wanted to convert an unfinished storage room into another bedroom, but finally walled it off completely. Leaving the main floor almost untouched, Wright enlarged the residential section by four bedrooms and two baths, enclosing the sleeping porch and corridor to the living room balcony, and adding a second floor over the servants' quarters and garage (fig. 14-8). He opened this floor up to views by creating three outdoor balconies, one facing the court on the east, and two on the west, on either side of the upper volume of the living room.

Pencil sketches over the elevations and several preliminary drawings reveal Wright's extensive alteration of the exterior with the addition of pattern, color, and a pronounced verticality. The strong horizontal lines of the roof cornice contrasted with the slanted walls of two attic stories placed over the living room and sleeping porch, probably for ventilation. The two volumes were visually united by a narrow slab wall. Wright enlivened the surface extensively along the balcony facing the court and around the upper volumes of the living room with wood boards set vertically rather than pitched. To further reinforce this detail, he added corbelled posts under the balcony (figs. 14-7, 14-9, 14-10, and 14-11) with stenciled ornament that repeated the orthogonal geometry of the plan, and a running strip along the lapped boards in a palette of rose, gray-blue, bronze, and pale yellow. By August 1923, Wright was far enough along with his plans to move out of his Harper Avenue studio and hire A.C. Parlee as the contractor for the remodeling.[5] Dividing his time between the Millard House in Pasadena and Olive Hill, Parlee proceeded slowly through the fall. Work began with the exterior and the enclosure of the north sleeping porches, before major work on the interior. Meanwhile, Barnsdall had renewed her interest in Norman Bel Geddes by sending the latest model of the theater to New York for his reaction. Holding onto the hope of reviving her theatrical company, she proposed that Bel Geddes and his family accompany her to France in August 1923. She believed they would be better able to reach an agreement without distractions. "I am not good at sustained effort," Barnsdall admitted to Bel Geddes. "I need time to fully understand. If you brought plans of the theatres and plays I am sure something would crystallize."[6] Bel Geddes recalled that their discussions went well until Barnsdall asked him to spend the fall in California rather than New York. He was unwavering in his decision not to leave New York during the height of the theater season and Barnsdall would not compromise.[7] With this disappointment, Barnsdall's efforts to rekindle her theater company abruptly ended.

While Barnsdall was still in Europe and Wright was on Olive Hill, for the first time in their long association, which now spanned eight years, Wright sat down to design a building for her under ideal conditions. With a view of the site from his window, refined details of a new structural system on his desk, and the client on an extended journey, Wright turned to a program that was reminiscent of the Oak Park Playroom and the Coonley Playhouse, two of his most inspired designs. His plans for the Barnsdall Community Playhouse, which he would call the Little Dipper, would surpass both of these in its lyrical interpretation of play.

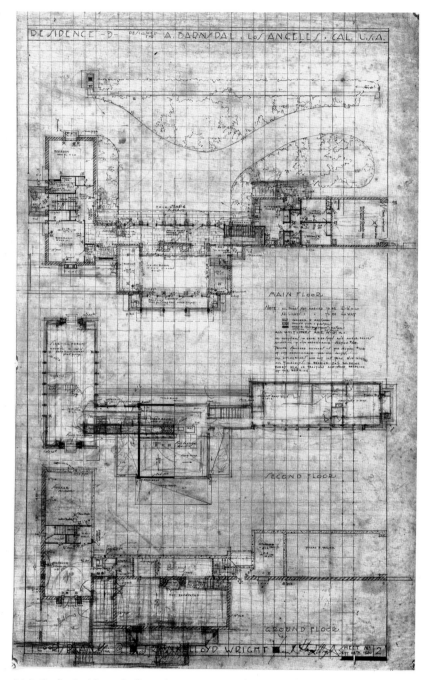

14-3. Studio Residence B, floor plans, 1923 revision (courtesy of the Frank Lloyd Wright Foundation). Wright's 1923 changes and additions were made in pencil over the 1920 ink-on-linen drawing (see fig. 10-5). The most extensive alteration was on the ground floor where Wright remodeled the basement as his studio and added a bedroom to the north (see fig. 14-5).

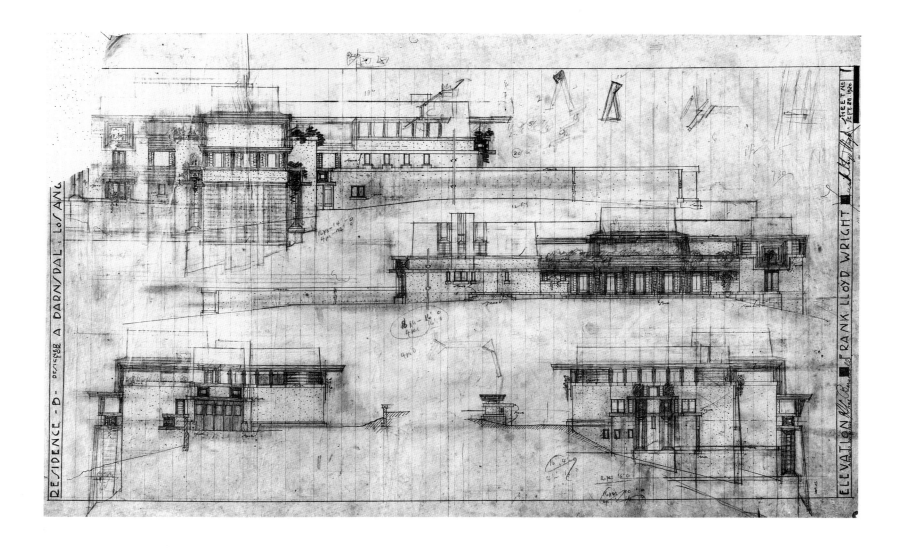

14-4. Studio Residence B, elevations, 1923 revisions (courtesy of the Frank Lloyd Wright Foundation). The drawing reveals the extensive 1923 pencil revisions over the ink-on-linen drawing (see fig. 10-6). The west elevation at the top of the drawing reveals Wright's concept for the studio, which included three floor-to-ceiling bays of louvered windows (see fig. 14-6) that were never built (see fig. 14-1). Wright also sketched the addition over the garage (see fig. 14-8).

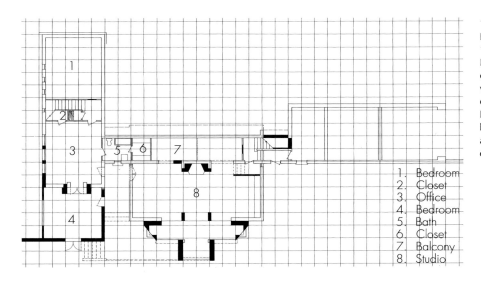

1.	Bedroom
2.	Closet
3.	Office
4.	Bedroom
5.	Bath
6.	Closet
7.	Balcony
8.	Studio

14-5. Studio Residence B, ground-floor plan, 1923 (drawing by Eulogio Guzman). Some conjectural decisions were made in the execution of this drawing. For example, the rear bedroom to the north appeared to be walled off.

14-6. Studio Residence B, Edgemont Street elevation, 1923 (collection of the City of Los Angeles Departments of Recreation and Parks and Cultural Affairs)

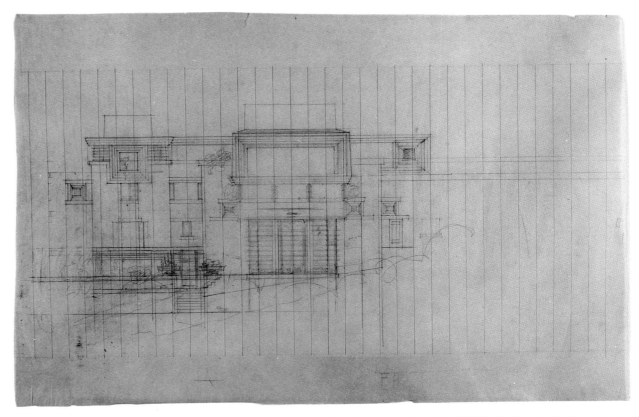

14-7. Studio Residence B, courtyard elevation, study for post under courtyard balcony (left), and study for lamp (right), 1923 (collection of the City of Los Angeles Departments of Recreation and Parks and Cultural Affairs). This sketch, almost certainly in Wright's own hand, indicates the corbel post and stencil pattern added in 1923 (see figs. 14-9 and 14-10).

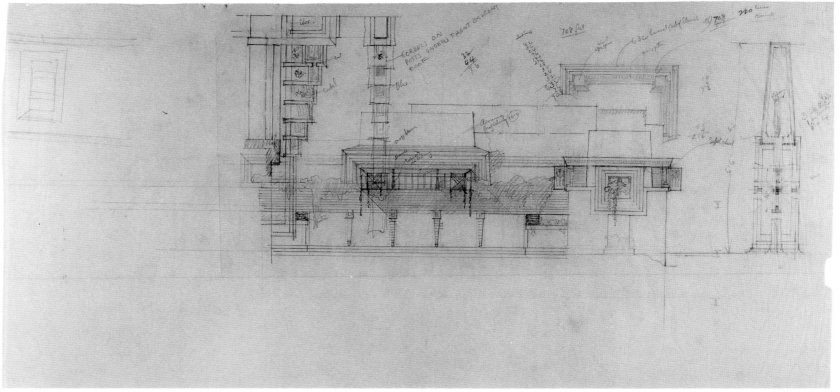

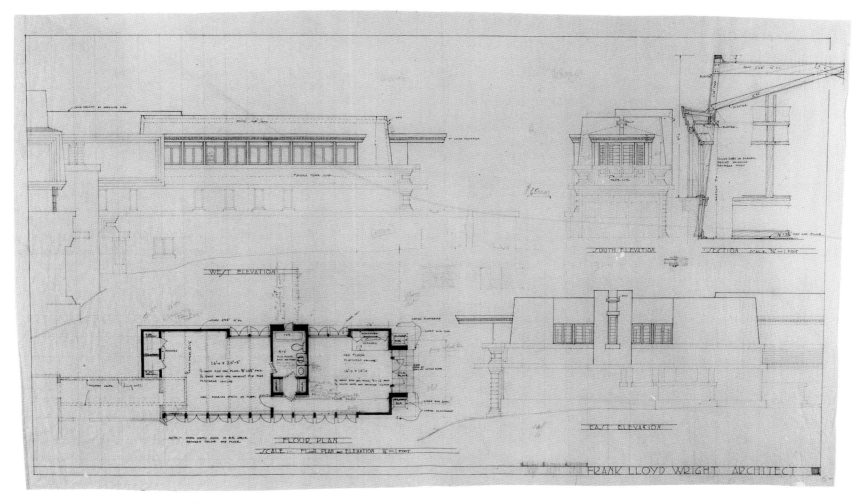

14-8. Studio Residence B, plan and elevations of bedroom addition, 1923 (collection of the City of Los Angeles, Departments of Recreation and Parks and Cultural Affairs)

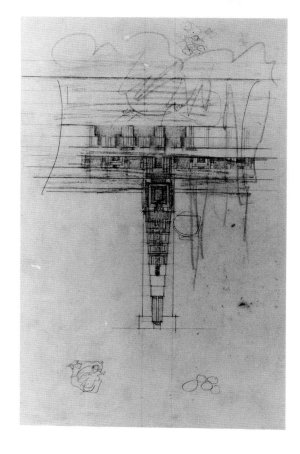

14-9. Studio Residence B, detail of
balcony posts, 1923–1928 (collection of
the author)

14-10. Studio Residence B, courtyard,
1923 (photo by Kameki Tsuchiura;
courtesy of Mr. and Mrs. Kameki
Tsuchiura). The courtyard as remodeled
by Wright in 1923. Compare with the
1921 scheme (fig. 12-21), and as
remodeled by Schindler, in 1928–1929
(fig. 16-16).

14-11. Studio Residence B, column
detail, 1923 (collection of the City of Los
Angeles Departments of Recreation and
Parks and Culural Affairs)

14-13. Studio Residence B, living room and library alcove, 1930 (courtesy of Lloyd Wright Studio)

14-12. Studio Residence B, living room and dining alcove, 1930 (courtesy Architectural Drawing Collection, University Art Museum, University of California, Santa Barbara). Although this photograph was taken after Schindler remodeled the house for Barnsdall, only minor changes were made in this room. With the exception of the furniture (note Barnsdall's use of the Hollyhock House dining table and chairs), the room appears substantially as Wright designed it in 1920.

15-1. Community Playhouse, the Little Dipper, perspective, 1923 (courtesy of the Frank Lloyd Wright Foundation). The swimming pool appears in this drawing, but does not appear elsewhere.

15-2. Aline and Betty Barnsdall, circa 1923 (courtesy of the Security Pacific Photograph Collection, Los Angeles Public Library)

CHAPTER 15

COMMUNITY PLAYHOUSE AND PARK MEMORIAL (THE LITTLE DIPPER)

Sometime before August 1923, when she departed for Europe, Aline Barnsdall made arrangements for the organization of her private school. The teacher, Helen E. Girvin, began to make plans for the term that was to begin on September 30 and end June 30, 1924. Wright had informed Barnsdall that the new building would not be ready for the opening, but assured her that it would be completed by the middle of November.[1] In the meantime, Barnsdall planned that the children, including her daughter, would meet in the unfinished rooms on the second floor of Hollyhock House. Barnsdall was taking steps to ensure that Betty would receive the right education.

The prospectus sent out that summer reveals that Barnsdall wanted a progressive curriculum that involved the children in the presentation of plays as a means of learning (fig. 15-3). In addition to lessons in English, arithmetic, and history, the students would make costumes and participate in "educational dramatics" and dancing that would aid them in learning subjects such as French and civics. To achieve this goal, the new building was to be "ideal in physical environment, artistically and practically adequate."[2]

The prospectus set forth the theme of the Barnsdall school:

Nature would have her children be children before they are men. Our tragic error is that we are so anxious for results of growth that we neglect the process of growth.

The project of Olive Hill has this spirit as its basis — not to provide another unit striving for new fads among the myriad schools organized and uprising throughout the country, but to help the children by the wisest and most gifted guidance to find themselves.[3]

It continued with the goals of the school:

Purpose—

To develop the child to the fullest.

To encourage spontaneity.

To free the child from self-consciousness.

To develop pride and character.

To develop skill in text analysis.

To develop skill in character analysis.[4]

By July 1923, Barnsdall and Wright were ready to pick a site. A freehand sketch over the 1920 general plan (fig. 9-1) indicates that the location chosen was west of Hollyhock House on a slope overlooking Residence B. Wright's first sketch was of a square rotated forty-five degrees, with the diagonal on the east-west axis of Olive Hill, intersecting a circle to the south.

Wright's notes for the playhouse outlined a school for twenty children in a big room (about forty by fifty feet) that could be divided into two sections. Barnsdall proposed that the room contain a fireplace, possibly a stage, and tables and chairs, with a coatroom and two toilets adjacent to the schoolroom, and a kitchen below.[5] Wright's notes mention "natural block" as the material, matching a sample in his studio (fig. 13-2), with a frieze of rose, pale gold, and Rocca blue.[6] On the reverse of this sheet of notes, Wright sketched a plan showing a forty-foot square, with its corner penetrating a fifty-six foot circle on center (fig. 15-4). From his earlier sketch on the plot plan, Wright rotated the square forty-five-degrees (so that its outer edge lay on the major axis of the hill) and flipped the plan 180 degrees, orienting the circular, shallow bowl to the north. The opposite corner of the square—the location of the fireplace and the stage—is sliced at a forty-five-degree angle, and Wright pasted a second sheet to the drawing to add an entrance housing the dressing rooms, coatroom, office, and interior stair down to the kitchen in a forty-five degree diagonal wing. The elevation (fig. 15-5) shows a solid rectangular volume of concrete block rising on a sloping hillside, capped by a band of glass and a flat roof.

After the plan (fig. 15-6) was laid out, using a sixteen-inch grid (the unit of the concrete block), the grid was numbered in threes producing a four-foot module. Each four-foot module was multiplied by five to make up the overall twenty-foot grid of the entire site. The elevation (fig. 15-7), similarly drawn on a sixteen-inch grid, follows Wright's first sketch, except that the roof line is now a gable. However, the verso of the plan shows that at this point the building was flipped 180 degrees so that the schoolroom faced southeast, receiving the optimum orientation to the sun.

The major ideas of the building were largely worked out before the plan was sketched in pencil over an inked survey (fig. 15-8), dated July 28, 1923. On the site (roughly 270 feet north to south, and 72 feet east to west), Wright laid out the plan with a pergola to the north containing a bas-relief portrait of Theodore Barnsdall (figs. 15-9 and 15-10). Flanked by a concrete block-paved terrace to the east and the natural slope to the west, the pergola was approached from the road by a stairway laid on a forty-five-degree angle to itself.

By August 1923, shortly after moving from the Harper Avenue studio to Studio Residence B, Wright's office completed the working drawing set of five inked sheets of linen showing the plans, elevations, sections, and block patterns (figs. 15-11, 15-12, 15-13, and 15-14). In the final plan (fig. 15-11), Wright clarified the entrance by consolidating all functions on one floor: the kitchen replaced the pantry, the bathroom replaced the office, and the dressing room and coatroom were combined as the wardrobe. The other major change was in the treatment of the roof. Wright created a lantern, an elongated hexagon with windows the full length of two sides (fig. 15-12), dematerializing the solidity of the massive block walls and creating a play of light that transformed the schoolroom into a powerful space.

From the road to the west of Hollyhock House, a narrow enclosed passage led down to the building entrance in the diagonal tail of the service wing. The entry, four steps above the oak floor of the schoolroom, opened on a direct axis looking south through folded glass doors to the circular bowl area for outdoor play. The square room was organized axially based on a composition of solids and voids. The mass of the chimney on the northwest balanced the triangular prow of glazed doors opening on the cross axis to the southeast, and the longitudinal northeast-southwest axis extended through two corner walls of glass set between solid walls. The ceiling rose over nineteen feet to the ridge of the trussed roof. Between the trusses, operable sash windows ventilated and lighted the room from above. Doors at the triangular prow could be folded to either side, creating a free flow of space between the indoors and outdoors and allowing the square to act as the stage and the circle as the auditorium for performances by

Creative Education

"Nature would have her children be children before they are men. Our tragic error is that we are so anxious for results of growth that we neglect the process of growth."

The project of Olive Hill has this spirit as its basis—not to provide another unit striving for new fads among the myriad schools organized and uprising throughout the country, but to help the children by the wisest and most gifted guidance available to find themselves.

To this end is planned a building, ideal in physical environment, artistically and practically adequate to such a purpose. Here the children will spend the major part of six days a week, deriving from their daily experience a learning of how to live together.

The curriculum will be so complete that no child will find it necessary to take up study of any kind elsewhere The full day of work and play will be supervised, hence constructive. Children will be given proper luncheons. rest-hours, exercise. Every child will receive individual instruction so that what is in embryo will be brought forth and developed.

The curriculum will consist of—

English—Reading, writing, grammar, letter-writing.
Arithmetic—Children discovering basic principles as they were discovered by the great scientists.
History—Story of the world from beginning with stereoptican views and talks.
Geography—Imaginary travels; moving pictures; trips to industries, etc.
Drawing and Construction—Creative.
Art—Lectures on great masters; great paintings. Visiting galleries; interviewing artists.
Music—Individual lessons on piano; on violin.
Dancing—Technique.
Physical training and games.
Rest period—Directly after luncheon.
French—Through games; songs; conversation; dramatization.
Sewing—Costumes for plays, dancing, etc.
Civics—Dramatization; talks; active participation.
Cooking.
Hygiene.
Character Building.
Educational Dramatics.

Purpose—

To develop the child to the fullest.
To encourage spontaneity.
To free the child from self-consciousness.
To develop poise and character.
To develop skill in text analysis.
To develop skill in character analysis.

One day each week (weather permitting) spent at the beach taking up the study of sea-life; swimming lessons; play.

Each Saturday devoted to Civics; nature-study; visit to Museum.

No wasteful holiday weeks observed; only legal holidays recognized.

Terms $1000. yearly; payable semi-annually in advance.
$ 500. yearly for young children attending half-days.

Pupils admitted at any time during school year. Proportionate discount made accordingly. No loss because of late entrance, as all instruction is to be individual.

Children will be called for and returned each day within a radius of five miles; arrangements made for greater distances.

School term—September 30th to June 30th.
Address after September 30th—Helen E. Girvin,
"The Little Dipper"
Olive Hill,
Hollywood Boulevard and Vermont Avenue, Hollywood.

Before September 30th   862 Plymouth Boulevard,
Los Angeles, California.

15-3. Prospectus for private school at the Little Dipper, 1923 (collection of the author)

15-4. Community Playhouse, the Little Dipper, preliminary plan, 1923 (courtesy of the Frank Lloyd Wright Foundation). Wright pasted a second sheet of paper to the plan which included the entrance. The notation, "Barnsdall Kindergarten Block House, FLW, 1920-21" was probably added in the 1930s.

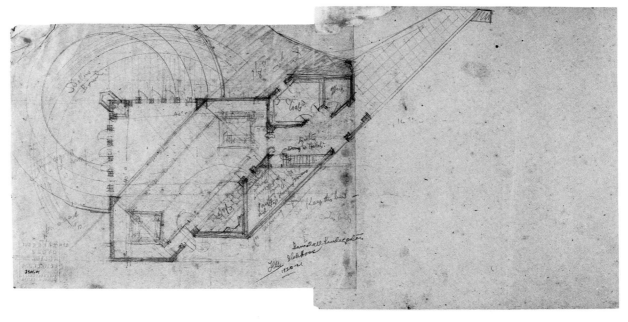

15-5. Community Playhouse, the Little Dipper, elevation, 1923 (courtesy of the Frank Lloyd Wright Foundation)

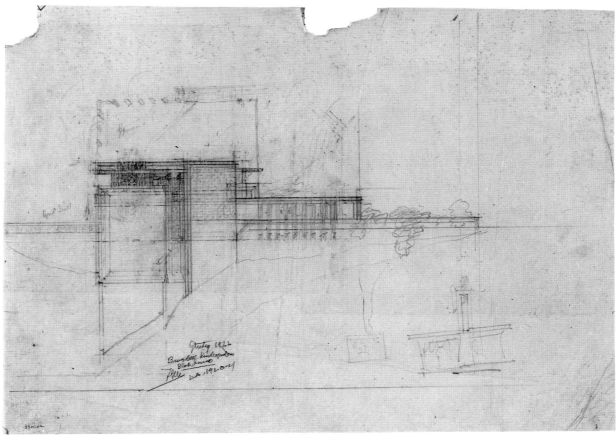

15-6. Community Playhouse, the Little Dipper, plan, 1923 (courtesy of the Frank Lloyd Wright Foundation). On the verso of this drawing, the plan has been drawn again and flipped 180 degrees so that the main room faces southeast.

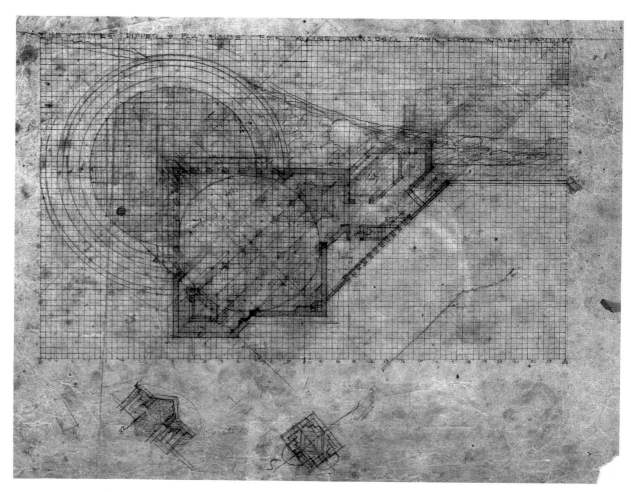

15-7. Community Playhouse, the Little Dipper, elevation, 1923 (courtesy of the Frank Lloyd Wright Foundation). The main room still faces northwest in this companion drawing to fig. 15-6.

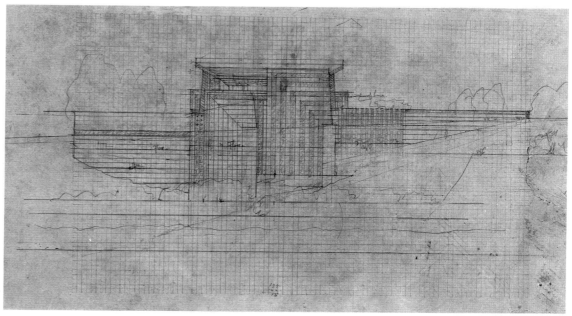

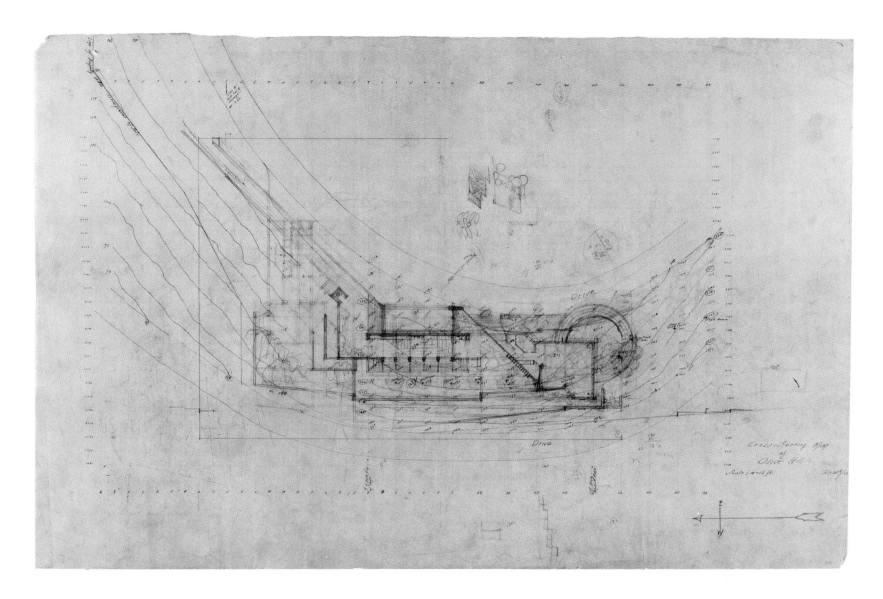

the children. The link between indoors and outdoors was reinforced at the corner, where Wright placed a hexagonal pool penetrating a rotated-square sand table. Anticipating his design for Herbert and Katherine Jacobs's second house in 1944, the pool extended from the outside to the inside.

In complete contrast to his use of structure and materials in Hollyhock House, Wright planned the Little Dipper as an experiment in what he later would term the textile block system. Going beyond the method used in the Millard House, Wright strove for structural innovation. The system called for the blocks to be made by mixing cement with decomposed granite found on the property. A dry mix was pressed into metal molds on site to produce a block. Each block was made with concave channels on all four sides so that when placed side by side and row upon row, cylindrical hollows were formed horizontally and vertically. In these channels were placed slender bars of steel that acted as reinforcing. When liquid concrete was poured into the empty channel from above, it coursed down and across until the entire wall was filled. Upon drying, the individual blocks were intended to form a monolithic structure. On-site fabrication and

15-8. Community Playhouse, the Little Dipper, plot plan over survey, July 28, 1923 (collection of the City of Los Angeles, Departments of Recreation and Parks and Cultural Affairs). The center of the circular bowl was on the major east-west axis of Olive Hill, which extended through the longitudinal axis of Hollyhock House.

185

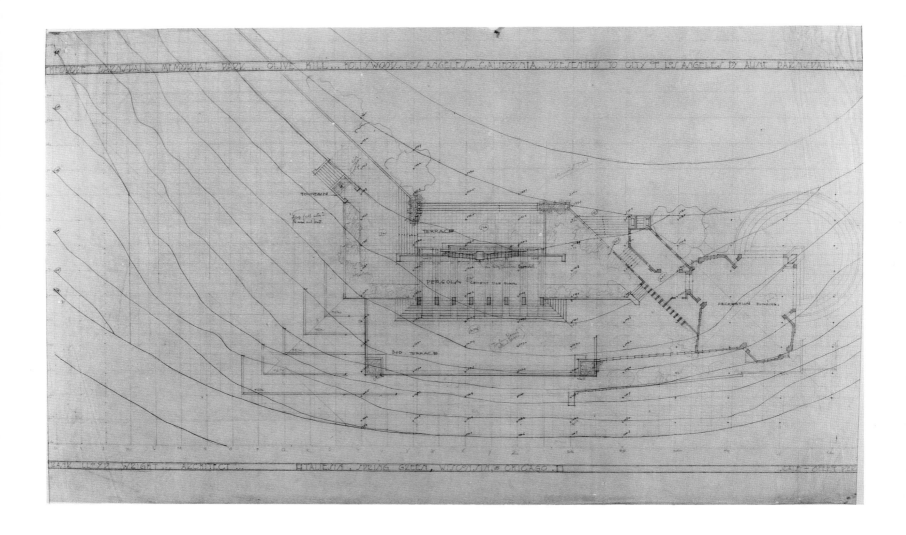

15-9. Barnsdall Memorial Park, plan, 1923 (collection of the City of Los Angeles, Departments of Recreation and Parks and Cultural Affairs)

construction was to be carried out by unskilled labor thus bypassing the trade unions. The blocks were used for both exterior and interior walls, and some were perforated as well as solid so that they became windows or vents or, with a sheet of opaque glass and an electrical outlet behind them, light fixtures.[7] In the square concrete block, Wright had found poetic unity of building and site, structure and material, ornament and wall plane.

There is no record of whether Barnsdall saw the working drawings before she departed for Europe. Although it is certain that she wanted to avoid the problems she had encountered in the construction of her house, her new understanding with Wright was less formal, and his powers of persuasion were more effective than a legal contract. However, a little more than two months elapsed before Wright was able to secure the building permit, which was dated November 7, 1923.[8] A.C. Parlee, the contractor for both the Millard House and the remodeling of Wright's Studio Residence B, was given the contract to build the Little Dipper, for $12,500.[9] It is unlikely that Wright was in Los Angeles when the permit was approved. Although his anticipated trip to Europe never materialized, after only a few months in Los Angeles he longed to return to Taliesin, if only for a visit.[10] After receiving word while still on Olive Hill that the Imperial

Hotel had survived the worst earthquake in Japanese history, Wright began to make plans to return to the Midwest. A divorce from his first wife, Catherine, was at long last about to become final, and he would have the opportunity to marry Miriam Noel after living with her for eight years.

Wright's departure also prevented him from receiving a letter from Barnsdall, written in Switzerland on October 19, and received on Olive Hill almost simultaneously with the issuance of the building permit.

And now what are you doing about my little house? Langey [Susan Lang, Barnsdall's secretary] says that on September 24 that there were only a few stakes on the ground, but it is absolutely promised for December 10th. I don't see 'The Miracle,' but I am 'having confidence' this time and watching 'warily' the result. She says you're a genius and not to worry. I am inclined to be skeptical and suggest that you speed up your genius a bit—

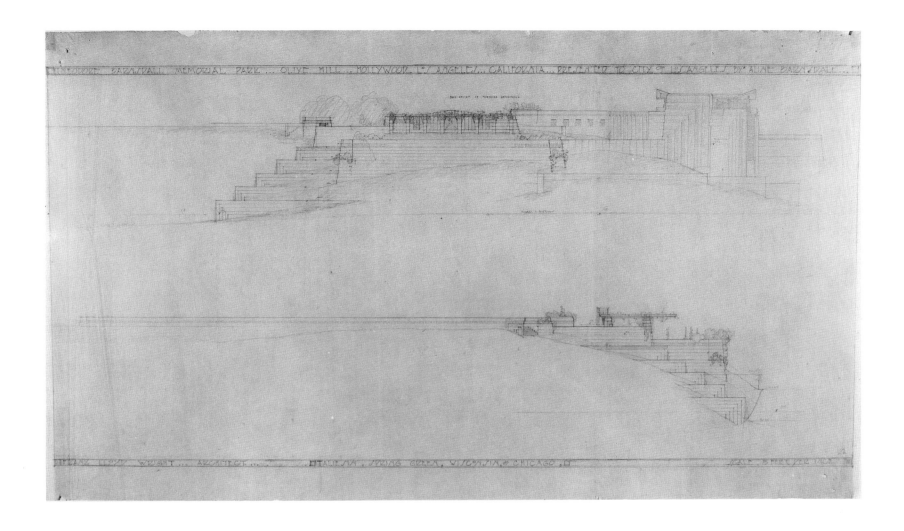

knowing how bad it is for the reputation of the school to have no permanent home. You will remember that you promised it for the middle of November when I left, and I made my plans accordingly so I must ask you to meet me on this; let the school have the use of one of the rooms and the upper porch in B from the middle of November until the school is completed. I'm sure you will do this for me as I would not have rented you the house but used it for the school had you told me it would be so long building. I won't have the school go off the hill and as I start to finish the upper part of my own house as soon as I return it won't be possible to keep it there—then Sugar needs her bedroom. It has occurred to me lately that I am a slave to the idea of doing something beautiful—and not being really free. I am making *life* ugly by it and life comes first. So I begin to practice the fine art of elimination and will do *nothing beautiful* or otherwise only as it enhances life for me. It doesn't enhance life for me to feel that you are putting the work on B before mine knowing how it jeopardizes the beginning of the school. I have only felt this since the last letters received from Miss Lang and you a few days ago and am willing to apologize if I find I am wrong. —if I am not, God help the future of our work on the hill.[11]

Barnsdall's message was sent to Wright at Taliesin on November 9 by Will Smith, in the form of an abbreviated telegram. But only a few days later, Barnsdall arrived in New York and cabled him twice suggesting that they meet to discuss the building plans.[12] On November 22, just three days after Wright's marriage to Miriam Noel at Taliesin, construction of the Little Dipper was halted because the building inspector required unrecorded changes made in the design.[13] In three weeks of construction, Parlee had proceeded through excavation, begun laying the foundations, made 7,508 blocks, and laid 226. Barnsdall, who evidently had finally had enough, refused to approve payment for the changes, and construction of the Little Dipper was canceled.

Meanwhile, Barnsdall had returned to Hollywood and made official her gift of Hollyhock House and the crown of the hill to the City of Los Angeles as a public library and park. Wright did not arrive in Hollywood until a week later, and

187

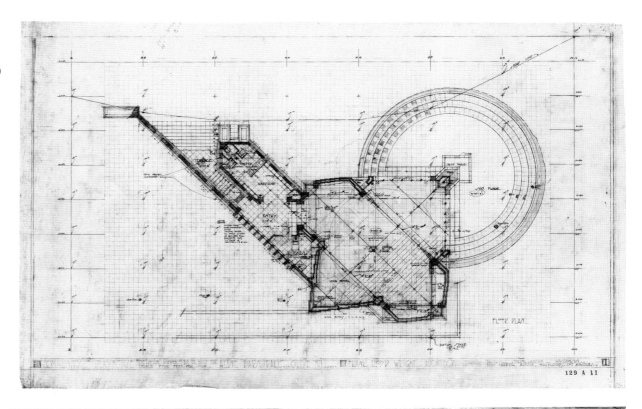

15-11. Community Playhouse, the Little Dipper, plan, August 1923 (collection of the City of Los Angeles, Departments of Recreation and Parks and Cultural Affairs)

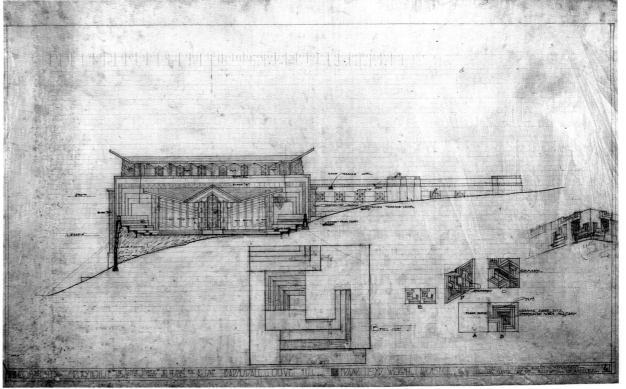

15-12. Community Playhouse, the Little Dipper, elevation, August 1923 (courtesy of the Frank Lloyd Wright Foundation)

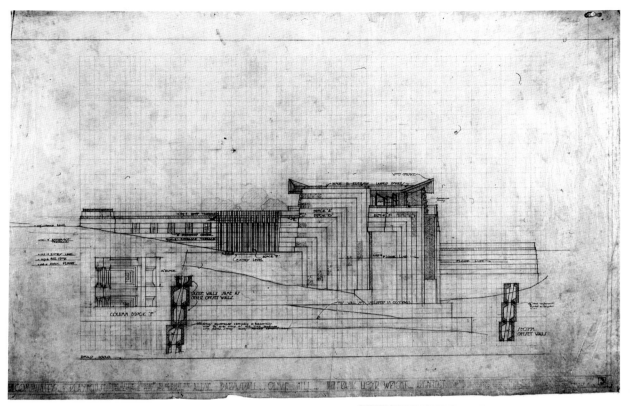

15-13. Community Playhouse, the Little Dipper, elevation, August 1923 (courtesy of the Frank Lloyd Wright Foundation)

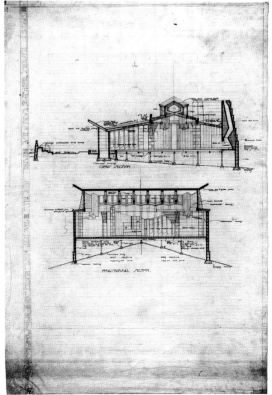

15-14. Community Playhouse, the Little Dipper, sections, August 1923 (courtesy of the Frank Lloyd Wright Foundation)

by December 13, 1923, he made out a check to Parlee for $1,515.48 for work executed on Residence B during his absence.[14] Within a few days, tempers began to flare, undoubtedly provoked by Barnsdall's reaction to Wright's mishandling of the construction of the Little Dipper. Wright moved out of Residence B into the Beverly Hills Hotel, stopping payment on his check to Parlee. After her disappointment over the construction of the Little Dipper and the disagreements surrounding Wright's remodelling of Residence B, Barnsdall's attitude toward Wright remained surprisingly equable. Her continued willingness to work with him is revealed in an undated letter, probably written around the holidays of 1923:

> I sincerely hope you never rent a house from [me] again or in any way do business outside of that as [an] architect. I feel sure that if we can ever get thru [sic] this present muddle that we can come to it later with more clearness, calmness and understanding. But to get thru [sic] this! I am so sure that you and I are only able to weave confusion just at present that I am eliminating only what must be done to pass this over to the city.
>
> The terraced garden: when can you submit plans for that?
> The list of thing[s] were [sic] have talked of in the living room:
> The petition [partition] taken away between living room and library
> Book cases put into music room—table and chair for librarian
> And window put in A.
> I am leaving the last of Febuary [sic] to sail for Spain so we should move as quickly as we can while I am here.[15]

PART FIVE

EPILOGUE TO HOLLYHOCK HOUSE AND OLIVE HILL

Olive Hill, aerial view looking northeast, April 7, 1947 (courtesy of Bruce Torrence Historical Collection, First Federal of Hollywood). Just a few months after Barnsdall's death, the entire site was still intact. The landscaping, including the Hill Grove massed behind Hollyhock House (center), had matured to realize Wright's original vision.

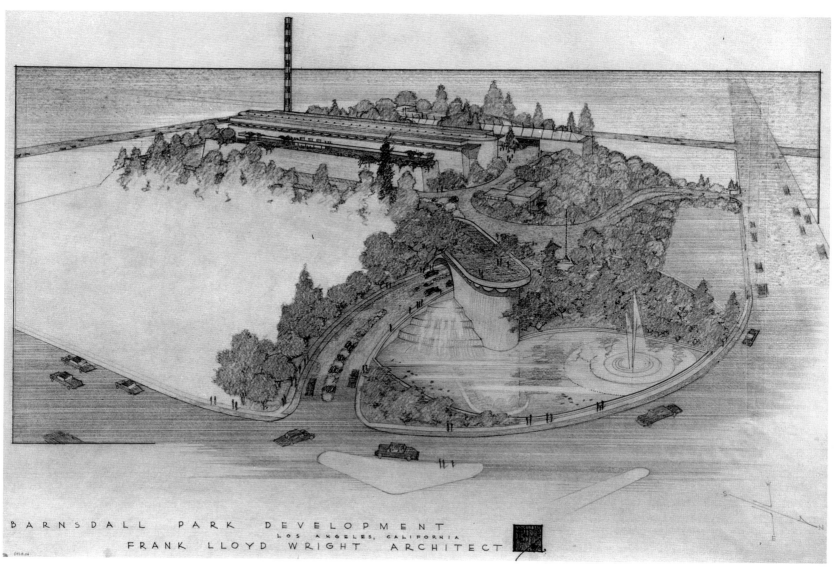

BARNSDALL PARK DEVELOPMENT
LOS ANGELES, CALIFORNIA
FRANK LLOYD WRIGHT ARCHITECT

CHAPTER 16

THE LAWSUITS AND AFTER

16-1. Barnsdall Park, perspective, 1959
(courtesy of the Frank Lloyd Wright
Foundation)

With the Little Dipper no further along in construction than the foundation walls, and Residence B halted before any of the major structural additions had been made, Barnsdall was hoping to reach an understanding with Wright that would allow them to sufficiently complete the work so that she could turn over the crown of the hill to the City of Los Angeles and put the remainder up for sale. However, by January 1924 it was clear that Wright and Barnsdall would never work together again.[1]

What followed in the weeks ahead was the filing of a series of lawsuits that were not completely settled for three years. First, A.C. Parlee filed suit against Wright on January 16, 1924, for $1,522.98 for labor and material outstanding against his contract on the remodeling of Residence B.[2] On February 28, 1924, Wright sued Barnsdall for the return of two Japanese screens, his investment in the remodeling of Residence B, and fees for the Beverly Hills house, the Little Dipper and Park Memorial, the furniture for the conversion of Hollyhock House to a library, the design of a window for Residence A, and the general plans and perspectives for Olive Hill, totaling $21,367.94.[3] And finally, on April 11, 1924, Parlee filed suit against Barnsdall for payment against his contract on the Little Dipper amounting to $11,857.62 less $4,000 advanced, for a total of $7,857.62.[4]

All of the lawsuits were either settled out of court or immediately dropped. As a result, it is not possible to determine the specific outcome of any one of them. Wright was never served with a notice of Parlee's suit over the remodeling of Residence B.[5] Parlee, however, was able to collect some monies owed on the construction of the Little Dipper when Barnsdall settled out of court for an unspecified amount on July 9, 1925.[6]

Wright and Barnsdall both took definite positions regarding their disagreement, which prolonged their legal entanglement until the beginning of 1927. Evidently, by 1923, Wright and Barnsdall had established a complex financial arrangement that intertwined their business and personal relationships and made the settlement more difficult. In addition to continuing as Barnsdall's architect on various projects, Wright had borrowed money from her in exchange for Japanese screens and a collection of Japanese prints. According to Wright's calculations, in addition to the $16,367.44 that Barnsdall owed him for architectural services and the remodeling of Residence B, she also held the two screens, which he valued at $2,683, and there was an additional $4,615.04 for causes unspecified but that may have been his estimate of the worth of the Japanese prints. Throughout his discussions with his lawyer, Wright continued to assert that Barnsdall owed him more than $23,000.

Barnsdall, however, maintained that she had paid Wright $2,588 toward Residence B and $5,000 in cash—probably the amount she had lent him—which she was deducting as an advance against his fee.[7] By February 1925 Barnsdall was willing to return the screens and prints, calculated at $2,600 and $5,000, respectively, and pay Wright $1,237.[8] Wright, who had returned to Taliesin permanently, found the offer completely ludicrous and cabled his lawyer, "Telegram mentions twelve hundred. Did you mean twelve thousand? Former amount absurd, latter nearer if screens returned."[9] By March 4, 1925, Wright wrote to Barnsdall from Wisconsin, where his deteriorating personal life with Miriam Noel was causing him increasing financial hardship.

Your notion of "fifty-fifty" is unique....

I decline to accept it now, of course, as you undoubtedly knew I would do. I consider your sense of "fifty-fifty" another expression of that genius of which you boast and are certainly a hard-boiled exemplar-, that is, your Irish ability to be a bit meaner and trickier than anybody else....

Hahn [Wright's lawyer] says you are as belligerent as ever and any effort to negotiate with you [is] only stupid. Both you and I, it seems have had a dirty-linen washing in public coming to us for some time, and this will be it. I don't think you mind very much, partly perhaps because you don't know what is coming to you and partly because, if you did care, you wouldn't be you.[10]

The trials were set for January 1927. By then, Wright had separated from Miriam Noel, met Olga Milanoff, the mother of his seventh child, been forced out of Taliesin, moved to Minneapolis, and been arrested on the Mann Act. With the threat of losing both Taliesin through a bank repossession and his Japanese print collection at an upcoming auction, Wright wrote Barnsdall a letter that has been lost. When she replied on December 10, 1926, she revealed what her experience with Wright had cost her.

The trouble goes deeper than a few thousand dollars. I admired you so much and I do now as a creative artist....It went deeper than money for it shocked me into fear of doing impulsive generous things. It was one of the things that shut me up like a clam and filled me with bitter resentment for several years. These things destroy more than bank accounts. One would have thought that after the trouble I had had with my house you might have made some effort to help me. But no your grand gesture was to sue. So go to it if you so want to instead of adjusting and meeting me and being a friend to one who is near enough like you in nature to understand many things that others can't....[11]

A few days before the trial, on January 24, 1927, Wright and Barnsdall reached an undisclosed, out-of-court settlement.[12] Evidence indicates that Barnsdall probably forgave his loan, estimated at $5,000, but kept the Japanese screens, set at $5,000 in Wright's suit, but estimated at $2,683 in his notes. If she were able to prove that she had made the payments she claimed, Wright would have received less than half the $21,367.94 he sued for, but more than the $1,237 Barnsdall had offered in 1925.

Before the settlement, Wright, at perhaps one of the lowest points in his life, wrote Barnsdall a letter that has been lost. She waited until February 4, 1927, after the legal documents had been signed to respond.

I hope we may not consider each other enemies and that we may never attempt to work together again. It can't be done. We are both too much of the same mould—egotistical, dictatorial and creative. As a man said whom I read your letter to, "He speaks of your being several different women. How many different men is he—just in that letter!"...you will never know me if you don't get this right...there is a new kind of woman in the world today.... You write, "And there is a third woman. A wistful, lonely one, none too sure of anyone, or anything around her—she having ventured too far

into the 'unchartered' than fortified by her knowledge of life or circumstances, driven sometimes to cover her fear by defiance and to buttress her woman weakness with a willfulness beyond parallel!" You will never know me if you don't come to realize that I have never known fear in that or any other moral sense, that I am only at home and interested on unchartered seas. My willfulness I was born with. I haven't that old fashioned thing called "womans [sic] weakness" and I doubt if many women ever really had it, rather they projected it to flatter the ego of men....

...I couldn't tell all the magic you can weave and I'm sorry you have been driven another way by circumstances.... As for the theatre you must trust that I will do my best with it as I trust you to give me the drawings as soon as you can and help me when you can....

My best wishes to your little family and I hope to see you when I am in New York in March. Will you be there?[13]

The settlement of the lawsuits closed a chapter in Barnsdall's life, coinciding as it did with renewed negotiations with the City of Los Angeles to donate Hollyhock House and the surrounding ten acres of land in memory of her father. Three years earlier, in March 1924, Barnsdall had faced another frustration when the City officially rejected her gift because she had imposed too many restrictions. Resolving to try again in a few years, Barnsdall had hired Schindler, to Wright's irritation, to complete the unfinished upstairs bedrooms in her house and turn the site of the Little Dipper into a park that she planned to open to the public.[14] She continued to travel abroad much of the year, and the projects with Schindler extended from April 1924 until March 1925.

The largest single change on Olive Hill had been the addition of a wading pool and pergola to the north of the Little Dipper where Wright had proposed a pergola and terrace (figs. 16-2 through 16-5). Using Barnsdall's stock of surplus concrete blocks, Schindler had integrated the new work with the existing foundation walls. Leaving the building outline intact, he made only minor changes, such as transforming the pool and sand table of the playhouse into a flower box and tiled fountain and adding a monumental flower box (five feet six inches square) cantilevered over the edge of the western wall.

Over the years, Barnsdall had difficulty making up her mind about how she wanted to complete the upstairs bedrooms. The room consistently referred to on plans as the Chamber was eventually plastered and completed with a bathroom and closet. The remainder of the floor was finished as a suite, including Barnsdall's bedroom, sleeping porch, dressing room, bathroom, and walk-in closet (fig. 16-8). The bedroom walls and ceiling were paneled in white oak, and the art glass doors, windows, skylight, and wood trim repeated details used in the original construction (figs. 16-6 and 16-7).

Although Barnsdall had continued to employ Schindler to make minor additions and changes to both Hollyhock House and Residence A, she had remained resolved to donate the buildings to the public. By 1927 she was successful in deeding both houses and the crown of Olive Hill to the City of Los Angeles in two separate gifts. Hollyhock House was leased to the California Art Club (an organization of local painters and sculptors) for fifteen years, and Barnsdall specified that Residence A was to be used for teaching of eurythmic dancing, a method devised by Jaques Delcroze, the Swiss associate of Adolphe Appia.

By August 31, 1927, the day the California Art Club held its formal opening, Barnsdall and Wright had begun to renew their friendship. Perhaps Wright was pleased when despite their past disagreements Barnsdall wrote him that she was donating her house and gardens to the public because she could not "bear to see a beautiful design destroyed."[15] Barnsdall's deed restrictions prevented any substantial alterations to Hollyhock House, but the Art Club adapted the house, without a complete remodeling, both for small gatherings and large functions. The only significant change involved the removal of the walls and bathrooms between the two guest bedrooms, creating one room for a gallery. On special occasions, theatrical and dance performances were given in the patio-theater.[16]

Within a few years, however, more exhibition space was needed. In 1932, at Aline Barnsdall's suggestion, Lloyd Wright became involved in preventing the club from enclosing the central courtyard as an exhibition hall. Writing to his father for advice, he proposed instead to extend the existing gallery out over the south terrace.[17] In a set of preliminary sketches that have been lost, the elder Wright responded by proposing to enclose the exedra and rear pool and cover the space with a copper roof fitted with a semicircular band of triangular skylights. He believed his scheme would make the house into "a real art museum" and "naturally complete the building for it's [sic] new purpose."[18]

Lloyd Wright quickly informed his father that the design did not meet either the budget or the full extent of the program. He suggested that Wright revise his scheme so that the area could serve as a lecture hall, banquet hall, and print gallery, and would provide a fourteen-foot-high space to view canvases from a distance of twenty-five feet. Although the club's needs were greater than Wright first realized, the budget was only $3,500.[19]

Through a sketch and additions made over the original working drawings, it is possible to reconstruct Wright's revised scheme (figs. 16-9, 16-10, 16-11, and 16-12). The design provides a transition between Hollyhock House and the circular plans of the 1930s and later; it relates both to Wright's ideas for a New Theater Circus drawn in 1931, and anticipates one of his last projects, the 1958 Spring Green Community Center. Retaining the basic form of his first proposal, Wright set a speaker's rostrum, which could double as a sculpture pedestal, over the circular pool. A hexagonal skylight over the rostrum was supported on either side by cantilevered concrete beams. The rostrum was to be enclosed by a rolling screen that would open the space to the courtyard when it was stored on either side of the piers. The outer ring of exhibit space would rise up to a continuous band of skylights, and the room would be finished like a garden enclosure with raked gravel floors, inexpensive walls, and composition roof. "I like the first scheme best—because it is a real gallery," Wright admitted. "I don't care much for combinations."[20] With limited funds and only ten years remaining on their lease, the Art Club eventually decided not to build Wright's scheme or any other.[21]

Barnsdall remained involved with plans for Hollyhock House and Barnsdall Park, because by October 1928 she had chosen to return to Olive Hill to live when she was in Los Angeles. She hired Schindler to remodel Residence B and design a second-story bedroom addition over the garage, creating a suite with a dressing room, wardrobe, and bath (figs. 16-14, 16-15, and 16-17).[22] The strong horizontal lines of the roof hovered over a band of windows on the east and west elevations. Although Schindler added strong geometric accents with sliding window screens, he repeated the stenciled ornament, visually uniting his addition with Wright's remodel of 1923.

Barnsdall and Wright remained friends throughout the years, growing close again in the early 1930s when Barnsdall's daughter, Betty, joined the Taliesin Fellowship. Although she talked of selling Olive Hill's remaining street frontages they were still in her possession and undeveloped when she died in Residence B on December 18, 1946 (fig. 16-13).[23]

Aline Barnsdall's death brought about the greatest change on Olive Hill in twenty-five years. By the early 1950s, Betty and her family began to sell off and develop the four street frontages creating two permanent, distinct zones: Barnsdall Park, on the crown of the hill, and a commercial zone that ultimately included a hospital, apartments, and a retail shopping center.

When the California Art Club vacated Hollyhock House in the early 1940s, the building was in need of serious maintenance and repair. The City of Los Angeles was discussing the problem when Dorothy Clune Murray stepped forward

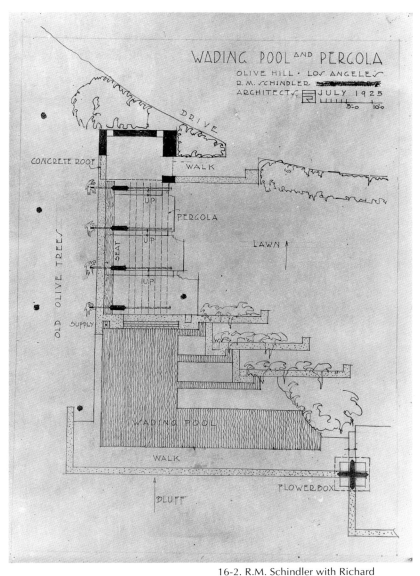

16-2. R.M. Schindler with Richard Neutra, wading pool and pergola, plan, 1925 (courtesy of the Architectural Drawing Collection, University Art Museum, University of California, Santa Barbara). In the legend at the upper right, Schindler crossed out Neutra's name next to his.

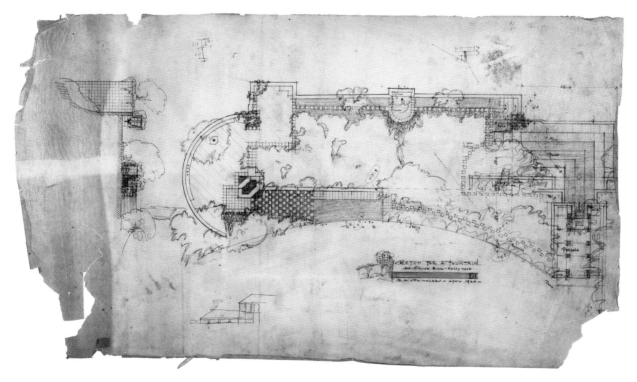

16-3. Schindler with Neutra, wading pool and pergola, perspective, 1925 (courtesy of the Architectural Drawing Collection, University Art Museum, University of California, Santa Barbara). Schindler used the surplus textile blocks remaining from the Little Dipper to build this structure.

16-4. Schindler with Neutra, wading pool and pergola, circa 1925 (courtesy of the Architectural Drawing Collection, University Art Museum, University of California, Santa Barbara)

16-5. R.M. Schindler, garden and fountain, April 1924 (courtesy of the Architectural Drawing Collection, University Art Museum, University of California, Santa Barbara). Before Neutra's arrival in Los Angeles in 1925, Schindler executed the plan for the conversion of the construction site of the Little Dipper into a garden. He retained the outline of the retaining walls for the Little Dipper and Barnsdall Memorial Park, converting the children's hexagonal sand table into a fountain, and the terrace of the park into a wading pool (compare with fig. 15-8). Note that Schindler drew an elevation (left).

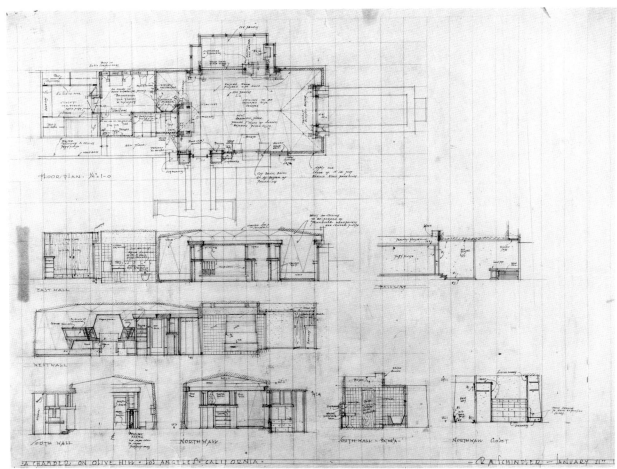

16-6. Schindler, Owner's Bedroom, circa 1925 (photo by Viroque Baker, (courtesy of the Architectural Drawing Collection, University Art Museum, University of California, Santa Barbara). Schindler finished the room with a white oak veneer tent applied in panels and the hexagonal bead detail used in the original construction.

16-7. Schindler, Owner's Bedroom, circa 1925 (photo by Viroque Baker; (courtesy of the Architectural Drawing Collection, University Art Museum, University of California, Santa Barbara). Barnsdall's sleeping porch is to the left behind the wood screen.

16-8. Schindler, Chamber (Owner's Bedroom), plan and interior elevations, 1925(courtesy of the Architectural Drawing Collection, University Art Museum, University of California, Santa Barbara). Schindler completed Barnsdall's bedroom primarily by adding finishes and fixtures.

1. Small Gallery/Stage
2. Large Gallery/Audience Hall
3. Beam
4. Skylight
5. Light Wood Ceiling
6. Skylight
7. Trench Filled With Broken Stucco

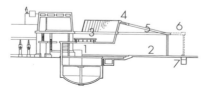

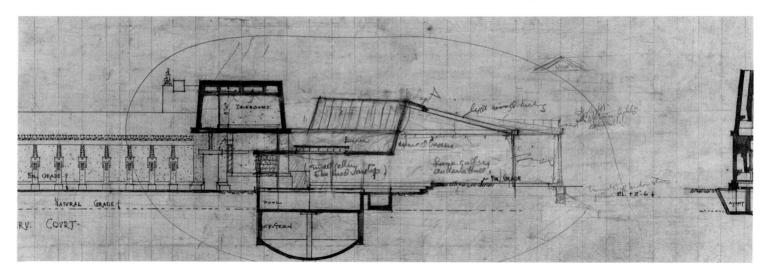

16-9. Art Gallery addition for California Art Club, section, 1932 (drawing by Eulogio Guzman). Wright's sketches represent a working-out of his ideas. As a result, they contain inconsistencies and contradictions that have been retained for the sake of accuracy in this redrawing.

16-10. Art Gallery addition for California Art Club, section, 1932 (courtesy of the Frank Lloyd Wright Foundation). This pencil sketch was drawn over the original ink-on-linen working drawing (see fig. 12-5).

16-11. Art Gallery addition for California Art Club, plan, 1932 (drawing by Eulogio Guzman). Wright's inconsistencies and contradictions have been retained.

16-12. Art Gallery addition for California Art Club, plan, 1932 (courtesy of the Frank Lloyd Wright Foundation). This sketch is all that has survived to record Wright's proposal. The drawings for the more ambitious first scheme have been lost. Note that on the lower edge of the drawing Wright has begun a section.

1. Light Board Wall
2. Composition Roof
3. Curved Beam
4. Skylight
5. Piers
6. Cantilevered Beam
7. Rostrum
8. Screen Wall
9. Open

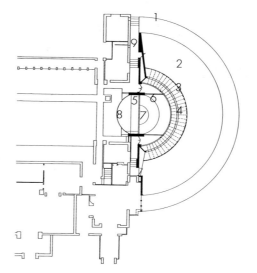

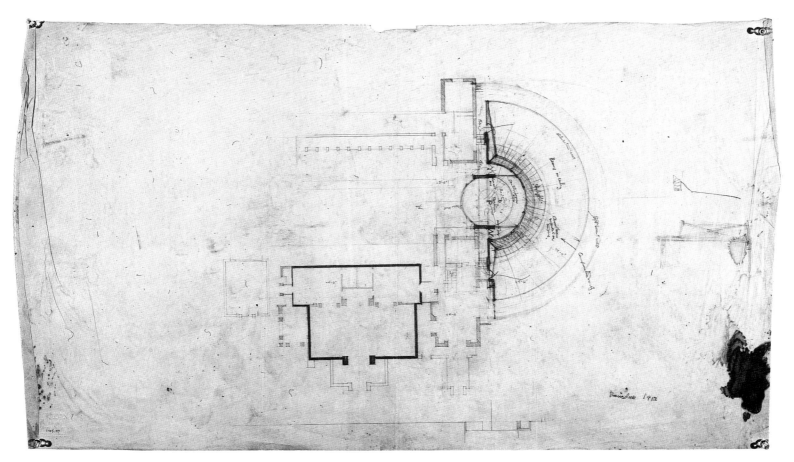

16-13. Schindler, Residence B, Edgemont Street elevation, after 1929 (courtesy Lloyd Wright Studio). Wright's enclosure of the sleeping porch and additions above and in front of the living room can be seen left and middle; Schindler's bedroom addition over the garage is visible to the right (compare with the 1921 elevation, figs. 12-19 and 12-20).

16-14. Schindler, Residence B, bedroom addition, after 1929 (courtesy of Barbara Giella). Barnsdall, who died here in 1946, made this her home when she was in Los Angeles.

16-15. Schindler, Residence B, bedroom addition interior, after 1929 (collection of the author). The wood screens are sliding panels that cover the windows.

16-16. Schindler, Residence B, entrance courtyard, after 1929 (collection of the author). Schindler added a window looking out onto the balcony. The insignia of the fraternity, Phi Kappa Sigma, has been removed from the balcony (see ch. 16, note 22).

16-17. Schindler, Residence B, bedroom addition, after 1929 (collection of the author). Although Schindler's window composition reflects his own style, the wood trim and stencils repeat those used by Wright in 1923.

with an offer to renovate it and lease it for ten years as the center for her Olive Hill Foundation. Working in collaboration with his father, Lloyd Wright supervised extensive rehabilitation work, which was completed in 1948.

With Frank Lloyd Wright's growing fame and international recognition, perhaps it was inevitable that he would be called upon to make recommendations about Hollyhock House and the planning of Barnsdall Park. In 1953, Wright, at the instigation of R. Kenneth Ross, director of the Municipal Art Department, designed an art pavilion that was located directly next to Hollyhock House (fig. 16-20). The $70,000 structure (230 feet long and 21 feet wide) was a translucent tent constructed of a pipe frame, Coralux, and Cemesto-Board (fig. 16-19). The pavilion, which added 8,000 square feet of exhibition space, was made possible through the private donations of the Municipal Art Patrons, and opened with Wright's traveling exhibition, "Sixty Years of Living Architecture," on June 2, 1954 (fig. 16-18). Ironically, the new Wright structure was completed just a few months after the demolition of Residence B. The house, still owned by the family, had fallen into a state of disrepair after many years of neglect.

The success of the art pavilion only emphasized the need for larger and more permanent facilities. By 1958, Ross called upon Wright to design a plan for an art gallery and administration building. In 1959, a few months before his death, Wright submitted a master plan that placed the entrance to the new cultural center at the corner of Vermont Avenue and Hollywood Boulevard (figs. 16-21 and 16-22). The administration building formed a bridge over the entrance drive that led to the three-story gallery to the east behind Hollyhock House (fig. 16-1). Underground parking was provided for visitors on the lower level of the gallery building. Recalling Wright's original landscape plans of 1919 and 1920, a reflecting pool with cascades and a water jet was placed at the entrance. Concerned about fund-raising, the City of Los Angeles rejected Wright's scheme.

Later proposals for new buildings resulted in the erection of the Junior Arts Center in 1967, and the Municipal Art Gallery, equipped with administration offices and a lecture hall, in 1971. Both buildings were designed by local firms.[24] Neither building contained space for parking, a problem that has yet to be adequately solved.

The historical significance of Hollyhock House gained public notice in 1963 when the Historic Preservation Committee of the American Institute of Architects included it in a list of seventeen Frank Lloyd Wright buildings recommended for preservation. The city took over operation of the house when Dorothy Clune Murray's lease expired in 1956, and by 1974 had carried out a major renovation under the supervision of Lloyd Wright with the assistance of his son Eric Wright, who had trained at Taliesin with his grandfather.

Although Hollyhock House is not one of Wright's best buildings, either in design or execution, it is certainly his most interesting. Many factors contributed to its flaws: Barnsdall's insistence on design before site acquisition; Wright's preoccupation with the Imperial Hotel and his dealings in Japanese prints; Barnsdall's need to make many of the important design decisions; Lloyd Wright's unrealistic optimism; the contractor's and subcontractor's lack of experience in experimental building; Barnsdall's strict financial limits; Schindler's inability to rescue the building from errors and omissions; and Barnsdall's ambivalence about having a home.

But more important was the fact that Hollyhock House was designed at a pivotal evolutionary moment in Wright's development. Turning his back on the Prairie house, one of his most perfect creations, he began to experiment with new ideas. While ignoring both structure and material, Wright sought new expression to give form to meaning. And while the various architectural elements of the building—its siting, plan, massing, exterior and interior, detailing, finishes, and fixtures—do not come together to create an artistic synthesis, each reveals Wright in his struggle to break away from the Prairie house grammar and

16-18. Exhibition Pavilion, interior, 1954 (photo by Edmund Teske). The installation is Wright's travelling exhibition "Sixty Years of Living Architecture."

to take a new direction. But perhaps more than anything else, Hollyhock House reveals Wright discarding the suburban type and reaching for a deeper, more universal symbol of the connection between dwelling and nature. Even the awkwardness of his choice of the literal imagery of the pre-Columbian temple shows Wright grasping for the essential, searching for beginnings. While Hollyhock House was then an end, it was also a beginning.

16-19. Exhibition Pavilion, elevation, 1953
(courtesy of the Frank Lloyd Wright
Foundation)

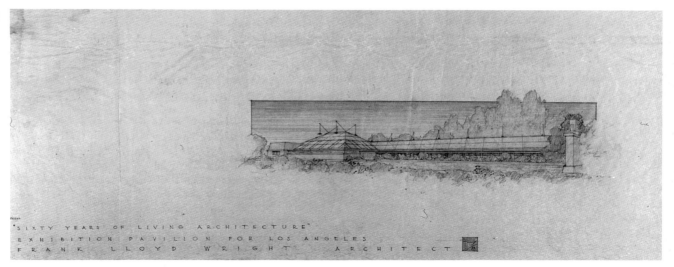

16-20. Exhibition Pavilion, plan, 1953
(courtesy of the Frank Lloyd Wright
Foundation)

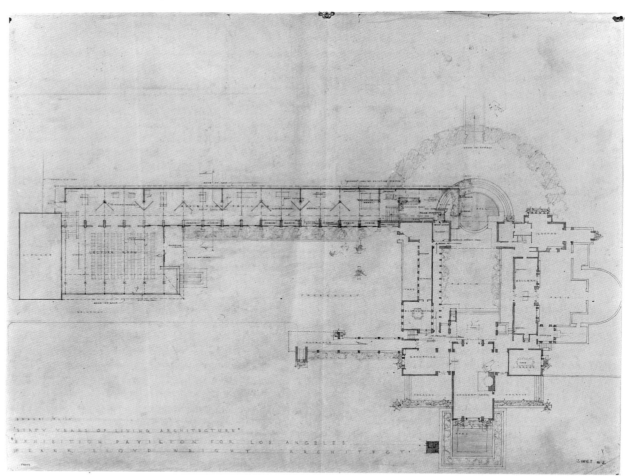

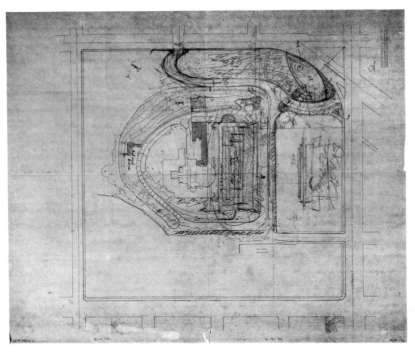

16-21. Barnsdall Park, preliminary plan, 1958-1959 (courtesy of the Frank Lloyd Wright Foundation)

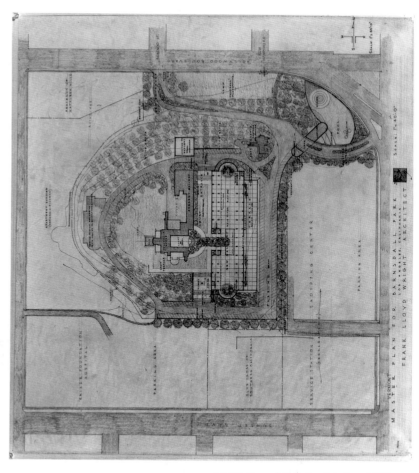

16-22. Barnsdall Park, plot plan, 1958-1959 (courtesy of the Frank Lloyd Wright Foundation)

Wright's design for Barnsdall's theater extended over a five-year period, from 1915 to 1920, and can be grouped roughly into four schemes:

Scheme I for the Chicago Little Theatre, circa 1915;
Scheme II, circa 1918;
Scheme III, circa 1919;
Scheme IV, circa 1920.

The surviving documentation for these designs consists of drawings for the buildings, photographs of models, and Olive Hill plot plans indicating the relationship of the building to the site. Many drawings were either discarded or lost, especially for Schemes III and IV, and what has survived reveals that the models, although very similar in general, introduced variations between schemes. The models themselves became intermediary schemes. Finally, for Schemes III and IV, the models do not correlate with the site plans. After Barnsdall purchased Olive Hill, Wright's attention was diverted by his client's shift in emphasis from the theater to the residential and commercial buildings, although problems presented by reworking the design to fit the hillside site required his utmost concentration. Unfortunately, there are few drawings that document this phase and those that survive are sketchy and incomplete. Acknowledging these limitations, it is possible to present an outline of the four main schemes.

SCHEME I, CIRCA 1915
See Chapter 1, figs. 1-1 and 1-4 through 1-7.

SCHEME II, CIRCA 1918
See Chapter 3, figs. 3-1 through 3-9, 3-14, and 3-17.

SCHEME III, CIRCA 1919
The surviving plans and sections indicate that Wright expanded the backstage area (figs. AP-1 and AP-2) and raised the ceiling over the main auditorium and stage, creating a vault. He moved the experimental theater into a square in the center and surrounded it with offices, a library, a gallery, and a restaurant that opened to the roof terrace through french doors (figs. AP-4, AP-5, AP-6, and AP-7). Barnsdall had decided to open "a popular priced cafe which she intended to supply from the produce on her ranch near Beverly Hills."[1] By January 1920, Barnsdall objected to the octagonal roof which was changed to a square.[2] Wright also changed the proportions of the exterior massing (AP-9).

SCHEME IV, CIRCA 1920
The two major sources of documentation for Scheme IV are photographs of the model and the site plans, which do not agree; separate drawings of the theater itself have not survived. The last model indicates that the square top had been redesigned (fig. AP-9) and the orchestra seating had been changed to semicircular rows, which improved sightlines (fig. AP-11).

The site plans (figs. 9-5 and 9-6) and perspective (fig. 9-3) reveal that the last scheme was the most substantially reworked. Wright closed off the front entrance with a landscaped, man-made lake. The plan was rotated 180 degrees, shifting the public entrance to the side, and opening up both the experimental theater and the lobby, now in the rear against the hill, with skylights.

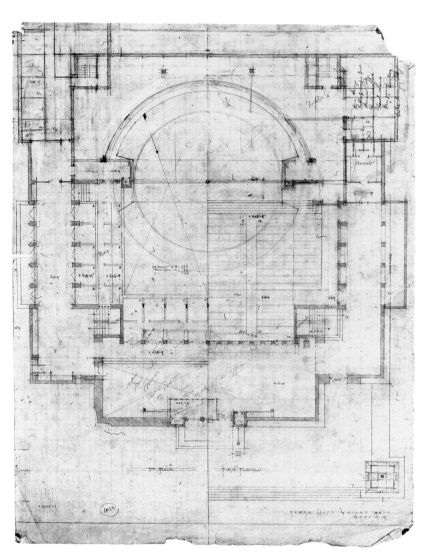

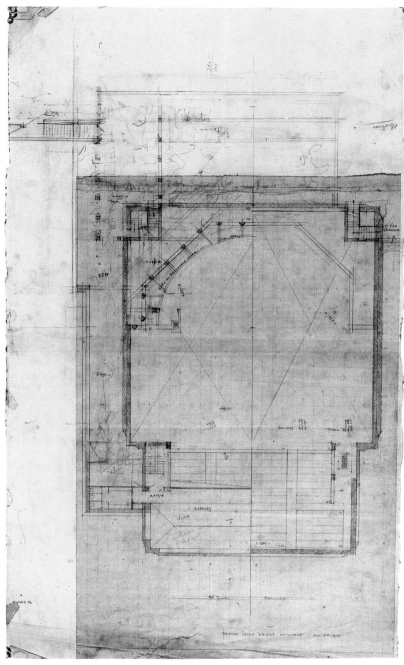

AP-1. Barnsdall Theater III, Hollywood,
1919, first and second floor plans
(courtesy of the Frank Lloyd Wright
Foundation)

AP-2. Barnsdall Theater III, Hollywood,
1919, balcony and third floor plans
(courtesy of the Frank Lloyd Wright
Foundation)

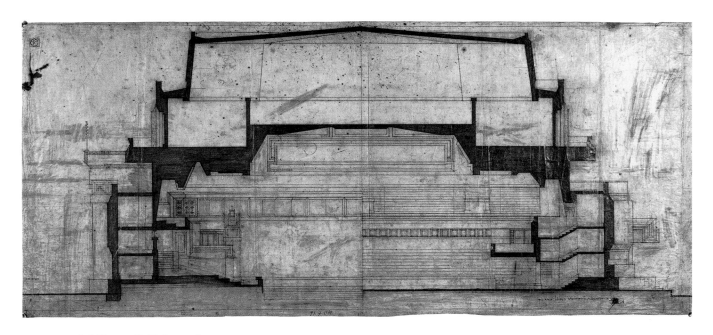

AP-3. Barnsdall Theater III, Hollywood,
circa 1919, cross section (courtesy of the
Frank Lloyd Wright Foundation)

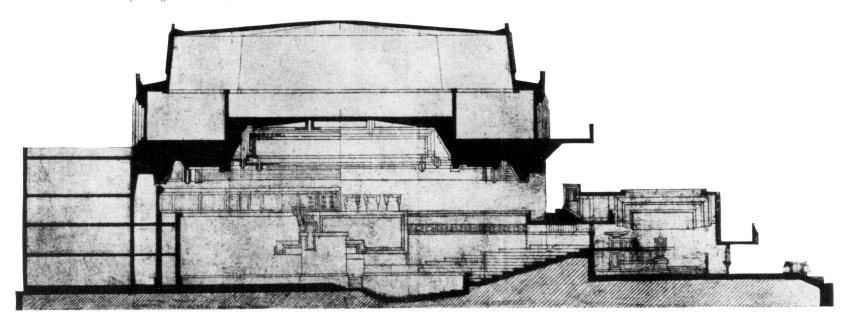

AP-4. Barnsdall Theater III, Hollywood,
circa 1919, longitudinal section (H.Th.
Wijdeveld, ed., *The Life-Work of Frank
Lloyd Wright*, 1925, 1965 reprint, pl.
156). This drawing has been lost. Many of
the drawings, as well as the 1919 model,
do not indicate adjustments to the topographical conditions of Olive Hill.

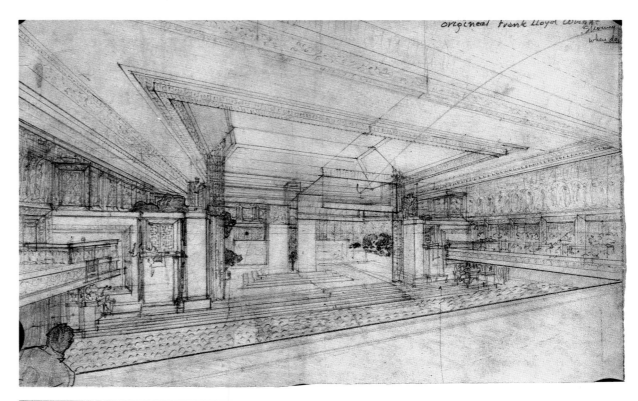

AP-5. Barnsdall Theater III, Hollywood, circa 1919, view toward stage (courtesy of the Dutch Architectural Institute, Amsterdam)

AP-6. Barnsdall Theater III, Hollywood, circa 1919, view toward stage (courtesy of the Dutch Architectural Institute, Amsterdam)

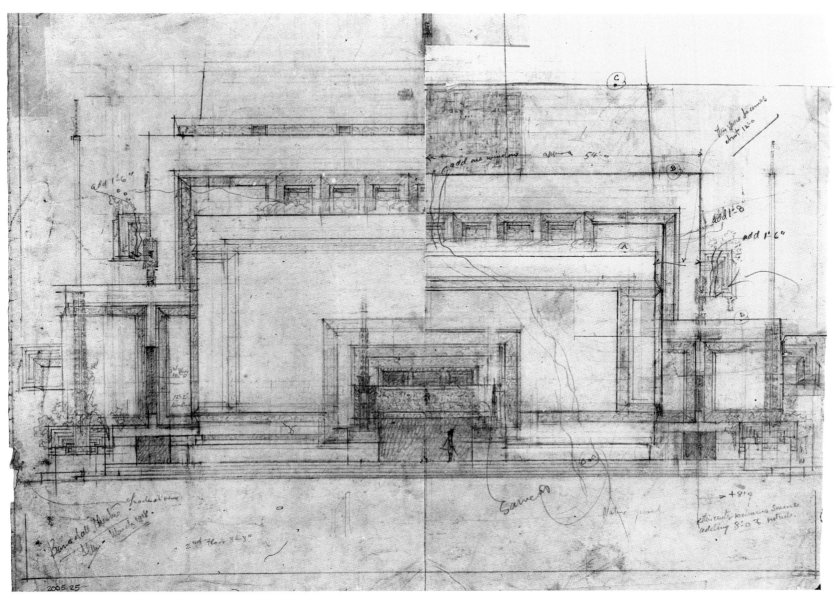

AP-7. Barnsdall Theater II to III, 1918–
1919, front elevation (courtesy of the
Frank Lloyd Wright Foundation)

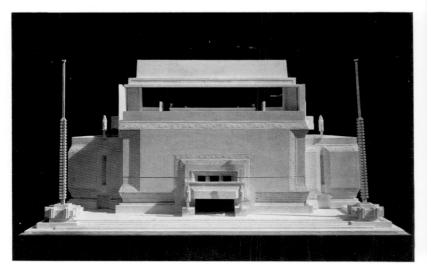

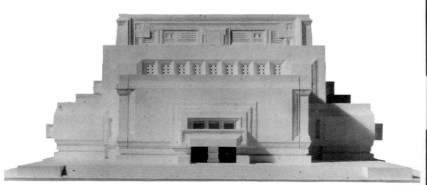

AP-8. Barnsdall Theater III, Hollywood, 1919, exterior of model (collection of the author). A portion of the model has been removed, providing a view into the floor housing the experimental theater. The crown has been changed from an octagon to a square, but there is no indication of ornamentation. This model does not indicate the slope conditions of Olive Hill.

AP-9. Barnsdall Theater IV, 1920, exterior of model (courtesy of the Frank Lloyd Wright Foundation). The octagonal top has been replaced by a square.

AP-10. Barnsdall Theater III, Hollywood, 1919, interior of model (collection of the author). The top floor has been removed and the ceiling over the main theater tipped back to reveal the interior.

AP-11. Barnsdall Theater IV, Hollywood, circa 1920, interior of model (courtesy of the Frank Lloyd Wright Foundation). The top and side sections have been removed to reveal the new seating configuration in relation to the stage.

Note: Wright's letter to Barnsdall has survived only in his original typed office copy. He revised this letter by hand in ink, subtly changing the meaning and thrust of his argument in certain passages. This is consistent with Wright's working method. He is known to have continuously revised drawings and manuscripts, and even his books after they were published. His additions and corrections have been preserved to provide the reader with his original thoughts and the means he used to persuade Barnsdall of his position. ## indicates words or punctuation crossed out and ( ) indicates words or punctuation added.

[Office copy]

Taliesin, June 27, 1921

Dear Miss Barnsdall:

After posting my letter to England yesterday I noticed your's [sic] bore a Bath postmark of May 25th and (was) forwarded from your office at the "Hill." (It) reached me at Taliesin June 26th.

If I would see you face to face before I sail for Japan, July 30th, I would not write. But somehow I don't believe I will see you. I think you would prefer to go quietly into your home alone #as# I expect to personally put the finishing work upon it from July 14th to July 30th.

You will marvel then, perhaps, as I do, that a thing so harmonious, strong and unlike anything of its kind in the world—should be there at all. That this creative thing should have survived the pretty [sic] personal strife that "dogged" its growth(,) step by step(,) is a miracle, #as# you will feel (this) yourself(,) perhaps(,) as the echoes reach you before you reach its threshold.

Order shall come out of chaos for you—because the principle at stake is dearer to me than my humiliations are bitter: and because your devotion to it was stronger than your own resentment or the power of misrepresentation and the alarmist advice of unwilling, unfaithful amateurs that threatened it during construction and #that is# crowding in upon it (even) now.

I have had to use weapons to do my part and am (ashamed,) not proud of my use of them. Even *this* (use of them) will be used against me as *proof* of the insulting references #that I am# morally oblique that caused me to use the weapons. I (did write) #wrote# a "hell-of-a-letter" to Clarence Thomas that #may have been# (was) oversized for his case. (B)ut it only mildly expressed my feeling. He has hindered my work, protecting himself by pretending to guard your interests. Alone(,) absolutely against the field I have all but achieved the impossible. I have battled the thing out *almost* to a finish.

(But) I have not had one man I could trust(,) from first to last(,) or that I could depend upon as expert to understand and push along behind me, #except Lloyd# since Robertson showed himself incompetent.

I needed a veteran builder familiar with this original type of building. I needed him because the whole thing is an invention, the details to the smallest, all inventions. Imagination and enthusiasm and experience and loyalty should meet in the builder at my back, or the difficulties of my work be turned against me as sins of omission or evasion or incompetence. You were led by #peripatetic# (amateurs') advice to assume that what amateurs could see and understand of the usual thing in the *usual* way was what should apply to me and my way of work. The superiority and distinction you sought when you came to me was to "happen" somehow, as a gift to you, no matter how you tied me up(?)

My "Arrogance" in disputing the (that) (pre)assumption offended you, and I not only had no man I could trust in my work, but (soon had) no client either who trusted me or that I could trust (to support me).

I made an initial mistake (in haste) which was unavoidable (in choosing Robertson) #in# (under) circumstances beyond my control—And—after doing all I could to rectify #it# (the mistake) you have held it over and against me ever since (by your own choice).

If you feel that you are justified (in this) and (that) this disgraceful ending for me of a great piece of work is justifiable in (the) circumstances—what I say here can only plead for a better understanding without much effect.

Some color was lent to your fears(, I admit,) and some apparent wisdom to the alarms of your advisors, by my mistake—#although I was innocent of "moral obliquity"# (But) you were out of hand on account of it just when I needed your help and confidence most. I could never get you back again. And since that time I have had no client (only a suspicious enemy).

Of Robertson I may have expected too much. He may yet be useful as his ignorance has probably been enlightened somewhat by his experience on this work. He is easy going—good natured and a politician: But when you refused to let me correct my mistake in (choosing) him and the (commissioned builder) method of building I advocated,—which could only succeed for us with a sympathetic veteran at its center,—you there and then tied a ball and chain to the progress of the work, #that# (It) all but wore #me# (us) out(.) #and that# (It) lies hidden now from your sight behind the (unfair) accusations of Robertson and Thomas(, in common interest,) dragging (in) helpless Senior Ray behind them. When you took that stand (with them) I was compelled to fight. #to# Fight nothing obvious, nothing open nor honest, but just to drag the whole thing behind me every step of the way: a way (made) so difficult that nothing in my whole varied experience in building 176 #different# unique buildings compares with it.

There was no interest in the life of the building (itself) on anyone's part but my own. You had taken the stand that my services #was# were one thing and building the building another (thing). The one was mine, the other was yours#,# (.) (B)ut I must be responsible for both. (Why this absurdity?)

You had flung my work to (both) clerks who were naturally envious or suspicious(.) (A)nd they were ignorant of my needs. The#y# (clerks) were privileged to smash me or my work when arbitrary (unreasonable) cost-limits were threatened.

You (probably) assumed that I would protect my work at any trouble or cost to me or at any cost to you. The building has come near to what you hoped and dreamed it would be only because, in this assumption, you were correct.

I did protect it as well as I could.

But has #it# (this) been (any) fair(er) to me (than yourself)? Has it been fair to you?—Is it even fair to the clerks?—It has awakened jealousy, mean-spirited restriction and suspicious competition (discovered) where firmest cooperation should have stood unshaken? My soul is sore and my mind stiff with #it# (this insult.) I have devoted (with you at the center) more personal time, energy and money to this work, three times over than was necessary: Crossed the Pacific twice to keep faith with you—at great sacrifice to other interests entrusted to me.

I knew your feelings too(,) better than you might imagine that I know them.

I am sorry for you#.#(r worry).

(The) only hope (I have is that) you may not be (finally) disappointed in my work.

The financial cost to you and to me and to everybody else has been greater because of #the# (this) friction and confusion. Perfunctory "rules of business" could no more gauge the *personal* equation of execution necessary to such creative work than it could gauge the nature of the conception (itself). The (arbitrary) requisitions made (by them,) like passing the "Terraces" through the Department before letting the general contract were #more# (mere) obstructions—as I can prove—of no possible benefit nor even protection to you. They have only abused the successful issue of a terrible struggle for that success.

It is no more possible to tell me how I shall get work done than it is to tell me how I shall conceive (it) nor is it any more reasonable.—Because the personal equation is present from first to last or else the result is (as) dead (as you see around you everywhere.)

I know it is (hard) to understand this.

It does seem as though the #one# (execution of the design) was business and the (conception of it) #other# art. But in my experience both are allied and both in a sense art.

(Therefore) I have to win the enthusiasm and confidence and esteem of my workmen. They(, too,) have to make sacrifices. I have to get them to do for me what they would not do under (the) usual circumstances (the workmen). If I do not get my work-fellows to do that in the spirit I desire, then confusion and dragging ensues that will soon eat up appropriations too fast and botch-work will stand where (")finish(") was essential. And then—too—"passing the buck" begins. The instinct of self-preservation is strong in human nature. I did secure this cooperation in this case (only) with Barker Brothers (toward the end) #only# to have my experts efforts (with them) during more than a month's time overthrown by senseless suspicions and (the) inferences #of moral obliquity# (from Thomas) that drew the "Hell of a letter"#.# (from me.)

COST!—EXTRAS! (They) loomed over your horizon like some terrible spetre [*sic*] of defeat. You took every measure to defend yourself, but (you) threw away the only one that could have protected you—#and# that one was the cooperation of your architect.

Do you (now) remember waving me aside when I pleaded with you for your confidence? You said, that (")you had no confidence in any #"#Artist". And (you) told me in no uncertain terms to get #when# (what) I could for my work(,) and

you would take care of yourself(?) You gave me then and there to understand that it was each one for himself or herself and a sporting chance for either to win through. (And in so many words.)

Well, my dear client(,) #Aline Barnsdall#—so far [*sic*] as getting our building built in the face of endless obstruction, restrictions to construction you (then) set up to protect yourself(,) instead of giving (to) me the help I needed—I HAVE GONE THROUGH:#—#

Although the cost (to you and to me) has been greater than necessary and the elapsed time in construction twice as long, still the net cost (to you) is not unreasonable(.) (N)or is the time elapsed so much longer than #necessary# (is reasonable in the circumstances.)

But #(when I returned from Japan)# I had to take a solid six weeks to stop the "drift" by every means in my power when I got to the scene (from Japan) or you would never have had anything like a furnished house (or one fit to live in.)

#The# (A)dditional cost(s) will all be attributed to my "changes" instead of to the bad-method and wasteful ignorance of the nature of the work on the part of the men you #expected# (forced) me to work with. I shall have something to say about that when the time comes.

I could not pick my help for fitness. #I had# (Having) made an initial mistake #and I was# (in choosing Robertson you) compelled (me) to go through with it. (Why?)

Los Angeles was a strange new field for me and I had to literally "break into" it. Apparently they did not want me out there (and do not want me now.)

#The# (D)iscord between owner and architect soon became known to the workmen and the fact also that the owner—"rich"—was "holding the bag" (building her own building) herself. "Why (then) should they worry"—and they didn't worry.—You did.—and I did.

Nobody (really) cared to (protect the rich woman or) understand the freak architect and his fool-work anyway; It was to laugh at him,—"(Q)ueer get up",—"(he's) no doubt a faker;" Stories about his private life on the Q.T., (and then)—"Say(,) the man must simply be a wonder to get away with it?" "Well, let him get it over on the woman if he can." (We'll see the fun!)

I lost my temper, (often) #sometimes#, I have a caustic way of meeting my adversaries. All this was made worse(,) #or# pulled out of drawing and carried to you, where and when it would suit their general purpose best to do it (and antagonize you.)

And you ran the gauntlet of peripatetic, chronic #advice#-selfseeking (advisors) #advice#, #often#, but ("A)dvice(") always.

The lone woman in business usually expires of #it# (such "advice") as a firecracker does of the damp.

You were frightened by (the "expert" opinions of the #paid# gratuitious expert) "Hicky" et all,—I know.

But you had sense and courage enough to go after what you wanted when you really wanted it, and get it.

My hat is off to you for your qualities.

(But) (S)uspicion (easily awakes) #awoke# in you(,) #and# (Y)our "man of business" (Thomas) #gave# (gives) it back to you redoubled.—He lives on it, thrives on it. (this is his job) I have never had one simple communication from him from the beginning until now not characterized by insolent implications no man would stand. #And he doesn't# (He may not) know it any more than a man is conscious of the color of his eyes when he looks out of them? His stupid egotism and personal animosity has gratified itself by irritating the sores made by arbitrary conditions imposed by yourself. He was the little picador mounted on his little "business" hobby that flung pigeon hole darts at the goaded bull and stepped nimbly behind your skirts as the maddened creature lunged by. "See" —he now cries" "I told you so"! "(H)e is dangerous," "kill him or he'll kill you!"

Some body will kill the (little) picador some day for the meanness and cowardice of his heart. He comes innocently and virtuously to you for protection, with no sense of his own offensiveness as the cause of all the "brutal" rage.

(But ...) If(,) in spite of all this sinful waste of strength(,) the quality of my work and endeavor stands up for you as I hope it may—(it is the only hope I have in the whole matter) and you listen to me again; #and# if in spite of what I have seen to be a disinclination on your part to stand the discipline of steady, sustained endeavor, you are still inclined to stand by your project for "Olive Hill", if you can break through the obstructions to any understanding with me you have yourself set up and fostered, then I shall stand up to my duty to myself and (to) my work and to you—as I have had no chance to do heretofore:

First, by insisting upon a real business-man in charge of affairs #with you# who is no hypocrite. #and# (A man) who knows how to trust men and inspire trust in them, getting the best thus, out of them, for you and for my work. No amateurs, however faithful to you, should be put in charge of great work done under high pressure with methods,—not stock and shop, but (methods) peculiar to the work itself.

Second, by refusing again to place my work for execution in any hands, but those I (myself) know (and agree) to be reliable, competent and sympathetic—a "builder" I can trust to get what I want when I want it with economic and scientific certainty.

Finally and Foremost, (execution of) a carefully worked (out) but general program scheme in all possible drawing-board-detail—understood and approved, —details of which you leave to me unreservedly. But I must also have privileges in the field to make such vital revisions as meet needs of form or function as they arise and power to make #the# (such) modifications (as) actual contact with the execution (of building) always inspires #in me#. Rightly as I think. And this matter should not be looked upon as "bad-faith" or any kind of weakness or crime— but must be recognized as the only way to insure greater harmony and integrity in the result. (A)s in truth it is.

The work I do is not #altogether# drawing-board Architecture. I must have my own privileges in the field where #any# (my) battle is inevitably fought (on) and (eventually) won or lost. This attempt to nail me fast to my "drawing-board", on suspicion, is unwise(.) (E)ven were it possible(.) (A)nd it is not possible.

For this margin in the field I should have a competent fund, which experience has taught me should be between fifteen and twenty per cent (on work like yours). This fund should be provided in some sensible way, fair to all concerned.

It is impossible for you to form any just idea of your architect from such sources and in such conditions as you have (yourself) set up (on Olive Hill). Failure was inevitable (to some degree).

And then (beside all else) there has been so much in this attempt on our (own) part that has been irrelevant and adverse to the real matter in hand. Instead of reasoning logically about the features as they arose(,) the flea-bites of personal rancour would often goad us into tangents that left the scheme and went wide of the mark: And too—I would often go bang or go hang against flat walls that no logic nor any power I had could pierce. Those walls were particular recollections, preferences or prejudices you had preconceived, perhaps not germane to the case at all, but nevertheless irrevocable. You confounded #this# (these idiosyncracies) with individuality (and defended them.)

In other words, the sweet reasonableness of the open mind did not meet me(,) in you(,) after I (")brutally(") took the stand that you were going to school to me in this building. I was perfectly right in the assumption but perfectly wrong in the assertion. You were out after me from that time on. I felt the change, knew you had either let your own self-love be wounded or had not seen the reasonableness of what I really meant—blinded by your resentment of my "arrogance". (Was it arrogance? Or only indiscretion!)

Just think for a moment of another phase—There was (")Kirah,(") Roy George, Clarence Thomas, Robertson-Hickey et all [*sic*], others you alluded to.—Ordynsky perhaps,—kind(,) fatuous old Mr. Ray.—(Y)our "Faithful Attorney", Norman Geddes et al, Miss Lang, Susan(, too,) and how many others all openly or subtly or tentatively or suggestively hostile to any real understanding between you and me.—all professing particolored fears for unprotected "ALINE" in the "Den of the wolf". I did not know what a really terrible fellow I was until it began to crop up and surround you in this heroic and genuinely purposeful efort [*sic*] of your life. And how futile! It hasn't saved you even the "Extras". It has *increased* them. (A)nd(, to boot,) it has worried you nearly to death;—robbed you of the delight in the effort, that ought to have been yours,—(A)nd left you all the while in jeopardy, because you struck at the only one who could have saved you, and that was *"the Wolf"* himself. Your whole fair project of the Hill poisoned at its source for you. I could not save you. By a miracle (only) I (will be able) save the building.

When I returned (from Japan) to resume the work at any cost to myself, (expecting to find you) I was informed that no communication from me would reach you—"you did not want to hear from me". A cablegram I desired forwarded at my own expense was denied me(.) #and# (Y)our address (was) withheld. Your (own) letter, delayed in transit, gave me your address or I wouldn't have it yet.

So(, cut off from communication,) I assumed that if I could be trusted to buy curtains in Japan I could be trusted to buy them for you in Los Angeles,—to save (further) delay(s) and get you into a completed house.—No very great presumption on my part under the circumstances? I bought them and the furniture too— to save you time. Why should I "consult" anyone? Who could judge anything about it but me? But #the whole work# (this effort too) was obstructed and would be (still) untouched #and# (or) mostly #still# unfinished had I accepted the stand your "man of business" took, and had I really dropped your interest in this construction as I #threatened I would do and# was requested to do. But I took care of you notwithstanding the ambiguous equivocal insulting situation I found myself in. I did it, as you will find, with an economy impossible to you otherwise— as any fair investigation will show.

Well—the building stands#,—#(.) (Y)our home.

It is yours for what it has cost you. It is mine for what it has cost me.

And it is for all mankind according to its cost in all its bearings.

Can we not pronounce benediction upon it(,) now(,) absolving #it# (the building itself) at least from rancour and false witness?

Whatever its birth pangs it will take its place as your contribution and mine to the vexed life of our time. What future it will have (—maimed as it is—)who can say?

Faithfully yours,
[unsigned]

R.M. SCHINDLER

1924   Garden bench (executed)

1924   Retaining wall (unexecuted)

1924–
1925   Fountain, flower box, wading pool, and pergola (assisted by Richard Neutra; executed)

1924–
1925   Chamber in Hollyhock House (executed)

1924–
1925   Light shades for Hollyhock House (executed)

1925   Owner's bedroom, bathroom, and closet in Hollyhock House (executed)

1925   Furniture (daybed, dressing table, chair, and table) for chamber, Hollyhock House (execution unknown)

1925   Sculpture stand for Hollyhock House (executed)

1925   Metal trim for front door of Hollyhock House (unexecuted)

1925   Lock cover for front door of Hollyhock House (executed)

1926   Various items for Hollyhock House: door handles, light fixtures, pool repair, picture frame, basement vents, floor repair, two screens with metal frames (executed)

1927   Residence A remodeling

1927   Poster exhibition at Hollyhock House (executed)

1928   Lamp post for Barnsdall Park (executed)

1928–
1929   Residence B, alterations and addition (executed)

CALIFORNIA ART CLUB

1927   Remodeling of Hollyhock House (removal of partition and bathrooms between two guest bedrooms to create gallery)

LLOYD WRIGHT

1931   Children's outdoor theater (unexecuted)

1932   Gallery addition for California Art Club (Lloyd Wright donation for Aline Barnsdall; drawings unseen, unexecuted)

1932   Billboards for Tom Mooney (executed)

1946–
1948   Rehabilitation of Hollyhock House for Dorothy Murray (executed)

1967   Renovation of Hollyhock House for Recreation and Parks Department (executed)

1974   Renovation of Hollyhock House for City of Los Angeles (executed)

FRANK LLOYD WRIGHT

1932   Gallery addition for California Art Club, Scheme I (at suggestion of Lloyd Wright for Aline Barnsdall; drawings lost, unexecuted)

Scheme II (unexecuted)

1953–
1954   Exhibition pavilion (erected for temporary exhibition of "Sixty Years of Living Architecture," but not demolished until 1974)

1958–
1959   Municipal Art Gallery (unexecuted)

NOTES

Unless otherwise noted, all letters to or from Frank Lloyd Wright are from the Frank Lloyd Wright Archives of the Frank Lloyd Wright Foundation, Taliesin West, Scottsdale, Arizona. Likewise, all letters to or from Norman Bel Geddes are from The Norman Bel Geddes Collection, Theatre Arts Collection, Harry Ransom Humanities Research Center, The University of Texas at Austin, by permission of Edith Lutyens Bel Geddes, executrix.

CHAPTER 1

1. Program notes for Zoe Akins's *Papa,* Norman Bel Geddes Collection, Theatre Arts Collection, Harry Ransom Humanities Research Center, The University of Texas at Austin (hereafter HRHRC), Dr. 31, m-1.

2. Lakeside City Directory, 1915.

3. Ellen Van Volkenburg, interview with author, Beverly Hills, California, April 18, 1974. Few of the Barnsdall Theater drawings in the Archives of the Frank Lloyd Wright Foundation are dated. I have attributed a cross section, #2005.25, dated "Feb. 7, 1915," to the Chicago Little Theatre commission.

4. Frank Lloyd Wright, *An Autobiography,* rev. ed. (New York: Duell, Sloan and Pearce, 1943), 224. Edmund Teske, interview with author, Hollywood, California, February 23, 1979. In an untitled statement written in 1977, Teske declared, "Miss Barnsdall knew genius when she encountered it—in a garage, a ballroom, or what have you—she herself being a fair daughter of that great liberating madness." Teske became an honorary member of the Fellowship in 1936 when Frank Lloyd Wright asked him to establish a photographic workshop at Taliesin. In 1944, Teske met Aline Barnsdall in Los Angeles and was invited to live in Studio Residence B while she traveled. Her remarks would have been made sometime between that date and her death in 1946. For Teske's reminiscences, see "Photography with Frank Lloyd Wright," *The Frank Lloyd Wright Newsletter* 2, no. 1 (1979): 10–16.

5. Aline Barnsdall compiled an album of her father's obituaries, "Theodore Newton Barnsdall, June 10, 1851 to Feb. 27, 1917," which is in the possession of her grandson Michael Devine.

6. Unpublished draft *MS* of Norman Bel Geddes, *Miracle in the Evening,* HRHRC.

7. Ibid.

8. Aline Barnsdall to Norman Bel Geddes, November 30, 1915.

9. Percy Hammond, "'Alice in Wonderland' at the Fine Arts," *Chicago Daily Tribune,* February 12, 1915.

10. *New York Times,* April 4, 1915, section VIII.

11. Wright, *An Autobiography,* 224.

12. Perry R. Duis, "'Where Is Athens Now?' The Fine Arts Building, 1898 to 1918," *Chicago History: The Magazine of the Chicago Historical Society* VI, no. 2 (Summer 1977): 66–78.

13. Wright to Barnsdall, n.d. [circa Fall 1916].

14. Ellen Van Volkenburg, interview with author, Beverly Hills, California, April 18, 1974. Oscar Brockett and Robert R. Findlay in *Century of Innovation: A History of European and American Theatre and Drama Since 1870* (Englewood Cliffs, New Jersey: Prentice-Hall, 1979), 230, point out that Sam Hume brought an exhibition of European stage design to Chicago in 1914 which featured Gordon Craig, among others.

CHAPTER 2

1. Ellen Van Volkenburg, interview with author, April 18, 1974.

2. Barnsdall to Bel Geddes, November 30, 1915.

3. Barnsdall to Bel Geddes, December 10, 1915.

4. Wright, *An Autobiography,* 228.

5. Henry Blackman Sell, "Interpretation, Not Imitation: Work of F.L. Wright," *International Studio* 55 (May 1915): 80.

6. On the history of the design and construction of the Imperial Hotel and the Imperial Hotel Annex, see my "Frank Lloyd Wright and the Imperial Hotel: A Postscript," *The Art Bulletin* 67, no. 2 (June 1985): 296–310; and my "Frank Lloyd Wright's Unknown Imperial Hotel Annex," *SD Space Design* 286, no. 7 (July 1988): 77–80.

7. Wright to Darwin Martin, February 28, 1916, Darwin D. Martin Papers, Department of Special Collections, Stanford University Libraries.

8. Antonin Raymond, *An Autobiography* (Rutland, Vermont: Charles E. Tuttle Company, 1973), 53, 49. In his memoirs, Raymond wrote that his stay at Taliesin was in the spring of 1916, coinciding with the visit of Hayashi and his wife from Tokyo. However, his letters to Wright indicate that he did not plan to arrive until May 15, and Hayashi had already departed for Japan on March 25. Raymond to Wright, February 2, 1916; Raymond to Wright, April 27, 1916; "Social and General," *Japan Advertiser*, April 14, 1916, 5.

9. Wright, *An Autobiography*, 194.

10. Barnsdall to Wright, July 27, 1916.

11. Barnsdall to Bel Geddes, October 22, 1915; Bel Geddes to Barnsdall, October 24, 1915; Barnsdall to Bel Geddes, November 2, 1915; Bel Geddes to Barnsdall, November 3, 1915; Barnsdall to Bel Geddes, November 30, 1915; Barnsdall to Bel Geddes, December 10, 1915; Bel Geddes to Barnsdall, December 14, 1915. Some forty years after the events, Bel Geddes published his version of meeting and working with Barnsdall in *Miracle in the Evening* (Garden City, New York: Doubleday and Company, 1960), 152–81, 268–81. The original correspondence at the University of Texas at Austin reveals that Bel Geddes abbreviated, condensed, and dramatized events. For Bel Geddes's version of his change of name see *Miracle in the Evening*, 154.

12. Unpublished draft *MS* of Norman Bel Geddes, *Miracle in the Evening*, HRHRC.

13. Ibid.

14. Ibid.

15. Ibid.

16. Elaine Hyman Wright (Kirah Markham) to Wright, February 7, 1917.

17. Theodore Newton Barnsdall died on February 27, 1917.

18. Barnsdall to Wright, January 4, 1917 (actually 1918: New Year's error).

19. Wright to Barnsdall, n.d. [circa 1916].

20. Barnsdall to Bel Geddes, October 24, 1917.

21. Constance D'Arcy Mackay, *The Little Theatre in the United States* (New York: Henry Holt and Company, 1917), 157.

22. Barnsdall to Bel Geddes, July 4, 1916.

23. Barnsdall to Bel Geddes, October 24, 1917.

24. Ibid.

25. Ibid.

26. Barnsdall to Wright, January 4, 1917 (actually 1918: New Year's error).

CHAPTER 3

1. Wright, *An Autobiography*, 446.

2. On the verso of a photograph showing the interior of the Barnsdall Theater II model, Wright wrote, "LOS ANGELES THEATRE, CEILING RAISED, showing Translucent Hemicycle and Musicians Gallery—with Foyer in front of Auditorium, FLW." I am indebted to Eulogio Guzman who brought this detail to my attention.

3. Barnsdall to Lloyd Wright, February 7, 1919, Lloyd Wright Collection, Special Collections, University of California, Los Angeles. Although Barnsdall's letter is dated 1919, internal evidence points to 1920 as the actual date. Barnsdall refers to the theater's new top, which was redesigned in late 1919. She wrote, "As I understand it the model of the theatre is to have the same perforated design at the top—only square, not octagonal."

4. Richard C. Beacham, *Adolphe Appia, Theatre Artist* (Cambridge: Cambridge University Press, 1987), 56–85.

5. Brockett and Findlay, *Century of Innovation*, 230.

6. Theatre #6 was originally published in the first issue of Bel Geddes's privately printed magazine, *Inwhich*, June 1915, HRHRC. The article included a short text, ground floor, and basement plans, and a section. The design was revised and published in

Claude Bragdon, "Towards a New Theatre," *The Architectural Record* 52 (September 1922): 171–82.

7. Barnsdall to Bel Geddes, May 16, 1916. Bel Geddes wrote of Wright's design of the Barnsdall Theater in his memoirs, *Miracle in the Evening*. However, this version of events is not corroborated by the correspondence. Bel Geddes wrote of two meetings with Barnsdall and Wright, one in Chicago and one in Los Angeles. He recounts the following conversation between Wright and himself (*Miracle in the Evening*, 162), when Wright presented his drawings to Barnsdall in Chicago:

> Mr. Wright, I have sketched out two or three different ways of solving these problems. They are yours, if you will accept them. I have them right here.
> Aline sent me a copy of your magazine with one of them in it. I don't think you went far enough.
> The theater and solution in the magazine is unrelated to yours. If you will please provide a means for handling lighting equipment and scenery, I will keep quiet.

The letters do not refer to any meetings with Wright where Bel Geddes was present, although they may have occurred. The correspondence indicates that Bel Geddes was hopeful that Barnsdall would commission his design for Theatre #6 and that he suspected, before meeting him, that Wright had stolen his ideas. His memoirs do not mention either of these facts.

8. Claude, "Towards a New Theatre," 171–82; R.M. Schindler to Claude Bragdon, September 18, 1922, HRHRC. The three ideas Schindler cited as similarities between the two schemes are: one ceiling for stage and auditorium, three-dimensional settings, and curtainless change of scenery in the basement.

9. Bel Geddes to Bragdon, October 2, 1922.

10. Narciso Menocal, *Architecture as Nature: The Transcendentalist Idea of Louis Sullivan* (Madison: University of Wisconsin Press, 1981), 36–42, and Dimitri Tselos, "The Chicago Fair and the Myth of the 'Lost Cause,'" *Journal of the Society of Architectural Historians* (December 1967): 264, 267. When Wright indicated three-dimensional stage sets for the Chicago Little Theatre scheme in 1915 he drew *qubba*. See figs. 1-1 (2005.31) and 1-7 (2005.23).

11. Barnsdall to Wright, May 30, 1918.

12. Ibid.

13. Barnsdall to Wright, October 8, 1918.

CHAPTER 4

1. Barnsdall to Bel Geddes, April 7, 1916.

2. See Bel Geddes, *Miracle in the Evening*, 155–57, 161–63. Antonin Raymond also recalled drawings of the Barnsdall House in the office during the summer of 1916. See Raymond, *An Autobiography*, 53.

3. Frank Lloyd Wright, *A Testament* (New York: Horizon Press, 1957), 111.

4. Wright, *An Autobiography*, 213.

5. Lecture by R.M. Schindler at the School of Architecture, University of Southern California, October 10, 1949, as reprinted in August Sarnitz, *R.M. Schindler, Architect, 1887–1953: A Pupil of Otto Wagner Between International Style and Space Architecture* (New York: Rizzoli, 1988), 68.

6. Frank Lloyd Wright, "In the Cause of Architecture: The Third Dimension," February 9, 1923, Wright Archive, Getty Center for the History of Art and the Humanities, Santa Monica, California. The manuscript version differs slightly from the published version which appeared as an article in H.Th. Wijdeveld, ed., *The Life-Work of the American Architect Frank Lloyd Wright* (1925; reprint, New York: Horizon Press, 1965), 48–65.

7. Wright to Louis Sullivan, April 10, 1919.

8. Schindler to Wright, June 9, 1919.

9. Telegram, Barnsdall to Wright, July 11, 1919; Wright to Miriam Noel, July 15, 1919, cited in *Important 19th and 20th Century Architectural Objects and Designs* (Chicago: Leslie Hindman Auctioneers, 1990), item #518.

CHAPTER 5

1. Costa Del Sur, "$300,000 Paid For 'Olive Hill,'" *Los Angeles Examiner*, July 1, 1919. The deed was signed on June 23, 1919, by the seller, Mary Harrison Spires, and recorded on June 30, 1919, at the Los Angeles County Hall of Records, Book 6870, 187, doc. no. 163 of DDS.

2. Monroe Lathrop, "Olive Hill Playhouse, Woman's Fine Project," *Los Angeles Express*, July 5, 1919.

3. Florence Lawrence, "Eminence to Be Made Rare Beauty Spot," *Los Angeles Examiner*, July 6, 1919.

4. Ibid.

5. Ibid.

6. "Patio House for Aline Barnsdall, Walker and Eisen, Architects, 1403 Hibernian Bldg., Los Angeles, Cal., Scale–1/8"=1'-0", August 15, 1919," blueprint, Collection of the City of Los Angeles, Departments of Recreation and Parks and Cultural Affairs. The one sheet contains a plan, front elevation, two side elevations, and a section through the patio. Also see *Los Angeles Times*, August 3, 1919, and *Architect and Engineer*, August 1919, 116. Barnsdall also offered a corner building site to the Hollywood Community Theater with the stipulation that the group pay the construction costs for their own theater. She gave them one year to accept or reject the offer. *Hollywood Citizen News*, August 8, 1919.

7. Wright to Darwin Martin, August 20, 1922, Darwin D. Martin Papers, Department of Special Collections, Stanford University Libraries.

8. Wright to Lloyd Wright, November 3, 1958, Lloyd Wright Collection, Special Collections, University of California, Los Angeles.

9. "Agreement, Frank Lloyd Wright, Architect, and Aline Barnsdall, Owner, Los Angeles, California, September 15th, 1919," Frank Lloyd Wright Archives, Taliesin West, Scottsdale, Arizona.

10. Barnsdall to Wright, January 7, 1920.

11. Barnsdall to Wright, September 24, 1919.

12. Ibid.

13. Barnsdall to Wright, n.d.

14. Telegram, Barnsdall to Wright, October 3, 1919; Barnsdall to Wright, October 23, 1919; Barnsdall to Wright, November 9, 1919; Barnsdall to Wright, January 7, 1920.

15. Sophie Pauline Gibling Schindler to parents, October 25, 1919, letter in the possession of her son Mark Schindler.

16. On the working drawings, this wall is not indicated as a bearing wall; there are no footings indicated. Marla Felber, who was working on the Historic Structures Report for Hollyhock House that was prepared by Martin Eli Weil, restoration architect, and Archiplan for the City of Los Angeles, Cultural Affairs Department, to author, January 17, 1992. In 1923 when Barnsdall was considering giving her house to the City of Los Angeles as a library, Wright and Barnsdall agreed to remove this partition. Wright and Barnsdall parted company before this change was executed. Barnsdall to Wright, n.d. [circa December 1923]. However, Wright in collaboration with his son, Lloyd Wright, prepared plans for a renovation in 1946. The plans do not call for the removal of the partition. This orientation was repeated at Taliesin West, which combines aspects of the siting of Olive Hill and the later Community Playhouse or The Little Dipper. The *parti* of Taliesin West, like that of The Little Dipper (see fig. 9-1), is based on a rotated square, and both have a diagonal axis. At Taliesin West, the major axis leads the eye to Thompson Peak, in the McDowell Mountains, whereas at Hollyhock House, the minor axis leads the line of vision to the Hollywood Hills, part of the Santa Monica Mountains. Vincent Scully discusses this aspect of the siting of Taliesin West in *Architecture: The Natural and the Manmade* (New York: St. Martin's Press, 1991), 344–45.

17. For a discussion of the history of the University Heights project see D.L. Johnson, "Frank Lloyd Wright's Architectural Projects in the Bitterroot Valley, 1909–1910," *Montana: The Magazine of Western History* 37, no. 3 (Summer 1987): 12–25.

18. Joseph Campbell, *The Hero with a Thousand Faces*, 2d ed. (Princeton: Princeton University Press, 1968), 239–40. The legend of Taliesin tells of a boy who metamorphoses into various creatures before he is discovered emerging headfirst from a leather bag. He grows up to be a poet and prophet.

19. "Wright Invents New Type of Dam," *Baraboo Weekly News*, January 4, 1912. In the nineteenth century, Wright's uncle, John Lloyd-Jones, had a flour mill upstream on the same site. See *Baraboo Weekly News*, May 25, 1911.

CHAPTER 6

1. Wright's prolonged absences in Japan during the teens and early twenties are comparable, with one crucial difference, to the period of 1909–1910 when he spent most of his time in Europe. While he was in Japan he did not close his office, and R.M. Schindler was left in charge. In 1931, an open dispute began to surface between Wright and Schindler over Schindler's role in Wright's office during his absences in Japan. In a letter that has been lost, but is quoted and paraphrased in Finis Farr, *Frank Lloyd Wright: A Biography* (London: Jonathan Cape, 1961), 194, Schindler claimed that he "drew up seven jobs without Wright's help." In addition to the evidence provided in Farr's biography, Wright mentioned the controversy in several 1931 letters to Lloyd Wright and made disclosures to Henry-Russell Hitchcock during the preparation of *In the Nature of Materials* (New York: Duell, Sloan and Pearce, 1942), as is evidenced in the "Chronological List of Executed Buildings and Projects."

In order to determine whether Schindler believed any of the Barnsdall buildings or projects was one of the seven disputed jobs, it is necessary to speculate what those jobs were. From drawings in the Architectural Drawing Collection, University Art Museum, University of California, Santa Barbara, and the Wright Archives at Taliesin, it is possible to compile the list as follows: (1) Thomas Hardy Monolith Homes, 1919, Racine, Wisconsin; (2) J.P. Shampay House, 1919, Chicago; (3) C.E. Staley House, 1919, Waukegan, Illinois; (4) Memorial Community Center, 1919, Wentachee, Washington; (5) J.B. Irving House, 1920, Wilmette, Illinois; (6) remodel of the A. Heurtley House for A. Porter, 1920, Oak Park, Illinois; (7) C.P. Lowes House, 1922, Eagle Rock, California. The Hardy, Shampay, and Staley projects are all confirmed by Hitchcock's research with Wright (see Hitchcock's *In the Nature of Materials*, 123). The Lowes project is more complicated because there were three schemes: (1) designed by Schindler for Frank Lloyd Wright, drawings carry legend with Wright's name and Schindler's initials, May 1922; (2) designed by Wright, drawings carry legend with Wright's name, December 1922; (3) designed by Schindler after he opened his own office, September 1923. The house was built according to this last scheme in 1924. Outside of the letter he wrote to Wright in 1931, Schindler never made any claims in writing for designs executed while he was with Wright, including the Barnsdall projects or even the Hardy Monolith.

2. The central core, which first appears in the Director's House, is one of the elements that Wright continued to refine until the Usonian house, when it became a major element in the service core for ventilating and lighting the kitchen and baths.

CHAPTER 8

1. Wright, *An Autobiography*, 228.

2. Frank Lloyd Wright, *In the Cause of Architecture* (1908; reprint, New York: Architectural Record Books, 1975), 117.

3. I am grateful to Eulogio Guzman who suggested this comparison.

4. In addition to the previous examples cited, Wright also used this plan type for the United States Embassy, Tokyo, 1914.

5. Wright and Barnsdall have left no documentary evidence that the court was designed as an outdoor theater. Several months after the departure of Barnsdall and the grand opening of the house for the California Art Club in August 1927, F.W. Vreeland in "New Art Centre for The Pacific Coast," *Arts & Decoration* 28 (November 1927): 64–65, described the court and its use as a patio-theater. Several cubicles of the pergola, which connects the house and the garage, were designated as "dressing rooms" on the plans. However, they could also have been designed to serve the swimming pool which, until its relocation in late 1920, was directly behind the pergola.

6. Barnsdall to Wright, January 7, 1920.

7. Holograph draft of Wright to Barnsdall, n.d., on margin of telegram, Barnsdall to Wright, December 9, 1919.

8. Lloyd Wright to Wright, n.d. [circa December 9–16, 1919].

9. Ibid.

10. Lloyd Wright to Wright, March 22, 1920.

11. Telegram, Barnsdall to Lloyd Wright, December 15, 1919, Lloyd Wright Collection, Special Collections, University of California, Los Angeles.

12. Barnsdall to Wright, January 7, 1920.

13. Barnsdall to Wright, January 29, 1920.

14. Lloyd Wright to Barnsdall, May 20, 1920, Lloyd Wright Collection, Special Collections, University of California, Los Angeles.

15. *Specifications Notes, Residence for Aline Barnsdall, Hollywood, Calif.,* n.d. [circa March–April 1920]. Frank Lloyd Wright Archives, Taliesin West, Scottsdale, Arizona.

16. Barnsdall to Wright, January 7, 1920.

17. Barnsdall to Wright, January 29, 1920.

18. Wright, *An Autobiography,* 225.

19. Barnsdall to Wright, January 29, 1920.

20. Barnsdall to Wright, January 7, 1920.

21. See my "Frank Lloyd Wright and the Imperial Hotel: A Postscript," 302.

22. *Planting Plan, Hill Grove, Olive Hill, property of Aline Barnsdall, Frank Lloyd Wright, Architect, January 27, 1920,* Architectural Drawing Collection, University Art Museum, University of California, Santa Barbara.

23. Wright, *An Autobiography,* 231.

24. Barnsdall to Lloyd Wright, February 7, 1920, Lloyd Wright Collection, Special Collections, University of California, Los Angeles.

25. The botanical names given were *Pinus pinae* and *Eucalyptus globus.* "List to Accompany Planting Plan for Aline Barnsdall," Lloyd Wright Collection, Special Collections, University of California, Los Angeles.

26. Telegram, Lloyd Wright to Barnsdall, n.d. [circa April 8–11, 1920], Lloyd Wright Collection, Special Collections, University of California, Los Angeles.

27. A set of blueprints in the Collection of the City of Los Angeles, Departments of Recreation and Parks and Cultural Affairs documents the design after Wright's revisions of early August 1920, but before more changes were made in late August and early September 1920 (and possibly after Wright's departure in December as well). The most noteworthy architectural changes occur in the dining room, where french doors were added which opened onto the court, replacing transom and casement windows that matched those on the north wall. The lighting called for six perforated wood ceiling grilles in patterns reminiscent of Wright's own dining room in Oak Park. These drawings also indicate an open porch off the north side of the room later known as the Chamber, a band of clerestory windows at roof level above the ornamental frieze on the north side of the guest bathrooms, and a series of plasterboard panels separated by leaded glass strips screening the music room from the entry hall. The study or library was not drawn until August 20, 1920; it does not appear on Sheet #7 before that date. Structural changes also appear on Sheet #6, "Living Room Details" (fig. 12-9), which clearly shows that the columns that now stand free of the wall plane did not appear on the drawings before August 16, 1920. Corresponding to other major drawings of the plan, such as Sheet #2, "First Floor Plan" (fig. 8-6), and the publication plan drawn for *In the Nature of Materials* (fig. 8-5), the east and west sides of the living room, the north side of the music room, and the south side of the study were to be supported by two inner columns flanked by two outer, larger columns, all on the same plane. Before August 16, the larger columns were drawn as hollow tile with hollow cores, and the smaller columns as concrete. After August 16, the larger columns were changed to concrete and the smaller columns to wood posts, and an additional concrete column was added in front of the window outside the wall plane, which matches as-built conditions. It is not clear whether Wright made this change, whether it was made by

28. Lloyd Wright to Wright, March 22, 1920.

29. Barnsdall to Wright, May 30, 1920.

30. Telegram, Barnsdall to Lloyd Wright, April 7, 1920, Lloyd Wright Collection, Special Collections, University of California, Los Angeles.

31. Telegram, Lloyd Wright to Barnsdall, n.d. [circa April 8–11, 1920], Lloyd Wright Collection, Special Collections, University of California, Los Angeles.

32. Lloyd Wright to Wright, March 22, 1920.

33. Frederick W. Gookin to Wright, June 27 and July 11, 1920.

34. Lloyd Wright to Barnsdall, May 3, 1920, Lloyd Wright Collection, Special Collections, University of California, Los Angeles.

35. Ibid.

36. Ibid.

37. *Southwest Builder and Contractor,* May 7, 1920, 12.

38. Barnsdall to Wright, May 30, 1920.

39. Telegram, Barnsdall to Wright, July 21, 1920; telegram, Barnsdall to Wright, July 22, 1920.

40. Telegram, Barnsdall to Wright, July 28, 1920; telegram, Barnsdall to Wright, July 31, 1920.

41. Typewritten draft of telegram, Wright to Barnsdall, August 6, 1920.

42. Holograph telegram, Barnsdall to Wright, August 9, 1920.

43. Telegram, Barnsdall to Wright, n.d. [circa August 10, 1920].

CHAPTER 9

1. Barnsdall to Wright, December 5, 1930.

2. Sophie Pauline Gibling Schindler to parents, August 13, 1920, letter in the possession of her son Mark Schindler.

3. Memorandum entitled "Programme," August 16, 1920, Lloyd Wright Collection, Special Collections, University of California, Los Angeles.

4. In the years following the Olive Hill project, Wright began to use water as a landscape element with increasing frequency. If the last element of the 1920 general plan is added to those of the 1919 general plan, a pattern is formed as follows: water flows from a spring (a), as a stream (b), which is dammed to create a pond (c) and a waterfall or two (d), and then continues as a stream (e) until it reaches a larger body of water such as a lake, river, or ocean (f). This pattern can be traced in whole or parts as a recurring motif for the remainder of Wright's career. All of the elements, a-f, were present in Wright's memory of his boyhood summers in his grandfather's valley, including the dam, pond, and waterfall of his Uncle John's mill. He then recreated them when he built Taliesin in 1911. In the decade after Olive Hill, Wright used water at Emerald Bay, Lake Tahoe (b-d-e-f), House C at Doheny Ranch (c-d-e), A.M. Johnson Compound (d-e-c), the Strong Automobile Objective (c-d-e), San-Marcos-in-the-Desert Hotel (c-d-e-c-d-e), and the House on the Mesa (c-b-e-f). The most famous example of this composition is Fallingwater, where Wright used an existing stream and double waterfall to recreate his own b-c-d-e, a reprise of the Olive Hill Director's House. The pattern continues with Florida Southern College (a-b-c-d-f), the Jester House (c-d-e), Usonia I (b-c), the Affleck House (b-c), the Hartford Estate (c-d-e-f-c-d-c), the Bailleres House (a-b-c-d-e-c-e-f), Broadacre City (b-c-e), and the Marin County Civic Center and Fairgrounds (a-b-c-d-e-d-c-e-f). In fact, the instances where water appears as a major and minor element in Wright's architecture are too numerous to be discussed here. With the Olive Hill general plan, Wright introduced an element of great symbolic power.

5. East elevations for both buildings are depicted in the Vermont Avenue perspective (fig. 9-3) drawn by Lloyd Wright between January and May 1921. The Director's House is clearly visible while the Apartment Building is almost totally obscured by landscaping.

6. Frank Lloyd Wright, *Experimenting with Human Lives* (Chicago: Ralph Fletcher Seymour, 1923).

7. General Conditions, Specifications, Residence "A," A. Barnsdall, Hollywood, California, with marginalia: "Finally Revised Dec. 7, 1920 FLLW." Gum was a term used for the wood of the eucalyptus tree. During the first decades of the century experiments were conducted in California to grow eucalyptus for commercial purposes such as wood trim, furniture, and firewood.

CHAPTER 10

1. Holograph draft of Wright to Barnsdall, n.d., on margin of telegram, Barnsdall to Wright, September 20, 1920.

2. Holograph draft of Wright to Barnsdall, n.d., on margin of telegram, Barnsdall to Wright, September 29, 1920.

CHAPTER 11

1. Sophie Pauline Gibling Schindler to parents, n.d. [circa October 5, 1920], letter in the possession of her son Mark Schindler.

2. Wright, *An Autobiography,* 530.

3. Of the seven jobs Schindler claimed he drew up without Wright's help (see Ch. 6, n. 1), the Hardy Monolith Homes were the most controversial. Farr, *Wright: A Biography,* 194, quotes a passage of a 1931 letter (which has since been lost) by Schindler to Wright: "You officially identified yourself with it [Schindler's work for Wright] by including my scheme and drawing of Mr. Hardy's working-man's colony unretouched in your personal exhibit as your own."
    Wright was furious. In letters to Schindler and to his son Lloyd Wright he denied all of Schindler's claims except for the Monolith Home. On June 19, 1931, in a letter to Lloyd Wright (in the possession of his son Eric), Frank Lloyd Wright explained:

    The only sketches R. S. made I know anything about are the Hardy cottages he refers to. He probably kept the rest, with some such purpose as the present in mind. That sketch gave my own stuff in my own style, and I put it in the show. But he "drew" it in my absence it is true and to avoid controversy I'll take it out. If drawing ideas and schemes of the Masters can make them the draughtsman's it is only necessary for the Master to turn his back and his help can steal him blind. They do.

    Eleven years later, Henry-Russell Hitchcock with Wright's cooperation compiled a "Chronological List of Executed Buildings and Projects" for the book *In the Nature of Materials.* This note on page 123 of that work was added to the listing for the Hardy Monolith Homes:

    (This scheme, as well as the C.E. Staley and J.P. Shampay house projects of this year, were developed by R.M. Schindler during Wright's absence in Japan. They are hardly to be considered Wright's work, though they issued from his office and the Monolith Homes drawings carry his signature.)

4. The degree of abstraction can be compared with Mies van der Rohe's two projects, the Brick Country House (1923) and the Concrete Country House (1924). Aside from Wright's redesign of this scheme for Barnsdall, the Monolith Homes had a decisive influence on Wright throughout the twenties and into the thirties when he synthesized it into his own vocabulary. The rectilinear character of the massing appears in the C.P. Lowes House (1922), the Storer House (1923), and the Freeman House (1923–1924), but it was not until 1927 that Wright digested the idea and reinterpreted it as the Block House for Chandler, Arizona. Tracing the complete evolution of the elements indicates the origins of the floor-to-ceiling corner window at Fallingwater.

5. Schindler may have written and/or sent plans to Wright in Japan. On August 18, 1919, Schindler copyrighted the plans in Wright's name either on his own initiative or at the direction of Wright. Application #4567, Office of Copyright, Library of Congress, Washington, D.C.

6. Sophie Pauline Gibling Schindler to parents, n.d. [circa October 5, 1920], letter in the possession of her son Mark Schindler.

7. Telegram, Barnsdall to Wright, October 6, 1920.

8. Sophie Pauline Gibling Schindler to parents, n.d. [circa October 20, 1920], letter in the possession of her son Mark Schindler.

9. Sophie Pauline Gibling Schindler to parents, n.d. [circa October 16, 1920], letter in the possession of her son Mark Schindler; telegram, Barnsdall to Wright, October 22, 1920.

10. Sophie Pauline Gibling Schindler to parents, October 1920 [circa October 28, 1920], letter in the possession of her son Mark Schindler.

11. Wright, *An Autobiography,* 229.

12. Ibid.

13. The only surviving record of this building is a model that Wright gave to Professor Goichi Takeda who donated it in August 1920 to the Department of Architecture, Kyoto University. Although it is known as a motion picture theater (1918), the model indicates that the plan is for a theater-in-the-round. No further information has been made available to explain the discrepancy. See Masami Tanigawa, *Measured Drawing: Frank Lloyd Wright in Japan* (Tokyo: Graphic Co., 1980), 66–75.

14. Barnsdall to Wright, November 12, 1920.

15. Sophie Pauline Gibling Schindler to parents, December 1920, letter in the possession of her son Mark Schindler.

16. Records in the Architectural Drawing Collection, University Art Museum, University of California, Santa Barbara, indicate that the bids dated December 9, 1920, for Residence A were: $23,997 versus $28,789; Residence B: $24,210+2,420=$26,630 versus $29,971. I am grateful to Barbara Giella for this information. In an unsigned telegram [n.d., circa December 13–15, 1920] addressed to Wright at Spring Green, Wisconsin, the bid for Residence A is recorded as $20,355.15, $1,275.90 over the estimate, with the following explanation:

    Due to additions to art stone, concrete floor, living room, garden walls, electric heating, plumbing not originally figured. Spec called for red gum trim. Bids & original estimate based on redwood. Difference 1100.

    Both Barton Spider Web System and Trucson Steel were considered as sources for the structural material for the Terrace Stores and Houses. Wright to Barton Spider Web System, December 16, 1920; telegram, Barton Spider Web System to R.M. Schindler, December 20, 1920; Schindler for Wright to Trucson Steel, January 5, 1921. Wright's office requested a variance to build into the sidewalk, Wright to P.P. O'Brien, December 6, 1920.

17. Lloyd Wright to Wright, n.d. [circa January 1921].

18. Wright to Barnsdall, November 18, 1930.

CHAPTER 12

1. See Ch. 8, n. 27 for details of the major differences between these drawings and the revised set.

2. Wright, *An Autobiography,* 228.

3. Foundation Plan, May 6, 1920, Collection of the City of Los Angeles, Departments of Recreation and Parks and Cultural Affairs. The foundation consisted of concrete footings and brick foundations, with the use of concrete where soil was retained.

4. Wright, *In the Cause of Architecture,* 209.

5. Lloyd Wright to Barnsdall, May 3, 1920, Lloyd Wright Collection, Special Collections, University of California, Los Angeles. The sizes of the rooms were as follows: living room, 24' x 44'; music room, 15'6" x 18'; library, 16' x 19'; dining room, 17' x 17'; guest rooms, 13'6" x 14'6" and 13'6" x 18'; breakfast room, 9'6" x 9'6"; own room, 10' x 14'6"; Sugar's room, 13' x 14'; upstairs north room, 10' x 16'. These dimensions correspond very closely to the rooms as built.

6. Telegram, Wright to Herbert Hahn, April 15, 1925.

7. Wright to Barnsdall, March 4, 1925.

8. Specifications, Residence, A. Barnsdall, Hollywood, California, n.d. "Millwork," 14, Frank Lloyd Wright Archives, Taliesin West, Scottsdale, Arizona.

9. Unfortunately, most of the original finish wood in the major rooms, except the dining room, was removed in 1946. No surviving documentation exists to indicate whether the millwork schedule was followed during the course of construction.

10. Robert Preston to Wright, January 25, 1921.

11. George Taylor for William Smith Architectural Stone to Wright, January 13, 1921.

12. George Taylor for William Smith Architectural Stone to Wright, January 5, 1921.

13. Schindler for Wright to William Smith Architectural Stone, January 14, 1921.

14. Lloyd Wright to Wright, n.d. [circa January 15, 1921].

15. Schindler for Wright to C.D. Goldthwaite, January 25, 1921; construction costs as quoted on building permit #25455 for Residence B, Department of Building and Safety, City of Los Angeles; Hitchcock, In the Nature of Materials, 123.

16. C.D. Goldthwaite to Wright, February 3, 1921; Schindler for Wright to C.D. Goldthwaite, February 7, 1921.

17. Barnsdall to Wright, January 24, 1921.

18. Telegram, Barnsdall to Lloyd Wright, January 16, 1921; unsigned memo, n.d. [circa December 1920–January 1921]; Lloyd Wright to Mr. Ray, President, Olive Hill Construction Company, March 29, 1921; List to Accompany Planting Plan for Cline [sic] Barnsdall, n.d., Lloyd Wright Collection, Special Collections, University of California, Los Angeles.

19. Schindler for Wright to Pioneer Roofing Co., February 4, 1921.

20. "Landscape Specifications, Olive Hill, Los Angeles, California, Property of Aline Barnsdall, Frank Lloyd Wright, Architect, 522 Homer Laughlin Building, Los Angeles," Lloyd Wright Collection, Special Collections, University of California, Los Angeles.

21. Lloyd Wright to Wright, n.d. [circa January 15, 1921].

22. Schindler to Richard Neutra, March 12, 1921, as quoted in Esther McCoy, Vienna to Los Angeles: Two Journeys (Santa Monica: Art + Architecture Press, 1979), 132.

23. Lloyd Wright to Wright, n.d. [circa January 15, 1920].

24. Sophie Pauline Gibling Schindler to parents, February 20, 1921, letter in the possession of her son Mark Schindler.

25. Lloyd Wright to Barnsdall, April 15, 1921.

26. Clarence Thomas to Schindler, March 10, 1921.

27. Schindler to Thomas, March 11, 1921.

28. Lloyd Wright to Wright, n.d. [circa February 1921].

29. E.O. Ward to Wright, April 27, 1921.

30. Schindler for Wright to Los Angeles Lime Co., September 6, 1921; Los Angeles Lime Co. to Schindler, September 8, 1921.

31. Smith, "Imperial Hotel," 306.

32. Telegram, Wright to Schindler, June 23, 1921.

33. "More Stores at Vermont," Holly Leaves, May 14, 1921; telegram, Schindler to Wright, June 26, 1921.

34. Wright, An Autobiography, 230.

35. Wright to Barnsdall, November 18, 1930.

36. Frank Lloyd Wright, Modern Architecture: Being the Kahn Lectures for 1930 (1931; reprint, Carbondale: Southern Illinois University Press, 1987): 21.

37. Lloyd Wright, interview with author, Beverly Hills, California, May 10, 1974.

38. I am grateful to Jonathan Lipman, who observed that Wright, as early as 1907 in the Meyer May house, began to shift the fireplace off center.

39. Comparisons with several examples of pre-Columbian architecture have been cited over the years. Dimitri Tselos discussed correspondences with the Temple of the Tigers at Chichen Itza in "Exotic Influences in the Architecture of Frank Lloyd Wright," Magazine of Art 46 (April 1953): 166; Vincent Scully compared it with Structure 33 at Yaxchilan in Frank Lloyd Wright (New York: George Braziller, 1960), 25 and illustration 62; Neil Levine traced parallels to the Nunnery at Uxmal in "Hollyhock House and the Romance of Southern California," Art in America 71, no. 8 (September 1983): 157–159. Comparisons can also be made with the Temple of the Sun at Palenque. I am grateful to Eulogio Guzman who suggested this example to me and who identified the ornamental design on the sides of the concrete columns as a pre-Columbian image depicting the rain god, Tlaloc.

40. Wright, In the Cause of Architecture, 63.

41. Telegram, Wright to Schindler, June 22, 1921; Barnsdall to Wright, January 24, 1921.

42. Wright to W. & J. Sloane, November 9, 1920.

43. W. & J. Sloane to Wright, March 1, 1921.

44. F.W. Vreeland, "A New Art Centre for The Pacific Coast," Arts & Decoration 28 (November 1927): 65; telegram, Schindler for Wright to W. & J. Sloane, March 7, 1921.

45. Telegram, Wright to Schindler, June 15, 1921.

46. Ibid.

47. Telegram (lost), quoted in Wright to Schindler, June 16, 1921.

48. Ibid.

49. Telegram, Wright to Schindler, June 20, 1921.

50. Ibid.

51. Telegram, Barnsdall to Wright, June 16, 1921.

52. Telegram, Wright to Schindler, June 22, 1921.

53. Telegram, Wright to Schindler, June 25, 1921.

54. Wright to Lloyd Wright, June 26, 1921.

55. Telegram, Wright to Schindler, July 1, 1921.

56. Wright to Barnsdall, June 27, 1921 (office copy).

57. Ibid.

58. Ibid.

59. Ibid.

60. Ibid. It is almost impossible to determine precisely what Wright found so objectionable about Hollyhock House. Very few photographs survive to document the building before 1922. The majority of photographs date from 1925–1926, after extensive rain damage in 1921–1922, the additions and corrections made during 1922–1923, and Schindler's changes and amendments made at Barnsdall's request, 1924–1926.

61. Telegram, Schindler to Wright, June 28, 1921.

62. Telegram, Wright to Schindler, June 27, 1921.

63. Telegram, Wright to Schindler, June 29, 1921.

64. Wright to Lloyd Wright, June 26, 1921, letter in the possession of Eric Lloyd Wright.

65. Telegram, Wright to Schindler, June 27, 1921; telegram, Schindler to Wright, June 28, 1921. It would be necessary to conduct scientific testing on the present plaster walls in order to determine the colors of the various layers of paint. Pertinent information is contained in two sets of specifications for remedial work which have been preserved. The first draft, Owner's Residence and Garage, dated July 24, 1922, and what appears to be the final draft, Olive Hill, Owner's Residence and Garage: Repairs and Additions, Work to be Done, n.d., indicate that in addition to extensive buckling of the floors, the exterior and interior plaster was damaged in the heavy rains of the winter of 1921–1922. Replastering and repainting "to match present interior walls" was specified. Lloyd Wright Collection, Special Collections, University of California, Los Angeles. Considering the condition of Hollyhock House by 1922, it is possible that Wright, according to his manner of work, would have carried out other changes while he was living in Los Angeles in 1923. However, there is no documentary evidence to support this speculation.

66. Schindler to Louis Sullivan, September 13, 1921, Architectural Drawing Collection, University Art Museum, University of California, Santa Barbara.

67. Telegram, Wright to Barnsdall, September 12, 1921.

68. "Agreement, Wright, Architect, and Barnsdall, Owner, September 15th, 1919." Memorandum (Pledge of Accounts Receivable) to the Bank of Wisconsin, December 30, 1921, Frank Lloyd Wright Archives, Taliesin West, Scottsdale, Arizona. The latter document, which was to be signed by the attorney-in-fact for Frank Lloyd Wright, is unsigned in the Archives' copy.

69. Memorandum, Bank of Wisconsin, December 30, 1921.

70. In 1924, Wright maintained that he had not been paid for the Olive Hill general plan, four perspectives, the apartment building. Wright versus Barnsdall, Case #138515, Superior Court of County of Los Angeles, *Notice to Produce Certain Documents and Writings*, n.d. I am indebted to Barbara Giella who furnished information from Schindler's records in the Architectural Drawing Collection, University Art Museum, University of California, Santa Barbara, concerning the construction cost of Hollyhock House.

71. Schindler to Neutra, November 19, 1921, as quoted in McCoy, *Vienna to Los Angeles*, 138.

72. "Will Spend One Million Dollars on Olive Hill Improvement," *Hollywood Citizen News*, July 8, 1921.

73. Lloyd Wright to Barnsdall, March 15, 1922, Lloyd Wright Collection, Special Collections, University of California, Los Angeles.

74. Barnsdall to Wright, August 9, 1943. Marla Felber, who worked on the Historic Structures Report for Hollyhock House prepared by restoration architect Martin Eli Weil and Archiplan for the City of Los Angeles, Cultural Affairs Department, pointed out that there was no roof flashing indicated in the specifications except over the porte cochere, sun room, owner's porch, and springhouse. "Sheet Metal Work," *Specifications*, Frank Lloyd Wright, Architect, Chicago, n.d., 25.

75. Wright to Barnsdall, May 28, 1943. The specifications, *Owner's Residence and Garage: Olive Hill*, July 24, 1922, called for "All roofs, except garage roof, pergola roof to garage and roof over entrance pergola, to have 6 x 8 tile, as selected, laid in a grouting of cement and to be made water tight." The undated second version of these specifications state: "Tile to be laid over present roofing, care being taken that same is made water-proof." Lloyd Wright Collection, Special Collections, University of California, Los Angeles.

76. Barnsdall to Wright, August 9, 1943.

77. Wright to Barnsdall, November 18, 1930.

78. Barnsdall to Tom Mooney, August 26, 1932, Tom Mooney Papers, Bancroft Library, University of California, Berkeley.

79. Barnsdall to Wright, December 5, 1930.

80. Barnsdall to Wright, August 9, 1943.

CHAPTER 13

1. Sophie Pauline Gibling Schindler to parents, August 22, 1922, letter in the possession of her son Mark Schindler.

2. Barnsdall to Bel Geddes, June 1, 1923.

3. Barnsdall to Wright, June 9, 1923.

4. Ibid.

5. "Donor of Olive Hill," *Holly Leaves* 12, no. 51 (December 21, 1923): 50.

6. Wright to Sullivan, November 30, 1922.

7. The seven articles were: J.J.P. Oud, "Architectonische beschouwing bij bijlage VIII," *de Stijl* 4 (1918): 38–41; Robert Van't Hoff, "Architectuur en haar ontwikkeling (bij bijlage VIII)," *de Stijl* 4 (1919): 40–43; Jan Wils, "De Nieuwe tijd: eenige gedachten bij het werk van Frank Lloyd Wright," *Wendingen* 2, no. 6 (1919): 14–15; H.P. Berlage, "Frank Lloyd Wright," *Wendingen* 4, no. 11 (1921): 2–18; Jan Wils, "Frank Lloyd

Wright," *Elsevier's Geïllustreerd Maandschrift* 61 (1921): 217–27; H.P. Berlage, "Frank Lloyd Wright," *Styl* (Prague) 4, no. 1 (1922): 10, 12–15; "Zpravy a Poznamky," *Styl* (Prague) 4, no. 2–3 (1922): 57–58. The two articles that appeared in the United States are: Fiske Kimball, "The American Country House, 1. Practical Conditions: Natural, Economic, Social," *Architectural Record* 46 (October 1919): 299–328, and Louis Christian Mullgardt, "A Building That Is Wrong," *Architect and Engineer* 71 (November 1922): 81–89.

8. Mullgardt, "A Building That Is Wrong," 86.

9. H.P. Berlage, "Frank Lloyd Wright," in *The Life-Work* (1965), 80–81. This article originally appeared in *Wendingen* 4, no. 11 (1921): 2–18.

10. Ibid., 84.

11. Ibid.

12. Wright to Berlage, November 30, 1922.

13. McCoy, *Vienna to Los Angeles*, 130.

14. Sarnitz, *Schindler*, 68. It is interesting to compare Schindler's quote with a similar one by Wright referring to Louis Sullivan: "Well, you may say that these frontal divisions were no less eclecticism for being fresh. But a new countenance had come to light! He had conceived [the Wainwright building] as still a column, as I came to see many years later. Base, shaft and capital were there with no direct or apparent relation to actual construction." Frank Lloyd Wright, *Genius and the Mobocracy* (New York: Duell, Sloan and Pearce, 1949), 59.

15. "Noted Architect Locates Here," *Holly Leaves* 12, no. 16 (April 20, 1923): 34.

16. I am grateful to Atsuko Tanaka who interviewed Kameki and Nobu Tsuchiura, Tokyo, Japan, May 1988.

17. Sophie Pauline Gibling Schindler to parents, February 26, 1923, and March 4, 1923. In the early years of his practice, Schindler kept a card file of each of his jobs. The Millard drawings are listed for February–March 1923. Architectural Drawing Collection, University Art Museum, University of California, Santa Barbara.

18. Wright, "In the Cause of Architecture," 12.

19. I am grateful to Robert Sweeney who has shared with me his extensive research and analysis of Wright's textile block system from his *Wright in Hollywood: Visions of a New Architecture* (New York and Cambridge: Architectural History Foundation/MIT, forthcoming 1993).

20. In an undated and unsigned memo in Barnsdall's hand, she listed the rooms by zone: "Guest House (Sugar's Dining Room and Sitting Room, Bedroom, Store Room and Sewing Room); Social Group (Living Room, Dinning [sic] Room, Music Room, Bedroom); Service Group (Kitchen, Service, Dining Room, Bedroom & bath, Bedroom, Bedroom & bath, Office, Store Room, Laundry, tub in front of Kennels); Own Group (Library, Bedroom, Gymnasium); S.T. [Sugar Top] Group (Two Bedrooms, two bath, Playroom)." Frank Lloyd Wright Archives, Taliesin West, Scottsdale, Arizona.

21. Wright, "In the Cause of Architecture," 10.

22. "Noted Architect Locates Here," *Holly Leaves* 12, no. 16 (April 20, 1923): 34; "Will Build in Beverly Hills," *Holly Leaves* 12, no. 20 (May 18, 1923): 28. Both articles referred to Barnsdall's site in Beverly Hills. The latter reported that the twenty-four acres adjoining Pickfair cost $60,000 and that the house was estimated at $150,000. I located the exact site by comparing the topographical elevations noted on Wright's working drawings of plans, elevations, and sections with the topographical contours in the vicinity of Pickfair that appear on the United States Geological Survey of the area for 1923 (Sawtelle Quadrangle) and the 1966 Survey, revised 1981 (Beverly Hills Quadrangle). The specific site was pinpointed by discovering the serpentine road (Summit Ridge Drive) that is visible in Wright's preliminary drawing (fig. 13-8). Corroboration was provided by the perspective (fig. 13-1). The land was surveyed in February 1919 by George A. Wright (who also surveyed Olive Hill in July; see figs. 5-1 and 5-2) and subdivided by the Beverly Hills Corporation on March 6, 1919. The house was sited on lot 4 of Tract 3357, which was sold, along with some adjoining property on June 11, 1924, to Abraham Lewenthal, Isaac Lewenthal, Myron M. Lewenthal, and Joseph Keho, County of Los Angeles, Property Deeds, Book 4425,

183–84. There is no record that Aline Barnsdall owned this property at the time she commissioned Wright.

23. Unsigned memo, n.d., "Catalogue–Rooms and Sizes–Barnsdall House," Frank Lloyd Wright Archives, Taliesin West, Scottsdale, Arizona.

24. "Will Build in Beverly Hills," *Holly Leaves* 12, no. 20 (May 18, 1923): 28.

25. Barnsdall to Wright, June 9, 1923.

26. Ibid.

CHAPTER 14

1. Barnsdall to Wright, June 9, 1923.

2. Barnsdall to Bel Geddes, July 23, 1923.

3. "Donor of Olive Hill," *Holly Leaves* 12, no. 51 (December 21, 1923): 50.

4. In an interview with Atsuko Tanaka in 1987, Kameki Tsuchiura recalled that Wright and Miriam Noel did not live at Harper Avenue; they resided elsewhere in Hollywood.

5. Closing bill (August 1923), Los Angeles Gas and Electric Corporation; A.C. Parlee vs. Frank Lloyd Wright, Case #135722, Superior Court of County of Los Angeles, *Complaint for Money,* January 16, 1924.

6. Barnsdall to Bel Geddes, April 24, 1923.

7. Bel Geddes, *Miracle in the Evening*, 279–80.

CHAPTER 15

1. Barnsdall to Wright, October 19, 1923.

2. "Creative Education," prospectus of the Barnsdall Olive Hill school.

3. Ibid.

4. Ibid.

5. An undated memo in the Barnsdall correspondence reads as follows:

> Equipment for Olive Hill School.
> 3 removable blackboards about 3 x 6 feet
> 24 chairs, two sizes, comfortable, straight chairs
> 10 small tables 2 x 3 feet
> 3 work tables about 7 x 2 1/2 feet
>
> Materials for construction of buildings, beaver board, etc.
> Carpenters tools [crossed out]
> Many blocks of all sizes
> Sand table and cover

6. These notes appear on the verso of drawing #2301.01, Wright Archives, Taliesin West, Scottsdale, Arizona.

7. Although pre-Columbian influence has been noted in the formal elements of the textile block system, a comparison can also be made with Islamic architecture. Wright's use of the perforated screen in the solid wall plane recalls the use of decorated grillage, *mashrabiya*, in the hot and sunny climates of the Middle East. See Fazlur R. Khan, "The Islamic Environment: Can the Future Learn from the Past?" in *Toward an Architecture in the Spirit of Islam*, The Aga Khan Awards, 1978: 25–26.

8. Permit #53782, Application for the Erection of Buildings, Class "C," Department of Building and Safety, City of Los Angeles.

9. Ibid.; A.C. Parlee vs. Aline Barnsdall, Case #143096, Superior Court of County of Los Angeles, *Complaint on Contract*, April 11, 1924.

10. Wright to Llewelyn Wright, June 8, 1923.

11. Barnsdall to Wright, October 19, 1923.

12. Telegrams, Barnsdall to Wright, November 12 and 16, 1923.

13. Parlee vs. Barnsdall, Case #143096, *Complaint on Contract*.

14. Parlee vs. Wright, Case #135722, *Complaint for Money*.

15. Barnsdall to Wright, n.d. [circa December 1923].

CHAPTER 16

1. Barnsdall to Wright, January 21, 1924.

2. Parlee vs. Wright, Case #135722, *Complaint for Money*. Parlee maintained that Wright had stopped payment on his check dated December 13, 1923, thus refusing to pay for outstanding labor and material.

3. Frank Lloyd Wright vs. Aline Barnsdall, Case #138514, Superior Court of County of Los Angeles, *Affidavit for Claim and Delivery of Personal Property*, February 28, 1924; Frank Lloyd Wright vs. Aline Barnsdall, Case #138515, *Complaint for Money and Notice to Produce Certain Documents and Writings*, February 28, 1924. Wright sued Barnsdall for $5,000 for "One pair of six-fold gold screens, ornamented with pine trees, mountain streams and white cranes"; $6,533.44 for the remodeling of Residence B; and $9,834.50 for past-due architectural services, for a total of $21,367.94. However, he calculated the monies owed on the back of a letter from his lawyer Herbert L. Hahn dated March 18, 1924, as follows: $6,533.44 for money paid out for labor and materials on the remodeling of Residence B; $9,834.50 for past-due fees; and $2,683 for Japanese screens; for a total of $19,150.44, in error by $100 over the correct amount.

4. Parlee vs. Barnsdall, Case #143096, *Complaint on Contract*. Parlee calculated his loss at $6,198.75 for labor and materials, $3,258.87 for equipment, and $2,400.00 profit, for a total of $11,857.62, less $4000.

5. Parlee vs. Wright, Case #135722, *Order Dismissing Action* pursuant Section 581-A (CCP), June 17, 1952.

6. Parlee vs. Barnsdall, Case #143096, *Settlement*, July 9, 1925.

7. Wright vs. Barnsdall, Case #138515, *Answer*, March 28, 1924.

8. Telegram, Herbert L. Hahn to Wright, February 11, 1925.

9. Holograph draft, Wright to Hahn, February 12, 1925.

10. Wright to Barnsdall, office copy, March 4, 1925.

11. Barnsdall to Wright, December 10, 1926.

12. Wright vs. Barnsdall, Case #138514 and #138515, *Release*, January 24, 1927.

13. Barnsdall to Wright, February 4, 1926 (actually 1927: error).

14. "Park Donor Explains," *Holly Leaves* 12, no. 17 (May 2, 1924): 29.

15. Barnsdall to Wright, December 10, 1926.

16. Vreeland, "A New Art Centre for the Pacific Coast," 65.

17. Lloyd Wright to Wright, n.d. [circa June 29, 1932].

18. Wright to Lloyd Wright, July 14, 1932.

19. Telegram, Lloyd Wright to Wright, July 18, 1932.

20. Wright to Lloyd Wright, July 15, 1932.

21. Lloyd Wright to Barnsdall, October 9, 1932.

22. Schindler's remodeling followed two years of occupancy by Phi Kappa Sigma, a fraternity of the University of California, Los Angeles. Newsletters, scrapbooks, and fraternity minutes of the Alpha Psi chapter of Phi Kappa Sigma, University of California, Los Angeles. I am grateful to Thomas Lorz, assistant director of the national organization of Phi Kappa Sigma, for his assistance in this research.

23. Certificate of Death #20179, Division of Vital Statistics, County of Los Angeles.

24. The Junior Arts Center was a joint venture of Hunter and Benedict with Kahn, Farrell and Associates. The Municipal Art Gallery was designed by Wehmueller and Stephens.

APPENDIX I

1. "Olive Hill Playhouse, Woman's Fine Project," *Los Angeles Express*, July 5, 1919.

2. Barnsdall to Wright, January 7, 1920.

INDEX

Note: Frank Lloyd Wright is abbreviated FLW.
Louise Aline Barnsdall is abbreviated LAB.